# Integrating Educational Systems for Successful Reform in Diverse Contexts

Linguistic, ethnic, and economic diversity are major factors influencing how school reform ought to be accomplished at local, state, and government levels. This book examines the issue of educational reform in diverse communities. It is the first to synthesize educational research on educational reform pertaining to racially and linguistically diverse students. It examines what is needed at the teacher, school, district, state, and federal levels for educational reform to be successful in multicultural, multilingual settings. Conclusions are based on a careful review of hundreds of recent quantitative and qualitative studies relating to educational reform in diverse communities. The authors conceptualize education as an interconnected and interdependent policy system and discuss the key policy, relational, political, and resource linkages that assist in achieving sustainable improvement in schools serving at-risk students.

Amanda Datnow is an Associate Professor of Education at the Rossier School of Education at the University of Southern California. At USC, she teaches in the Ed.D. and Ph.D. programs and is also the Associate Director of the Center on Educational Governance. She received her Ph.D. from UCLA and was formerly a faculty member at the Ontario Institute for Studies in Education at the University of Toronto and at Johns Hopkins University. Her research focuses on the politics and policies of school reform, particularly with regard to the professional lives of educators and issues of equity.

Sue Lasky is an Assistant Professor in the College of Education and Human Development at the University of Louisville. She is also a Spencer Fellow. Her areas of specialization are in systemic reform and school-family partnerships. Her current research focuses on identifying systemic linkages across the education policy system. She has worked in evaluation at the Ontario Institute for Studies in Education at the University of Toronto, where she earned her doctorate, and at the Center for Social Organization of Schools at Johns Hopkins University.

Sam Stringfield is a Distinguished University Scholar and Co-Director of the Nystrand Center for Excellence in Education in the College of Education and Human Development at the University of Louisville. He is a founding editor of the *Journal of Education for Students Placed At Risk* (*JESPAR*), and he is currently serving as the acting chair of the Educational and Psychological Counseling Department. His research focuses on designs for improving programs within schools, for improving whole schools, for improving systemic supports for schools serving disadvantaged children, and international comparisons of school effects.

Charles Teddlie is the Jo Ellen Levy Yates Distinguished Professor of Education at Louisiana State University (LSU). He received his Ph.D. in Social Psychology from the University of North Carolina at Chapel Hill. He is currently a Guest Professor at the Research Institute of Educational Economics and Administration at Shenyang Normal University in China. He also served as the Assistant Superintendent for Research and Development at the Louisiana Department of Education. Teddlie's major writing interests are social science research methodology and school effectiveness research. He has taught research methods courses for more than twenty years, including statistics and qualitative research methods.

# Integrating Educational Systems for Successful Reform in Diverse Contexts

**AMANDA DATNOW**

*University of Southern California*

**SUE LASKY**

*University of Louisville*

**SAM STRINGFIELD**

*University of Louisville*

**CHARLES TEDDLIE**

*Louisiana State University*

**CAMBRIDGE**
UNIVERSITY PRESS

CAMBRIDGE UNIVERSITY PRESS
Cambridge, New York, Melbourne, Madrid, Cape Town, Singapore, São Paulo

Cambridge University Press
32 Avenue of the Americas, New York, NY 10013-2473, USA

www.cambridge.org
Information on this title: www.cambridge.org/9780521857567

First published 2006

Printed in the United States of America

*A catalog record for this publication is available from the British Library.*

*Library of Congress Cataloging in Publication Data*

Integrating educational systems : for successful reform in diverse
contexts / Amanda Datnow ... [et al.].
p. cm.
Includes bibliographical references and index.
ISBN 0-521-85756-2 (hardcover) – ISBN 0-521-67434-4 (pbk.)
1. School improvement programs – United States – Longitudinal
studies. 2. Educational change – United States – Longitudinal studies.
3. Multicultural education – United States – Longitudinal studies.
I. Datnow, Amanda. II. Title.
LB2822.82.I58 2006
371.200973 – dc22        2006016304

ISBN-13   978-0-521-85756-7 hardback
ISBN-10   0-521-85756-2 hardback

ISBN-13   978-0-521-67434-8 paperback
ISBN-10   0-521-67434-4 paperback

# Contents

# List of Figures and Tables

## TABLES

# Acknowledgments

This book reports on a research synthesis project that was part of the federally funded Center for Research on Education, Diversity, and Excellence (CREDE) of the University of California, Santa Cruz. Although we authored this review ourselves, we benefited from the advice of a highly esteemed and expert advisory board who provided very useful comments and advice on the first draft of this report. Thus, while we are greatly indebted to them for their input, the members of the advisory board should not be held responsible for the contents of this document. The members of the advisory board included:

Larry Cuban, Stanford University
Ron Gallimore, UCLA Graduate School of Education
Libia Gil, American Institutes for Research
David Grissmer, RAND Corporation
Rosemary Henze, San Jose State University
Lea Hubbard, University of San Diego
Sharon Lewis, Council of the Great City Schools
Hugh Mehan, University of California, San Diego
Joseph Murphy, Vanderbilt University
Jeannie Oakes, UCLA Graduate School of Education
Lauren Resnick, University of Pittsburgh
Robert Slavin, Johns Hopkins University and Success for All Foundation
Hersh Waxman, University of Houston College of Education

The work reported herein was supported under the Educational Research and Development Centers Program, PR/award number R306A60001, as administered by the Institute for Education Sciences, U.S. Department of Education. However, the contents do not necessarily represent the positions or policies of the National Institute on the Education of At-Risk Students, the Institute for Education Science, or the U.S. Department of Education, and endorsement by the federal government should not be assumed. We also express our appreciation to Kirsten Sundell at the University of Louisville, who assisted with the bibliography. We are also greatly indebted to Roland Tharp for his comments on an earlier draft and Catherine Murphy for her expert editing.

# 1

# Introduction

This book reports the findings of an extensive review of literature of research on educational reform in school systems serving racially and linguistic minority youth. Our aim is to identify strategies for supporting reform in educational settings serving these students. In doing so, we place particular emphasis on identifying the linkages between systemic levels (e.g., school, district, community) that are important in the process of school improvement.

Thus, the purpose of the volume is to develop an understanding of what might be needed at the teacher, school, district, state, and federal levels for educational reform to be successful in multicultural, multilingual settings. We define reform as an innovation intended to improve education (e.g., standards-based reform, site-based management, school reconstitution), rather than simply a change for change sake. We know from prior research that reform will rarely succeed without coordinated support from multiple levels (e.g., school, district, state), and that reform is rarely sustained if built on technical models alone. Political support and belief changes are required at multiple levels of the system. Instead of trying to identify "one best system," the goal of this volume is to identify approaches that are adaptable and contextually sensitive. In particular, our aim is to identify strategies for supporting reform in school systems serving culturally and linguistically diverse communities.

## RULES OF EVIDENCE AND INCLUSION

This review of research covers studies that were conducted between 1983 and 2004. However, the majority of research reviewed was conducted between the mid-1990s and 2003. We chose 1983 as the beginning point because that is the year in which *A Nation At Risk* was published, a report that placed school reform on national, state, and local agendas. Another significant marker for the research we are reviewing is O'Day and Smith's (1993) proposal for systemic reform, which sparked a significant amount of research and policy change across the country. We include primarily research conducted in the United States.

We reviewed both quantitative and qualitative research. We attempted to apply rigorous, yet practical standards for inclusion. In terms of quantitative research, we attempted to focus on quasi-experimental studies of student achievement that use matched control group designs. However, the number of studies that fit this criterion is limited, and we have also included a limited number of other quantitative studies that meet relatively high standards of quality. We have also included survey research, where applicable.

In terms of qualitative research, we included longitudinal case studies or shorter but rigorous ethnographic studies. We did not include qualitative studies that involve very limited time spent in schools or with very limited numbers of interviews and/or observations or those that were journalistic in nature. We did not include purely theoretical or opinion pieces, but included thoroughly researched historical studies.

Finally, some of the scholarship that addresses policy-level issues, particularly regarding federal policy, is primarily descriptive. For example, the creation of the federal Elementary and Secondary Education Act (ESEA), including Titles I and VII, the series of federal special education suits, and their historic funding levels are simply matters of public record.

Given that we are seeking to focus on reform in multilingual or multicultural contexts, we only included research that took place in settings that are racially and/or linguistically diverse. Most urban areas in the United States are racially diverse; thus, we did not find our criteria for racial diversity to be a limiting factor. However, the research on reform in linguistically diverse settings is much more limited. As Goldenberg (1996) pointed out in his review of effective schooling for limited-English-proficient (LEP) students,

The biggest gap seems to be in studies that examine processes, substance, and outcomes of strategies for making schools more effective and successful for LEP students. The paucity of such research is striking, particularly if we consider the vast literature on effective schools and school change that has emerged since the 1970s and the concomitant rise in LEP students in U.S. schools. Even studies with the potential to shed light on issues of successful schooling for LEP students often do not do so. For example, Chasin and Levin (1995) provide a case study of an "Accelerated School" (elementary level) where 13 different languages were spoken, but they do not report students' English-learning status, address concerns that are specific to their educational experiences, nor report changes in any outcomes for these students. Similarly, Wilson and Corcoran (1988) report on secondary schools that are successful with "at risk" – poor and minority – students. Since the schools had sizable Asian and Latino populations, it is almost certain that many of these students were LEP, but again, language backgrounds and English-learning status of students are not addressed. (Goldenberg 1996, p. 1)

We found the same to be true in this review of literature a decade later. Goldenberg (1996) said, "However, findings from the more 'generic' effective schools research are probably applicable to LEP students, even if LEP issues are not specifically highlighted nor directly addressed. Indeed, these findings probably serve as reasonable starting points, although obviously a number of other factors related to language, culture, or immigration experience are also likely to come into play for LEP students" (p. 1). We proceeded with our review in a similar fashion, highlighting the diverse contexts in which the research took place, even if the authors of the studies did not see them as salient to their findings.

We have generally limited our review to research that focuses on *reform*, with the exception of research focused on the school level because we believed there was important research on school effectiveness that needed to be included. Also, the chapter on the role of the reform design team addresses issues of school-level reform. We also tried to find as many studies as possible that deal with at least two levels of the system (e.g., state and district, district and school). Our focus is such because our synthesis team activity focused on identifying linkages between levels; hence, we reviewed research that speaks to these linkages. The linkages are perhaps most explicit in the chapters that address the state, district, and community, where the majority of studies were found.

We hypothesize that examining linkages across policy domains will provide insights that can inform the fields of educational research, policy development, and evaluation. However, in trying to identify the linkages between the domains that make up the policy system, it became readily apparent that there is a dearth of empirical research that has as its primary goal identifying or describing such linkages. This gap in the reform literature reflects a systemic weakness in understanding why reform efforts have not been more successfully sustained.

A linkage is in essence a bridge between at least two policy domains. It creates the connection between two otherwise disconnected points. It is an expression of existing capacity, while also being a potential aspect of capacity building. Linkages can be formal, as in official mandates or policies, or informal, as in telephone communications or e-mails between colleagues. Linkages can also be structural, as with funding that comes from states or the federal government to support schools. They can also be relational, as when district leaders work with friends or professional colleagues in the community as a way to develop partnerships.

Linkages can be ideological. This is especially important when reform stakeholders hold different beliefs or ideologies about the purposes of reform, how reform should look, or how it should be achieved. Linkages can be created, destroyed, or simply not used when implementing reform. Coordination of the movement of human and material resources across the linkage is as important as the linkage between two policy domains. A linkage is only a passageway or pathway between two or more policy domains; it is not necessarily reflective of how it is (or is not) used, nor is it reflective of the quality of the resources or communications that cross it.

Our volume begins with a conceptual framework. We then proceed to a review of research on reform by level (e.g., school, district, community, state, design team, federal). In each case, we use the particular level as a lens through which to review linkages with other levels and to identify key areas of capacity building to support reform implementation. In all cases, the effect on the school level is highlighted because this is the arena of central interest. We then discuss the methodological issues in the study of systemic integration for effective reform and close with a review of key points, implications, and directions for future research.

## CONCEPTUAL FRAMEWORK

This review presumes that educational reform is a co-constructed process (Datnow, Hubbard, and Mehan 2002). Clearly, educational reform involves formal structures. We propose that it also involves both formal and informal linkages among those structures. Yet, reform involves a dynamic relationship, not just among structures but also among cultures and people's actions in many interlocking settings. In the following paragraphs, we first will present a model of formal structure and then a discussion of the more complex sense of the co-constructive processes of reform adaptation and implementation.

### FORMAL STRUCTURES LINKING LEVELS OF EDUCATION

We begin with a static model of the systemic-school-teacher space. The model does not explain change or reform but provides a series of reference points for each of the levels of review (e.g., federal, school, classroom) that follow. The model also demonstrates the complexity of the task of reform, underscoring the importance of a human organizational/creative role in creating and sustaining any change from stasis.

The U.S. education system is nothing if not colorfully complex. The federal Department of Education is intended to support the education of young people. These include, but are certainly not limited to, Title I (known as "No Child Left Behind"), migrant and bilingual education, special education legislation and court rulings, Perkins-III funding to support career and technical education (formerly known as vocational education), and Head Start. The latter two programs illustrate that complexity: Head Start is funded and administered through the U.S. Department of Health and Human Services, while career and technical education are funded through the Department of Education. A third example of the complexity of federal involvement in the education system is special education. Federal courts have ruled on several special education issues, in effect making special education a very substantial source of required action for local educators.

Fifty state governments as well as the educational governing bodies of the District of Columbia, the schools of the U.S. military, and the schools in various U.S. protectorates all have separate governance organizations. For simplicity's sake, we will discuss these as "state government," while noting that other structures exist within the United States. The term "state department of education" has a range of meanings. For example, in terms of geographic size and number of students, Rhode Island could fit inside Dade County, Florida; yet, the latter is one school district. There are fewer students in all of Wyoming than in the Denver school system, and fewer students in all of Colorado, Wyoming, Idaho, and Montana combined than in the Los Angeles Unified School District. Hawaii operates all of its schools within a single, unified school district spread across several islands. Montana, like Hawaii, has fewer than 1 million residents, but more than 700 school districts.

Local school districts (or local education authorities, LEAs) are even more diverse than state education agencies (or SEAs). There are more than fifteen thousand LEAs in the United States. Some are reputed to have more school board members than employees and serve under 100 students, while New York City's school system serves over 1 million students. Within the United States, approximately twenty-five LEAs each serve more than one hundred thousand students. Some districts serve only elementary schools, others only high schools, and a few serve pre-K through community college populations. Many districts serve entire counties, while others serve carefully gerrymandered, very small communities. There are more than ninety thousand public schools in the United States. They range from one-room, K–12 facilities to campuses serving several thousand students in only two to four grades.

The most cursory examination of Figure 1 makes clear that while each of over a half-dozen sources of influence on students' education affect their achievement, no single source can lay rational claim to

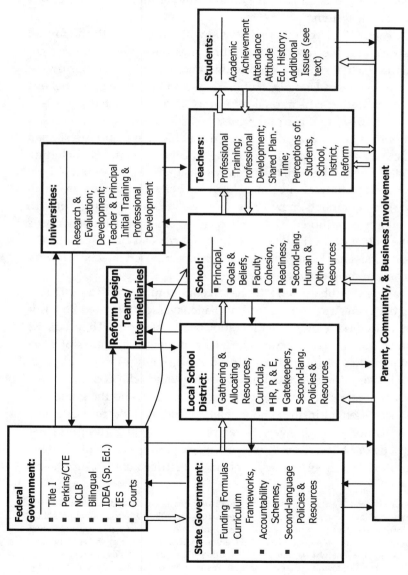

FIGURE 1. A Static Representation of the Relationships of Educational Organization Types and Their Potential Influences on Students

7

being "the major" or "controlling" influence.[1] Rather, as will be discussed below, virtually any educational change process that is likely to be long-lived is, in part, negotiated among multiple levels of our educational system.

At each "level" of this review, we will return to both the formal structure and the research indicating that reform stakeholders co-construct actual reforms, both within and among levels. Borrowing from the work of Datnow, Hubbard, and Mehan (2002), we believe that formulating educational reform as a co-constructed process is helpful in making sense of the complex, and often messy, process of school change. Educators' actions in schools shape and are shaped by actions simultaneously occurring in diverse contexts, including the classroom, school, district, reform design team, state, and federal levels. Interactions at one policy level can generate "outcomes," such as policy statements, new rules, or new procedures, which in turn potentially condition the interactions of other actors in other contexts in the policy chain (Hall and McGinty 1997). This book looks at the possibilities enabled by and the constraints imposed on school reform by conditions in these various settings.

Datnow, Hubbard, and Mehan (2002) emphasized the relationship between structure, culture, and agency and illustrated how this dynamic works in the implementation of school reform. They took the premise that social structures are the contingent outcomes of practical activities of individuals. Real people – confronting real problems in classrooms, school board meetings, and reform design labs – interact together and produce the texts, the rules, and the guidelines that are essential in the school change process. Reform implementation is not an exclusively linear process by which design teams, districts, or states "insert" reforms or policies into schools. Rather, educators in schools, policy makers in districts, and design teams

---

[1] Before examining the major components in Figure 1, we should be clear that this review is not intended to be definitive regarding each plausible component of school reform in the context of multicultural and multilingual education. There were seven "synthesis team" reviews within the Center for Research on Education, Diversity, & Excellence (see www.crede.org). The other six focus primarily on relationships between students and either curriculum, instruction, or family/community. Therefore, none of those areas will be examined in this review. Rather, we examine the institutional and organizational effects on students and teachers, and how people working within those organizations create, or fail to create, meaningful reforms.

co-construct reform adoption, implementation, and sustainability. Whether reforms "succeed" is a joint accomplishment of actors at various levels, operating within their own particular constraints.

The theoretical framework guiding the work of Datnow, Hubbard, and Mehan (2002) was somewhat similar to Fullan's (1999) use of complexity theory as a vehicle for understanding school change, as well as Helsby's (1999) use of structure, culture, and agency as a vehicle for addressing how reforms change teachers' work. Both Fullan and Helsby argued that change unfolds in unpredictable and nonlinear ways through the interaction of individuals in different settings under conditions of uncertainty, diversity, and instability.

In addition to finding a defense for these tenets of change, Datnow, Hubbard, and Mehan (2002) paid attention to the role of power and perspective in shaping reform implementation. They acknowledged that educators in schools must sometimes respond to realities that are created among powerful people and organizations – some who may have accrued power due to their institutional, race, class, or gender position (Erickson and Shultz 1982; Mehan, Hertweck, and Meihls 1986). They also acknowledged that the meaning of reform varies according to a person's or organization's perspective (Bakhtin 1981; Garfinkel 1967).

Contexts are inevitably connected to other contexts (Sarason 1997) *throughout* the social system. By necessity, in this review and in most studies of reform, the interaction among social actors in one context is foregrounded, and by necessity, the other contexts are backgrounded. In the sections that follow, we foreground particular levels of the system – school, district, community, state, federal, and design team – while backgrounding the linkages at other levels.

## ORGANIZATION OF THIS VOLUME

This volume is organized into nine chapters. Chapter 2, which was written primarily by Charles Teddlie, foregrounds the school level and identifies what we mean by effective school practices for racially and linguistically diverse students. Chapter 3, authored primarily by Sue Lasky, focuses on the district as a policy domain and explores linkages across the policy system from a district perspective. Chapter 4, also written primarily by Lasky, examines the community context and community linkages that can affect school reform processes. Chapter 5, also written primarily by Lasky, foregrounds the state as a policy domain and explores linkages across the policy system through a state lens. Chapter 6, written primarily by Amanda Datnow, high-lights comprehensive school reform designs as key linkages between the federal government and schools. Chapter 7, written primarily by Sam Stringfield, foregrounds the role of the federal government in directing and supporting school reform and discusses linkages through the federal lens. Chapter 8, authored primarily by Charles Teddlie, focuses on methodological issues in the study of systemic integration for effective school reform. Chapter 9 provides a final discussion and identifies areas for future research.

2

# School Effectiveness and Improvement

This chapter presents research specifically related to how factors at the school level affect education in schools serving racially and linguistically diverse students. Although there has been little research devoted exclusively to this topic, we review three bodies of research that speak to this issue in a variety of ways: (1) generic school effectiveness research (SER); (2) contextually sensitive school effectiveness research; and (3) school and classroom research conducted with an equity orientation.

Figure 2 shows the school at the center of many important linkages in our framework.

We propose that practices associated with the creation of equity in schooling are likely to be closely related to those factors that produce good learning environments for racially and linguistically diverse students. There have been more effective schools research studies conducted in low socioeconomic status (SES) and urban settings than in environments serving culturally and linguistically diverse students, although there is obviously an overlap between the sets of research.[1] Therefore, findings from research conducted in low-SES

---

[1] The similarity between the two groups of students (low-SES, urban students; linguistically and culturally diverse students) is twofold: (1) there is an obvious overlap in that African American students are part of the culturally diverse student group in the United States, and much of the SER conducted in low-SES urban environments has been in schools with a high percentage of African American students, and (2) many linguistically and culturally diverse students come from homes that would be classified as disadvantaged or low-SES.

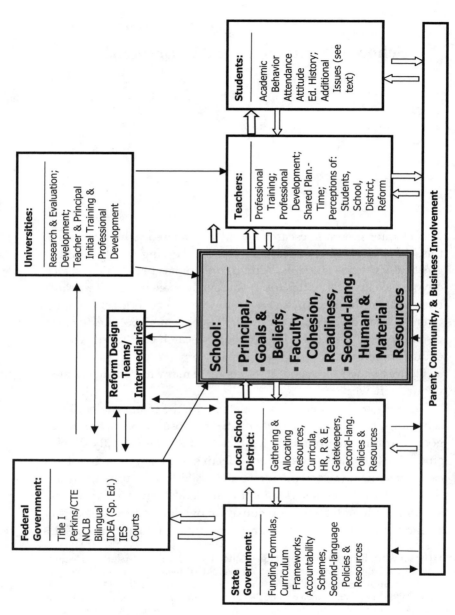

FIGURE 2. School Involvement and Connections to Educational Reform

12

and urban schools are applied (where appropriate) to the education of culturally and linguistically diverse students because different types of disadvantaged students often face similar educational challenges. That said, the challenges that English language learners (ELLs) face are obviously unique.

## THE PROCESSES OF EFFECTIVE SCHOOLING

Much of the evidence about effective schooling has been summarized in lists of correlates (e.g., Edmonds 1979), characteristics (e.g., Levine and Lezotte 1990), or processes (e.g., Reynolds and Teddlie 2000). Although the research that initially produced these lists was severely criticized for methodological deficiencies (e.g., Ralph and Fennessey 1983; Rowan 1984; Rowan, Bossert, and Dwyer 1983), the replicability of the results, on the basis of evidence from numerous studies conducted over the past twenty years, has muted most of that criticism.

Cawelti (2003, p. 18) declared Edmonds' (1979) research to be one of the eleven studies that has had "the greatest impact on education" over the past fifty years, to a large degree because the initial results have often been replicated:

Edmonds showed that high achievement correlated very strongly with strong administration, high expectations for student achievement, an orderly atmosphere conducive to learning, an emphasis on basic skills acquisition, and frequent monitoring of student progress. Although some scholars scoffed at this research's lack of rigor, several investigators replicated the research by using these findings, and the study influenced thousands of educators working in schools in which students from low-income families tended to achieve less well than others. (p. 19)

The processes of effective schools[2] presented in this section have been reported from a wide variety of settings (e.g., in schools serving

---

[2] The effective schools literature is based to a large degree on evidence from case studies (e.g., Brookover and Lezotte 1979; Edmonds 1979; Lezotte and Bancroft 1985; Taylor 1990; Venezky and Winfield 1979; Weber 1971). In addition to these case studies, several large-scale, longitudinal studies (using scientifically defensible sampling and analysis strategies) have confirmed the importance of the characteristics of effective schooling (e.g., Brookover et al. 1979; Mortimore et al. 1988; Reynolds et al. 2002; Rutter et al. 1979; Teddlie and Stringfield 1993).

low- and middle-SES students; in rural, suburban, and urban community types; in countries as diverse as the United States, the United Kingdom, and the Netherlands), but we report primarily on U.S. findings. These processes represent the "ground zero" of effective schooling for all students. They can serve as a springboard on which to study systematically what constitutes sound schooling for racially and linguistically diverse students.

The specific list of the "processes of effective schooling" contained in this chapter was taken from the *International Handbook of School Effectiveness Research* (Reynolds and Teddlie 2000, p. 144). There are nine effective schools processes listed below, together with subcomponents that further delineate each process. These subcomponents may or may not appear in the results from any given study, but all of the characteristics have been found with enough frequency to be included in this summary of the effective schools research. Where possible, we have provided some detail on the specific subcomponents associated with each of the effective schools processes, but a complete discussion of each of them is beyond the scope of this review, which focuses on those factors most related to the education of culturally and linguistically diverse students.

In describing these generic processes, which are relevant to the effective schooling of all students, it is important to remember that the original five correlates were developed from research that concentrated primarily on one specific school context: elementary schools serving low-SES students in urban areas. This early effective school research had an advocacy tone to it and was concerned with equity issues.[3] The original five correlates were "broadened out" and made applicable to a wider variety of school settings, as more effective schools research accumulated from an expanding literature during the 1980–2000 period. The addition of the four new effective schools processes was also made possible through the incorporation of information from allied fields (e.g., teacher effectiveness research) into SER.

---

[3] The importance of the equity ideal to early effective schools research has been detailed in Teddlie and Stringfield (1993), pp. 3–5 and Reynolds et al. (2000), pp. 10–11.

Research focused on low-SES, urban schools (which generated the original five correlate model) is more relevant to the specific education of culturally and linguistically diverse students than the generic SER. Nevertheless, both equity-driven SER and the more recent generic SER are related to the education of culturally and linguistically diverse students, and we thus discuss results from both throughout this review.

### (1) The Processes of Effective Leadership

Processes of effective leadership are one of the most ubiquitous findings across SER literature. The five subcomponents associated with the processes of effective leadership are: (a) being firm and purposeful, (b) involving others in the process, (c) exhibiting instructional leadership, (d) frequent, personal monitoring, and (e) selecting and replacing staff. Some of these subcomponents appear to be more relevant in schools with students from disadvantaged backgrounds. The principal being "firm and purposeful" has been frequently cited as a requirement of effective leadership in schools serving the disadvantaged (e.g., Hallinger and Murphy 1986; Mortimore et al. 1988; Rutter et al. 1979; Sammons, Hillman, and Mortimore 1995; Teddlie and Stringfield 1993). Effective principals in schools serving disadvantaged students develop a limited number of well-defined goals and communicate them effectively to the various school constituencies, instead of pursuing a large number of diverse goals simultaneously (e.g., Teddlie 2003; Teddlie and Meza 1999). Personal monitoring has emerged as an important factor in many studies, especially in schools serving disadvantaged students (e.g., Armor et al. 1976; Austin and Holowenzak 1985; Brookover et al. 1979; Mortimore et al. 1988; Teddlie, Kirby, and Stringfield 1989). Deal and Peterson (1990) conclude that this is a major technique through which principals can shape school culture. Similarly, the ability to select and replace staff is very important in schools serving disadvantaged students because it is typically difficult to recruit competent faculty members, and staff turnover is high (e.g., Austin and Holowenzak 1985; Reynolds et al. 2002). The process of effective leadership has been expanded beyond the principal in recent school reform research to include leadership teams composed of teachers (e.g., Chrispeels, Castillo, and Brown 2000; Chrispeels and Martin 2002).

### (2) *Developing and Maintaining a Pervasive Focus on Learning*
Schools that focus on student learning have consistently been reported to be more effective in producing learning outcomes than those that do not. The two subcomponents associated with a "pervasive focus on learning" are (a) focusing on academics and (b) maximizing school learning time. Marzano (2003) has given this effective schools process the broader label of a "guaranteed and viable curriculum." In schools serving the disadvantaged, this guaranteed and viable curriculum typically involves a commitment to the mastery of central learning skills. Maximizing learning time is especially important for schools serving low-SES students because they "require much instructional support and climate considerations frequently distract from efficiency" (Levine and Lezotte 1990, p. 14).

### (3) *Producing a Positive School Culture*
A positive school culture is frequently identified as a feature of effective schools. The three subcomponents associated with a positive school culture are (a) creating a shared vision, (b) creating an orderly environment, and (c) emphasizing positive reinforcement. There is evidence that the creation of an orderly environment is especially important in schools that serve low-SES students and in urban environments (e.g., Edmonds 1979; Lezotte 1989; Reynolds et al. 2002; Reynolds and Teddlie 2000; Taylor 1990; Teddlie and Stringfield 1993). Order within the school is important because without social control at the school level it would be very difficult for staff to attain high levels of student attention and engagement within classrooms. Similarly, the use of positive reinforcement is especially important in schools serving the disadvantaged. Early SER (e.g., Mortimore et al. 1988; Reynolds 1976; Reynolds and Murgatroyd 1977; Rutter et al. 1979) has indicated that hostile pupil cultures are established in schools serving disadvantaged students when staffs at those schools use harsh punishment and overly strict control. The appropriate use of positive reinforcement often involves the use of visible external academic reward structures, such as posted honor rolls and banners proclaiming schoolwide scholastic goals (e.g., Hallinger and Murphy, 1986; Reynolds et al. 2002; Teddlie and Stringfield 1993).

### (4) Creating High (and Appropriate) Expectations for All

Holding high expectations for students has been one of the most consistent findings in SER, together with the communication of such expectations so that students and faculty members know them (e.g., Brookover et al. 1979; Edmonds 1979, 1981; Reynolds et al. 2002; Stringfield and Teddlie 1991; Teddlie and Stringfield 1993; Venezky and Winfield 1979; Weber 1971). Teachers who truly believe that schools can outweigh the effects of coming from disadvantaged family backgrounds must communicate these high expectations to students through verbal and behavioral reinforcement.

### (5) Monitoring Progress at All Levels

The monitoring of student progress is an effective schools process emphasized in most SER, including all of the major reviews listed throughout this chapter (e.g., Levine and Lezotte 1990; Dyer, Linn, and Patton 1969; Marco 1974; Teddlie, Lang, and Oescher 1995). Levine and Lezotte (1990) similarly concluded that "identification and assessment of school effectiveness should be in accordance with data disaggregated by student SES and race/ethnicity" (p. 7). They based this conclusion on the concern that aggregated school averages may result in classifying some schools as effective, even though their disadvantaged students may have considerably lower achievement levels. This equity issue is also known as "mean masking" and has been demonstrated in several studies going back to the early days of SER (e.g., Dyer, Linn, and Patton 1969; Marco 1974; Teddlie, Lang, and Oescher 1995). In addition to assessing overall program success for the entire school and for subgroups of students, student-level achievement data can be used to identify and give relevant feedback to those students who need remedial instruction and reteaching (Airasian 1994; Bangert-Downs et al. 1991; Madaus et al. 1979; Marzano 2003; McMillan 2000).

### (6) The Processes of Effective Teaching

Processes of effective teaching are another frequently identified feature of effective schools. As SER expanded during the 1980s and 1990s, it incorporated related research from other allied fields into its list of effective schools correlates. The most obvious, and valuable, inclusion was teacher effectiveness research (TER). The importance of TER to SER has been frequently discussed (e.g., Levine and Lezotte 1990; Reynolds and Teddlie 2000; Sammons et al. 1995; Teddlie 1994), and several authors have called for the merger of the two areas into one called "educational effectiveness" (e.g., Creemers and Reezigt 1996; Creemers and Scheerens 1994; Scheerens and Bosker 1997).

There are numerous reviews of TER (e.g., Brophy 1996; Creemers 1994; Marzano, Pickering, and Pollock 2001; Richardson 2002; Rosenshine 1983), each of which features somewhat different aspects of the literature. By the mid-1980s, a substantial body of literature concerning effective teaching characteristics was fully developed, including quantity and pacing of instruction, opportunity to learn, time allocation, classroom management, active teaching, whole-class versus small-group versus individual instruction, redundancy/sequencing, clarity, proper use of praise, pacing/wait time, and questioning skills. The four subcomponents that are the most relevant to effective schooling are maximizing class time, exhibiting best teaching practices, successful grouping and organization, and adapting practice to the particulars of the classroom (Levine and Lezotte 1990; Reynolds and Teddlie 2000).

### (7) Involving Parents in Productive and Appropriate Ways

School effectiveness research in general indicates that parental involvement is positively related to effective schooling (e.g., Armor et al. 1976; Levine and Lezotte 1990; Slavin 1996). Parents' direct involvement in schoolwork (Epstein 1997) has particularly beneficial effects, while involvement in extracurricular activities has little effect. Several accounts of rapid school improvement show principals increasing parental involvement to generate momentum and change (National Commission on Education 1995). Reynolds and colleagues (2002) reported that differentially effective low-SES schools were distinguishable in terms of parental influence, with parents in more effective low-SES schools being more involved and in positive ways (Teddlie et al. 2002).

### Other Effective Schools Processes

Two final processes often identified in the SER literature, (8) developing staff skills and (9) emphasizing student responsibilities and rights, are important to effective schooling in general, but there has been little research concerning their relevance to schools serving disadvantaged students. Research indicates that effective staff development is (a) practical, (b) an integral part of school activities rather than an "add on," and (c) is school-site based (e.g., Reynolds and Teddlie 2000). Mortimore and colleagues (1988) concluded that staff attending in-service courses indiscriminately and unrelated to the core mission of the school is, in fact, associated with ineffectiveness. "One-off" presentations by outside experts or consultants used as "hired guns" are also likely to have negligible consequences or be counterproductive (Levine and Lezotte 1990).

The process entitled "emphasizing student responsibilities and rights" has also not been researched separately for schools serving disadvantaged students or culturally and linguistically diverse students. There is evidence that giving students greater responsibility for their own work and more control over their learning situation may be associated with positive outcomes (Mortimore et al. 1988). This increased responsibility may be particularly important for low-SES students, who typically score lower on indices of internal locus of control (Cotton 1995; Teddlie and Stringfield 1993).

### STRATEGIES FOR CREATING EFFECTIVE SCHOOLS FOR DISADVANTAGED STUDENTS

This section focuses on the results from a pair of "contextually sensitive" studies (Hallinger and Murphy, 1986; Teddlie and Stringfield 1985, 1993) of effective schooling. While the first part of this chapter described the nine generic effective schools processes separately, the following section describes an overall strategy employed in creating effective schools for students from low-SES backgrounds. Studies indicate that the staffs of effective schools have implemented somewhat different strategies, depending on the SES context of their particular school (e.g., either primarily middle-SES or primarily low-SES), for educating their students. We examine the strategies for creating effective schools for the disadvantaged for their relevance to the education of linguistically and racially diverse students.

#### Conducting Contextually Sensitive SER

Teddlie, Stringfield, and Reynolds (2000) reviewed over 150 contextually sensitive studies in four major areas (SES of students attending schools, community type, grade-level configuration, governance structure of schools). These studies have two basic methodological components: purposively sampling subgroups of schools from the general population, rather than selecting a representative sample of schools and setting up contrasts between different levels of the "context" variable (e.g., contrasting rural with suburban with urban schools).

Context variables[4] have been studied extensively throughout the social sciences (e.g., Fiedler 1967, 1973; McLaughlin 1990; McLaughlin and Talbert 1993). For example, McLaughlin and Talbert (1993) have described the types of contexts that are required for effective teaching to occur. McLaughlin (1990) urged researchers to focus first on the local context in which an educational innovation is to be implemented and second on the innovation itself (or the policy related to it). Hargreaves and Hopkins (1991) discussed the adaptive approach to change, which is concerned with developing the capacity for change within the specific school context, rather than a particular change model.

Levine and Lezotte (1990) and Scheerens (1992) found that there have been two comprehensive process-product studies using SES as a context variable conducted in the United States: one by Hallinger and Murphy (1986) in California and one by Teddlie and Stringfield (1985, 1993) and their colleagues in Louisiana. The most interesting aspect of these two studies was that many of their results were congruent, despite significant differences in methodologies and study populations.

The California study involved case studies of eight elementary schools selected from a population of schools that had scored above prediction for three consecutive years on a standardized achievement test. Two of these schools were classified as low-SES, two as lower-middle, two as middle income, and two as upper-middle class (Hallinger and Murphy 1986). The Louisiana School Effectiveness Study included seventy-six schools that were divided along two dimensions: (a) effectiveness status (more effective, typical, less

---

[4] For instance, Fiedler (1967, 1973) conducted psychological research guided by contingency theory as it relates to leadership, concluding that the effectiveness of leadership depends on situational (contingency) factors.

effective); and (b) SES of student body (middle-, low-SES). Hallinger and Murphy were able to identify four distinct levels of SES communities for their study in the relatively affluent state of California, while Teddlie and Stringfield used only two levels because Louisiana has fewer affluent communities.

Results from both studies confirmed that there were some characteristics that distinguished effective from ineffective schools, regardless of the SES of the schools: clear academic mission and focus, orderly environment, high academic engaged time-on-task, and frequent monitoring of student progress. While there were definite similarities between effective middle- and low-SES schools, there were a number of very interesting differences between the two groups of schools. The Teddlie and Stringfield (1985, 1993) research indicated that effective schools had implemented somewhat different strategies, depending on the SES context of the particular school under examination.

These differences in characteristics associated with effectiveness in middle- and low-SES schools revolve around six areas:

### Promotion of Educational Expectations

Middle-SES schools promoted both high present and future educational expectations, while low-SES schools emphasized present educational expectations only. These results indicate that schools serving primarily low-SES students may want to focus particularly on raising expectations for mastery of academic subjects taught in the grade level the students are currently attending.

### Principal Leadership Style

Effective principals in schools serving low-SES students tended to be initiators who wanted to make changes in the schools, while effective principals in schools serving middle-SES students tended to be good *managers*. Follow-up studies (e.g., Evans and Teddlie 1995) replicated these results and explained them using the terminology of Hall and colleagues (1984) concerning principals' change facilitator styles: *initiators* (make it happen), *managers* (help it happen), and *responders* (let it happen). Thus, there is evidence that principals with a certain leadership style (i.e., change initiators) are more likely to be successful, at least initially, at schools serving disadvantaged (low-SES) students.

### The Use of External Reward Structures

Visible external academic rewards were emphasized in low-SES schools, while they were downplayed in middle-SES schools. These results relate to aspects of producing a positive school culture emphasizing positive reinforcement.

### Emphasis in the School Curriculum

Curricular offerings were centered on the basic skills in effective low-SES schools, while effective middle-SES schools had an expanded curriculum. These results relate to developing and maintaining a pervasive focus on learning and may be part of a two-stage process in low-SES schools in which basic skills are emphasized first, followed by an expanded curriculum.

### Parental Contact with the School

Parental involvement was encouraged in middle-SES schools, while principals and staff in many low-SES schools created boundaries to buffer the school from negative community influences. These results relate to involving parents in productive and appropriate ways and may also be part of a two-stage course of action in schools serving low-SES students: (a) in the first stage, negative parental influences (e.g., excessive criticism of teachers or unannounced visits to classrooms) are buffered, and (b) in the second stage, more positive parental interactions (e.g., assistance with homework) are encouraged.

### Experience Level of Teachers

Effective middle-SES schools had more experienced teachers, while effective low-SES schools had less experienced teachers. These results are indirectly related to processes of effective teaching and developing staff skills at the school site. Reynolds and Teddlie (2000) have discussed the "additive effect," which involves (among other consequences) the likelihood of more experienced and effective teachers avoiding schools serving students from lower-SES backgrounds because these schools are more stressful environments in which to work.

The study conducted in California (Hallinger and Murphy 1986) confirmed the differences between schools with students from different SES backgrounds, especially with regard to

1. *Differences in curriculum.* Curriculum in low-SES schools was narrow, focusing on basic skills; curriculum in high-SES schools was broad, concentrating on a variety of academic skills.
2. *Differential student expectations.* The source of expectations in low-SES schools was the school itself and tended to be moderate; in high-SES schools, the sources were the home and school and tended to be very high.
3. *Differences in principal leadership style.* Principal leadership style in effective low-SES schools was high with regard to control of instruction and task orientation; in effective high-SES schools, it was low to moderate with regard to control of instruction and moderate with regard to task orientation.
4. *Differential parental involvement.* Home links were weak in effective low-SES schools and strong in effective high-SES schools.

### Parallel Results from School Improvement Studies

Similar results have been reported in studies describing improvement in schools serving students from low-SES backgrounds, as opposed to those serving middle-SES students. Cuban (1993) succinctly described this difference with regard to results from the Louisiana School Effectiveness Study as follows:

Similarly, they found that the context – where students went to school, their background, and grade level – can have a large effect on which school improvement strategies are successful. Context matters. (p. x)

It appears that schools serving disadvantaged students have to first contend with several negative, contextually determined variables that schools serving more affluent students typically do not. These factors include a lack of basic order and control in the school and classrooms, less experienced teachers, low expectation levels for student performance, ineffective administrative practices, and perceived or real problems with parents and the community.

For example, Chrispeels (1992) studied the creation of cultures for improvement in eight schools undergoing restructuring programs in southern California. One of the major considerations of the Chrispeels case studies concerned the effect of the social context of the school community on the form and the success of the restructuring efforts. In two of the school restructuring programs in low-SES communities, the principals and staffs perceived parents and their lack of concern as one of the major barriers to improvement. At two other more afflu-ent schools, the principals and staff did not have to expend energy overcoming real or perceived parent/community difficulties before addressing the demands of their school reform.

These results are similar to those reported by Lightfoot (1983) in her qualitative "portraits" of urban, suburban, and elite schools. Her portrait of a low-SES urban school in Atlanta describes an improved, tightly administered school but one that did not appear to have a plan for generating instructional excellence. It appeared that significant progress had been made toward the baseline components for school improvement but that the vision for the next phase of the school trans-formation had not materialized. Similarly, Teddlie and Stringfield's (1993) description of a low-SES rural school in Louisiana presented the image of an improving school that was being driven by a new principal intent on correcting disciplinary problems and creating a very public reward structure for academic achievement in his school, yet who did not have a clear idea of the long-term academic goals for the school.

## Phases in the Development of Effective Schools
## for Disadvantaged Students

A common thread runs through the results from these studies of effective and improving low-SES schools. The staffs at these low-SES schools typically have to spend more time creating certain baseline components of school success (e.g., high expectation levels, reward structures for academic success, safe and orderly climates, curricu-lum oriented toward acquisition of basic skills) than do their counter-parts at middle-SES schools, where the community has often already generated these components.

Thus, fundamental elements of school reform programs often differ between schools located in middle- and low-SES communities, with schools in the low-SES communities making considerable efforts to create certain baseline conditions that may already exist in more affluent communities. The effort required to create these baseline components of successful schooling in low-SES communities necessarily detracts (at least in the short term) from other aspects of school improvement, such as the generation of a comprehensive instructional system and of long-term academic goals.

This analysis of the differences between schools in low-SES and middle-SES contexts implies that the creation of effective schools in the former environments often calls for an initial compensatory stage in which communities deficient in educational resources make up this lack at the school, sometimes working in conjunction with the home in what Chrispeels (1992) called "home-school relations." Wimpelberg, Teddlie, and Stringfield (1989) used an economic term, "cumulative resource effects," to account for, among other factors, the effects of student-body SES on the ability of schools to accumulate resources, which then often "pay off" in achievement gain. In low-SES communities, more time and effort has to be expended by the school staff, perhaps in conjunction with concerned parents and community leaders, in generating these cumulative resources than is the case in more affluent communities.

In low-SES schools, then, it appears that change occurs in two stages, sometimes blended together:

1. A compensatory phase, in which certain baseline conditions are met (e.g., safe, orderly environment; high expectations from students, parents, staff members; tangible reward structures for the reinforcement of academic success; the creation of academic "press" at the school).
2. A long-term phase, emphasizing systemic process change at both the school and teacher levels.

In middle-SES schools, where these baseline conditions are often already met, resources can be marshaled with regard to the long-term phase almost from the beginning.

RESEARCH RELATED TO EQUITY ISSUES
AT THE SCHOOL LEVEL

The literature summarized in this part of the volume was taken from a review (Cotton 1995) entitled *Effective Schooling Practices: A Research Synthesis*, which was produced by the Northwest Regional Educational Laboratory (NWREL) in the mid-1990s. This review of over 1,100 sources was the third edition of a research synthesis that was first published in the mid-1980s and included sources from SER, TER, and related fields. The synthesis was divided into two sections, one on school practices and the other on classroom practices.

The NWREL report identifies twenty-five specific practices that promote educational equity at the school level. These fall under four categories of practice: Providing Programs/Support to Help High-Needs Students Achieve Success; Working to Achieve Equity in Learning Opportunities and Outcomes; Providing Multicultural Education Activities as Integral Part of School Life; Providing Challenging Academic Content and English-Language Skills for English-Language Learners.

PROVIDING PROGRAMS/SUPPORT TO HELP HIGH-NEEDS STUDENTS
ACHIEVE SUCCESS

- Focus on prevention of learning problems rather than remediation.
- Emphasize exploration, language development, and play in programs for preschoolers; kindergarten programs feature structured, comprehensive approaches.
- Place high-needs students in comprehensive programs featuring detailed teachers' manuals, curriculum materials, lesson guides, and other support materials.
- Place high-needs students in small classes (twenty-two or fewer students) whenever possible.
- Use proven methods such as continuous progress and cooperative learning to promote these students' learning success.
- Carefully coordinate programs and activities for high-needs students with regular classroom activities.
- Provide high-needs students instruction in test-taking skills and provide them with activities to reduce test-taking anxiety.

- Provide alternative learning arrangements that engage the special interests of older students (e.g., "school-within-a-school," off-campus activities).
- Provide programs for older students that incorporate validated approaches such as peer, cross-age, and volunteer tutoring and computer-assisted instruction.
- Avoid retention in-grade until all other alternatives have been considered.
- Use pull-out programs judiciously, if at all, ensuring that they are intensive, brief, and designed to return students to regular classrooms, not to support them indefinitely.[5]

WORKING TO ACHIEVE EQUITY IN LEARNING OPPORTUNITIES AND OUTCOMES

- Make equitable distribution of achievement and other student outcomes a clearly stated and vigorously pursued school goal.
- Disaggregate achievement and behavioral data (by race, gender, SES level, etc.) to achieve clear understanding of how students of different groups are performing.
- Gather information on ways to meet the needs of underserved groups.
- Implement practices identified as promoting the achievement of high-needs groups.[6]

PROVIDING MULTICULTURAL EDUCATION ACTIVITIES AS INTEGRAL PART OF SCHOOL LIFE

- Integrate multicultural activities fully into the school curriculum, rather than restricting them to one-shot sessions.

[5] References in the Cotton (1995) review included Brophy (1982); Cuban (1989); Druian and Butler (1987); Griswold, Cotton, and Hansen (1986); Knapp, Turnbull, and Shields (1990); Levine, Levine, and Eubanks (1987); Madden et al. (1993); Nye et al. (1992); Robinson (1990); Slavin (1987, 1994); Slavin and Madden (1989); Slavin, Karweit, and Madden (1989); Slavin, Karweit, and Wasik (1994); Stein, Leinhardt, and Bickel (1989).
[6] References in the Cotton (1995) review included Baker (1992); Dreeben (1987); Lee and Smith (1993); Moore (1988); Murphy and Hallinger (1989); Rumberger and Douglas (1992).

- Involve all students in multicultural activities, not just those students belonging to minority cultural groups.
- Make multicultural activities a norm from the beginning of children's school experience.
- Communicate respect for cultural plurality by recognizing and responding to culturally based differences in learning style.[7]

PROVIDING CHALLENGING ACADEMIC CONTENT AND ENGLISH-LANGUAGE SKILLS FOR ENGLISH-LANGUAGE LEARNERS

- Offer language minority students a strong academic core program, as provided for other students.
- Conduct assessment of English- and native-language proficiency as students enroll in the school and periodically thereafter.
- Provide ELL students intensive English-as-a-second language instruction.
- Provide ELL students with instruction in their native languages for their core classes whenever possible.
- Provide ELL students a combination of instruction in their native languages and instruction in English.
- Group students heterogeneously by ability and language so that they can learn from one another.[8]

These practices are presented here to complement the generic and context-specific effective schools processes presented in the previous parts of the chapter and because they are relevant to the overall goal of this volume, which is to summarize factors that are involved in the creation of positive learning environments for racially and linguistically diverse students. These findings are particularly relevant because they address activities related to multicultural education and to language minority students, respectively. It is beyond the scope of this review to discuss all of the twenty-five practices.

---

[7] References in the Cotton (1995) review included Byrnes and Kiger (1987); Campbell and Farrell (1985); Darder and Upshur (1992); Gimmestad and DeChiara (1982); Grant, Sleeter, and Anderson (1986); Levine and Lezotte (1990); Merrick (1988); Pate (1981, 1988); Pine and Hilliard (1990); Rich (1987); Swisher (1990); Valverde (1988).

[8] References in the Cotton (1995) review included Ascher (1985); Collier (1992); Cummins (1986); Darder and Upshur (1992); Fillmore and Valadez (1986); Garcia (1988); Lucas, Henz, and Donato (1990); Reyes (1992); Saldate, Mishra, and Medina (1985); Tikunoff (1985).

Instead, we focus on how these specific equity practices relate to, and complement, the more generic processes discussed in the previous sections.

Practices that help high-needs students achieve success are certainly relevant to racially and linguistically diverse students because many of these students are at risk of educational failure. Two very important practices are (1) focusing on the prevention of learning problems, rather than their remediation and (2) avoiding retention in-grade until all other alternatives have been considered. In recent years, high-stakes accountability systems in several states have led to higher remediation and retention rates, thereby increasing the current relevance of these equity-related school practices.

### RESULTS FROM RESEARCH STUDYING THE SCHOOL AND CLASSROOM LEVELS SIMULTANEOUSLY

Hopkins (2002) recently stated the importance of the school and classroom levels to the school change process:

In the early phases of a school improvement effort, the process of initiation, implementation, and institutionalization will be going on at least two levels. The first is the classroom level: putting into practice changes in curriculum focus and teaching strategy. The second is the school level, where the cycle of initiation, implementation, and institutionalization is concerned with capacity building: the process of learning how to change, in particular, the way in which in-service activities, planning, and inquiry are organized to support the school improvement initiative. (pp. 277–278)

While the link between school and classroom processes is obviously important, the teacher and school effectiveness research areas emerged separately during the 1960s, 1970s, and into the 1980s. For example, reviews of the two areas written in the mid-1980s (Brophy and Good 1986; Good and Brophy 1986) revealed only a 3 percent overlap between their respective reference lists.

There is recognition now among researchers working in several allied fields (e.g., effectiveness research, restructuring literature, school change literature) that the simultaneous study of classroom and school processes, and their interactions, is essential (e.g., Bickel 1998; Fullan 1993; Good and Brophy 1986; Teddlie and Reynolds

2000). This school-classroom link is especially important to the education of disadvantaged students because the links between these levels in the schools they attend are often weak or inconsistent.

Good and Brophy (1986) summarized the research on the school-classroom link in the mid-1980s as follows:

> To date not a single naturalistic study of effective schools provides basic data (means and standard deviations for each classroom) to demonstrate that the behavior of individual teachers in one school differs from the behavior of teachers in other schools. (p. 586)

Fortunately, this statement is no longer true because numerous studies have now explored the school-classroom link both qualitatively and quantitatively. Researchers conducting sophisticated school effectiveness research began exploring classroom processes over twenty years ago due to dissatisfaction with the explanatory power of extant economic and sociological models (e.g., Brookover et al. 1979; Mortimore et al. 1988; Rutter et al. 1979; Stringfield, Teddlie, and Suarez 1985). These researchers used informal observations and survey proxies for teacher effectiveness variables in their studies, and they were rewarded by being able to describe and explain aspects of the schooling process that had not been previously examined in school effectiveness research.

Starting in the mid-1980s, researchers began explicitly including classroom observations (and consequently TER variables) in their SER (e.g., Crone and Teddlie 1995; Reynolds et al. 2002; Teddlie and Stringfield 1993; Virgilio, Teddlie, and Oescher 1991). These studies of TER variables within the context of SER revealed consistent mean and standard deviation differences in classroom teaching between schools that were differentially effective. For example, results from Teddlie, Kirby, and Stringfield (1989) indicated that teachers in effective schools were more successful in keeping students on task, spent more time presenting new material, provided more independent practice, demonstrated higher expectations for students, provided more positive reinforcement, and so forth, than did their peers in matched ineffective schools.

In addition to these mean differences in teaching behaviors between differentially effective schools, interesting distinctions in patterns of variation were also found: the standard deviations reported for teaching behavior were smaller in more effective schools than they were in less effective ones. This result indicates that there are processes occurring at more effective schools (e.g., informed selection of new teachers, effective socialization processes) that result in more homogeneous, or consistent, behavior among teachers in which the "trailing edge" of teaching is somehow eliminated.

While reviewing the results from this research, Bickel (1998) concluded that "what is needed is more careful research on how school- and classroom-level variables interact to influence effectiveness" (p. 966). At least five areas of this school-classroom level linkage require more research:

- The method and selection of teachers.
- The type of classroom monitoring feedback.
- The type of support for individual teacher improvement provided by the administration.
- Instructional leadership provided by the administration, including allocating and protecting academic time.
- Instructional leadership to promote a positive academic climate at the school level, which translates to higher expectations and standards at the classroom level. (Teddlie and Stringfield 1993, pp. 200–201)

Research into each of these five areas may yield results of particular importance in schools that serve culturally and linguistically diverse students. For instance, staff development activities at schools serving a diverse student body might productively focus on multicultural activities, as described in the next part of this chapter.

## RESEARCH RELATED TO EQUITY ISSUES AT THE CLASSROOM LEVEL

Dalton (1998) and Tharp and colleagues (2000) reported five pedagogical standards[9] that were taken from research conducted with students at risk of educational failure due to various contextual factors (e.g., cultural, language, racial, geographic, economic). Development

[9] These standards are discussed in detail at the CREDE Web site: http://www.crede. org/standards/standards.html.

of these standards is grounded in over twenty years of empirical school-based intervention research. These standards are as follows:

- Teachers and students producing together: facilitating learning through joint productive activity among teachers and students.
- Developing language and literacy across the curriculum: developing competence in the language and literacy of instruction across the curriculum.
- Making meaning: contextualizing teaching and curriculum in the experiences and skills of students' homes and communities.
- Teaching complex thinking – challenging students toward cognitive complexity.
- Teaching through conversation – engaging students through dialogue, especially instructional conversation.

As Chrispeels (2002b) noted, these standards are directly related to staff development, especially in schools that serve diverse student bodies. For instance, staff development activities related to "making meaning" might involve intensive training regarding the cultural characteristics of the diverse communities from which the students come.

The literature summarized in this section was taken from *Effective Schooling Practices: A Research Synthesis*, produced by NWREL in 1995. The literature in this section focuses on one part of the NWREL synthesis: classroom characteristics/practices that promote educational equity. These specific practices are presented here to complement the generic effective teaching behaviors previously described.

PROVIDING HIGH-NEEDS STUDENTS THE EXTRA TIME/INSTRUCTION THEY NEED TO SUCCEED

- Use approaches such as tutoring, continuous progress, and cooperative learning with young children to reduce the incidence of later academic difficulties.
- Monitor student learning carefully to maintain awareness of students having frequent academic difficulty.
- Communicate high learning and behavioral expectations to high-needs students and hold them accountable for meeting classroom standards.

- Provide high-needs students with instruction in study skills and in the kinds of learning strategies used by successful students.
- Give high-needs students additional learning time for priority objectives whenever possible; students should spend this time in interactive learning activities.[10]

SUPPORTING THE SOCIAL AND ACADEMIC RESILIENCY OF HIGH-NEEDS STUDENTS

- Communicate warmth and encouragement to high-needs students, comparing their learning with the students' own past performance rather than making comparisons with other students.
- Work together to ensure that each high-needs student has an ongoing supportive relationship with at least one school staff member.
- Create opportunities for these students to develop supportive peer relationships and serve as peer resources to one another.
- Teach problem-solving skills and provide opportunities for students to practice real-life application of these skills.
- Help each student to develop an internal locus of control by calling attention to the relationship between individual effort and results.
- Encourage family members and other key persons in the lives of high-needs students to continually express high expectations for their behavior and school achievement.[11]

PROMOTING RESPECT AMONG STUDENTS OF DIFFERENT SES/CULTURAL BACKGROUNDS

- Work to ensure equity in learning opportunity and achievement for all SES and cultural groups.
- Provide multicultural education activities as an integral part of classroom learning.

[10] References in the Cotton (1995) review included Anderson (1983); Bamburg (1994); Brophy (1986, 1988); Brown and Saks (1986); Druian and Butler (1987); Gettinger (1984, 1989); Good (1987); Griswold, Cotton, and Hansen (1986); Lumpkins, Parker, and Hall (1991); Madden et al. (1993); Sammons, Hillman, and Mortimore (1995); Slavin (1987, 1988); Slavin, Karweit, and Madden (1989); Slavin, Karweit, and Wasik (1994); Slavin and Madden (1989); Stein, Leinhardt, and Bickel (1989); Waxman et al. (1985).
[11] References in the Cotton (1995) review included Benard (1993); Glaser (1992); Grossman et al. (1992); Luthar (1991); Midgley, Feldlaufer, and Eccles (1988).

- Make use of culturally heterogeneous cooperative learning structures in which there is individual accountability and group recognition.
- Provide learning activities designed to reduce prejudice and increase empathy among cultures, races, genders, SES levels, and other groups.
- Teach critical thinking skills in relation to intercultural issues.
- Contribute to the development of students' self-esteem by treating them with warmth and respect and offering them opportunities for academic success.
- Avoid using practices known to be detrimental to intercultural relations (e.g., long-term ability grouping).[12]

Previous sections have contained reviews of three bodies of literature as they relate to the role of the school in the education of racially and linguistically diverse students. While there has been little research devoted exclusively to this topic, many studies have yielded relevant results. The research included in this chapter spans over twenty years of school effectiveness and school improvement research and clearly shows that there are specific processes and practices that are present in effective schools. These findings beg the question of why these practices have not become more pervasive throughout the educational system. They also clearly indicate that students who attend schools where these practices are not in place will experience compromised learning.

---

[12] References in the Cotton (1995) review included Byrnes (1988); Davis (1985); DeVries, Edwards, and Slavin (1978); Gabelko (1988); Gallo (1989); Gimmestad and DeChiara (1982); McGregor (1993); Moore (1988); Oakes (1985); Pate (1981, 1988); Rogers, Miller, and Hennigan (1981); Slavin (1985, 1987, 1988, 1990); Walberg and Genova (1983); Warring et al. (1985).

# 3

# District-Level Reform Efforts

This chapter focuses on the role of the district in developing, implementing, and supporting urban school reform. Figure 3 orients the district in our conceptual framework:

Along with studies of districts, we have included three current reviews of districts and school boards in educational reform: Anderson (2003); Land (2002); and Mac Iver and Farley (2003). These are among the most current and comprehensive reviews.

Much of the research on district-level reform efforts relies on case study research methods. Few of the studies, however, link district involvement in school reform with student achievement. For instance, one of the largest studies, conducted by Massell and Goertz (2002), examined the capacity-building strategies of twenty-three districts, yet did not link them to student achievement. Most studies describe key policies and deliberate actions taken at the district level that are associated with high levels of student performance. They also tell the story of how the districts moved from lower to higher performing, as measured by student results on standardized assessments or teacher, principal, and district reports of implementation. While there are differences in emphasis and detail across studies of the roles that districts hold in standards-based school reform, there is a notable convergence in findings, such as common strategic principles and policy-linked actions associated with "success" (Anderson 2003). There is thus much to be learned from this body of work, including what linkages exist across policy domains and the

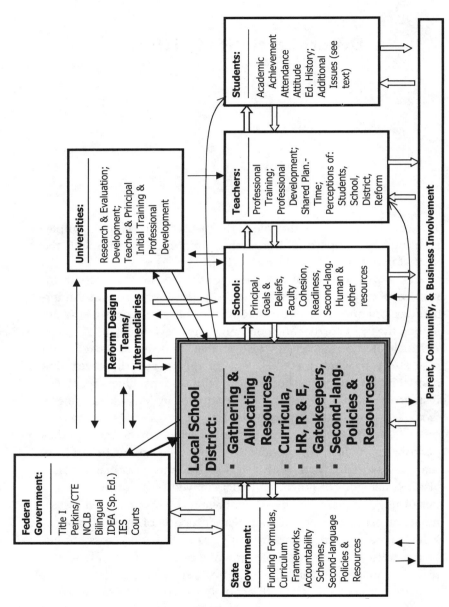

FIGURE 3. District Involvement and Connections to School Reform

**Federal Government:**

Title I
Perkins/CTE
NCLB
Bilingual
IDEA (Sp. Ed.)
IES
Courts

**Universities:**

Research & Evaluation;
Development;
Teacher & Principal
Initial Training &
Professional
Development

**Reform Design Teams/ Intermediaries**

**Local School District:**

- Gathering & Allocating Resources,
- Curricula,
- HR, R & E,
- Gatekeepers,
- Second-lang. Policies & Resources

**School:**

Principal,
Goals &
Beliefs,
Faculty
Cohesion,
Readiness,
Second-lang.
Human &
other
resources

**Teachers:**

Professional
Training;
Professional
Development;
Shared Plan.-
Time;
Perceptions of:
Students,
School,
District,
Reform

**Students:**

Academic
Achievement
Attendance
Attitude
Ed. History;
Additional
Issues (see
text)

**State Government:**

Funding Formulas,
Curriculum
Frameworks,
Accountability
Schemes,
Second-language
Policies &
Resources

**Parent, Community, & Business Involvement**

strategies midlevel leaders have used to develop districtwide capacity for improved teaching and learning. Studies that more directly link district improvement strategies to improved classroom teaching and increased student learning are needed.

## THE ROLE OF THE DISTRICT

While it is clear that the district serves various functions (Togneri and Anderson 2003) and is a key political policy domain (Elmore 1993), the actual power of this midlevel organization to control school affairs and affect reform is contested (Newman et al. 2001). For instance, Comprehensive School Reform resources can bypass the district central office and go directly to schools (Datnow and Kemper 2003). Schools can lead reform efforts themselves (Lusi 1997). Conversely, schools can also have such low capacity to reform fundamental aspects of learning conditions within their walls that district reforms do not get off the ground (Elmore and Burney 1998).

Some research describes the roles that districts play in reform implementation less than positively. Districts are described in these works as a key policy domain where reforms are diluted and where schools' ability to achieve the externally developed design vision and plans are thwarted primarily because of (a) district demands for immediate results; (b) lack of resources dedicated for professional development; (c) lack of incentives for teacher sharing; (d) policies that encourage the rapid turnover of teachers in reform activities; and (e) a lack of slack resources for innovation and improvement (Bodilly 2001, p. 128).

There is mounting evidence that the district can be a pivotal policy domain. Increasing evidence suggests that efforts to improve both individual and large groups of schools are unlikely to be successful for any length of time without district support (Chrispeels 1992; Smylie and Wenzel 2003). Although there is also evidence that districts are not always involved in school reform efforts, or sometimes they lack capacity or will to affect improved student learning outcomes in the schools under their charge, the district is increasingly being recognized as a key player. The roles that districts play are diverse and complex. Some of their functions include (a) mediating state and federal policies and distributing external funding;

(b) generating and implementing policy initiatives; (c) establishing the normative culture and expectations for schools under their jurisdiction; (d) providing material and human resources to schools, including professional development; (e) and pursuing resources for schools in the forms of grants and community partnerships (Bryk et al. 1998; Christman 2001; D'Amico et al. 2001; Elmore and Burney 1997, 1998; Foley 1998, 2001; Hightower 2002a, 2002b; Mac Iver and Farley 2003; Porter and Chester, 2001; Snipes, Doolittle, and Herlihy 2002; Togneri and Anderson 2003). Historically, federal and state policies have focused on schools as the primary domain to be changed. It is only in recent years that educational reformers have begun to pay much attention to the role of districts in school improvement efforts (Marsh 2002).

Recently, the role of the district in instructional improvement has been redefined because of changes in federal, state, and community contexts. There is mounting evidence that the success of districts that have begun to focus on improving student learning depends on more than tight coupling between the district and the school (Spillane and Jennings 1997). It is also more complex than suggesting that the presence or absence of linkages between the district and the school is a key factor in sustained reform because it is possible to have a policy system that is relatively tightly coupled or that is linked closely to other policy domains while still having low capacity to improve student learning (Lasky and Foster 2003).

Research indicates that districts that have begun to improve classroom teaching and student learning are characterized by the following:

1.  Stable leadership across the school board, district office, and school that is focused on one primary purpose – improving student learning. Those districts provide quality resources and skillfully coordinated resource distribution. School leadership is networked across sites.
2.  Systemwide capacity – particularly content and process knowledge, problem-solving skills, and planning ability.
3.  Material and human resources, including sustained and appropriate professional development.

4. A history of trust and cooperation among multiple stakehold-ers. Minimal crisis situations exist. School-level authority is legitimated, and efforts are made to ensure union support.

5. High-quality research and multiple kinds of data used for plan-ning, problem solving, and decision making.

6. A systemwide curriculum tied to state standards with clear expectations (Bodilly 1998; Elmore and Burney 1997, 1998; Hightower 2002a, 2002b; Kirby, Berends, and Naftel 2001; Mac Iver and Farley 2003; Resnick and Glennan 2002; Snipes et al. 2002; Togneri and Anderson 2003).

Before discussing how these districts improved conditions for stu-dent learning, we will first examine preconditions for district reform.

## PRECONDITIONS FOR DISTRICT REFORM

Snipes and colleagues (2002) identified several political and orga-nizational preconditions at the district level that increase the likeli-hood of coordinating and sustaining reform efforts. These were (a) creating a new role for school boards; (b) crafting a shared board and superintendent vision of reform; (c) diagnosing the local educa-tional situation; (d) fleshing out the reform vision and selling it to district stakeholders; (e) improving business operations; and (f) pur-suing new funding to support reform strategies. Each of their case study sites – Sacramento City Unified School District, Houston Inde-pendent School District (HISD), Charlotte-Mecklenburg Schools, and New York City Chancellor's District – took different approaches in putting each of these preconditions in place.

There were two elements to redefining the board role. In each dis-trict, a major shake-up of the school board in which a new board majority, with a focus on improved student learning outcomes, was elected or appointed. Once reform-oriented board members were in place, the boards began to shift their focus and priorities. As their pri-orities became more focused on student achievement, and they could articulate a vision or set of priorities for reform, the boards actively sought a superintendent who shared their vision and values. Boards also held the new superintendents personally responsible for achiev-ing their collectively decided on and instituted goals.

Diagnosing the local educational situation was a core element in board and superintendent problem-solving strategies. It facilitated not only understanding the realities in their districts and communities but also gave focus to their problem solving, goal setting, and planning. Once boards and superintendents had a shared, concrete, vision for reform and a solid understanding of their local situation, they worked to create linkages with local stakeholders. This included establishing visibility in the community, rebuilding trust and support for schools, and building political capacity to see reform efforts through. A key precondition for creating linkages with stakeholders was restructuring districts' infrastructures and establishing new central office and board norms that were focused on serving schools. Each district first took care of the most pressing problems in their schools such as improving physical plants and providing classroom materials as a way to build good faith between schools and the central office.

All of the districts in this study also secured increased funding to pursue their goals and did not pursue funding or start new programs that were inconsistent with their objectives. These linkages took several forms. In all of the case study districts, bond elections were an important source of additional funding. Districts were also proactive in seeking resources from private and public groups. For instance, Sacramento received a $1.5 million grant from the Packard Foundation for teacher coaches and to implement its reading program. Increasing local taxes was a strategy used in Charlotte-Mecklenberg.

These preconditions relied on several kinds of linkages. Electing or appointing reform-oriented school boards meant using both formal and informal relational networks (e.g., in Sacramento, the mayor backed a slate of school board candidates, thus creating a majority voting block aligned with the mayor). Choosing a reform-oriented superintendent also meant relying on political alliances and community networks. In 1995, when the Charlotte-Mecklenburg school board was looking for a new district superintendent, board members went to the community for advice.

Creating a shared vision can also be a process of involving multiple stakeholders. In Houston, the superintendent used a less-than-positive state audit of HISD to establish "Peer Examination, Evaluation, and Redesign" (PEER) committees to bring former district critics and outside experts into core decision-making and planning processes. Therefore, he was able to move controversial initiatives through the district's political system. Along with starting a public media campaign, he was able to significantly change the community's perception of HISD and establish the conditions for further financial and human support from external partners.

The findings from the Snipes and colleagues (2002) study are important because they begin to explicate the multiple dimensions of creating the preconditions necessary within districts to support reform. They also point to a significant gap in the empirical literature. Virtually all research on the role of the district in urban reform begins once reform efforts are under way and does not examine or identify the steps that preceded reform.

## THE ROLE OF SCHOOL BOARDS

Increasing evidence suggests that robust working relationships between school boards, district superintendents, and other reform stakeholders enhance the likelihood of sustained school reform efforts within districts (Land 2002; Snipes et al. 2002; Tognieri and Anderson 2003). For this reason, we include a brief review of board-level research and school reform. We see from the previous discussion some of the ways in which boards create the preconditions for reform to take hold in districts. In this section, we draw from a review of the role of school boards in school reform over the past twenty years by Deborah Land (2002), as well as on a more recent five-district study by Togneri and Anderson (2003).

School boards have seen their traditional roles changing quite significantly since the beginning of standards-based reform in the United States. They have also come under criticism, pressure, and public scrutiny in recent years. There is, however, scant research focused on how school boards can operate most effectively in new governance structures. Likewise, there is virtually no research that can substantiate that characteristics for effective governance are essential for student academic achievement (Land 2002). Land pointed out that districts with quality governance tended to have greater student achievement as measured by dropout rates, the percentage of students going to college, and aptitude tests. Drawing from the work of

Land (2002), Snipes and colleagues (2002), and Togneri and Anderson (2003), we have compiled a list of effective governance practices of school boards:

- Focus on student achievement and policy.
- Effective management of the district by the board without micromanagement.
- Trusting and collaborative relationship between the board and superintendent.
- Evaluation of the superintendent according to mutually agreed upon procedures.
- Effective communication between the board chair and superintendent and among board members.
- Effective board communication with the community.
- Board adoption of a budget that provides needed resources.
- Long-term service of board members and the superintendent.
- Shared leadership.
- Continuous improvement and shared decision making.
- Staff development and other learning opportunities at the district level.
- Understanding conditions that facilitate school improvement and having articulated, clear improvement strategies in place.

School boards played several roles in supporting improved teaching and learning in Aldine Independent School District, Chula Vista Elementary School District, Kent County Public Schools, Minneapolis, and Providence, Rhode Island (Tognieri and Anderson 2003). These boards had a focus on accountability and policy. In short, they were driven by the goal of improving student achievement and disseminated policies that supported instructional reform. Board members strove for consensus and collegiality and took a problem-solving, rather than blaming, stance toward achieving their primary objective. Publicly, they placed a high priority on speaking with one voice. They also held the superintendent or chief administrator of the district accountable for results but did not micromanage day-to-day management decisions (Togneri and Anderson 2003, p. 32). Relational linkages were also a core aspect of these reforms. Good relationships among several stakeholders proved important, including superintendent/board relations, board member relations, interagency collaboration, and linkages to state governmental agencies (Snipes et al. 2002; Togneri and Anderson 2003).

DISTRICT CAPACITY

As midlevel organizations in the policy system, districts can be key mediators of federal or state policies. When district leaders have a strong and articulated theory of change, reform goals are clear; then resources – human and material – can be coordinated throughout the system to support implementation. Districts can also buffer schools from fast-changing or inconsistent state and federal policies, and the demands from multiple and possibly inconsistent accountability systems can be coordinated (Elmore and Burney 1997; Hightower 2002a; Snipes et al. 2002; Stein, Hubbard, and Mehan 2002; Togneri and Anderson 2003).

Districts coordinate a multidirectional flow of communication. They both receive and direct communication and resources to agencies to whom they are accountable and to schools under their supervision. There is a clear interdependence, particularly at the district and school levels, between all individuals and groups involved in the reform process (Lusi 1997; Snipes et al. 2002; Togneri and Anderson 2003).

In analyzing district reform efforts, it is important to make a distinction between change and continuous improvement. Change is basically implementing new policies or programs on top of older ones. It tends to be uncoordinated, piecemeal, or disconnected in understanding and planning. Continuous improvement is the adaptation, extension, and deepening of a district's instructional improvement strategy over time. It requires coordinated planning and a clear direction to guide action. There are several assumptions about district capacity inherent in the notion of continuous improvement. These include (a) a well-worked-out systemwide strategy for influencing classroom instruction; (b) clear district goals against which to judge whether it is improving or not; (c) a district institutional structure for monitoring performance that makes possible adjusting its overall strategy to new information; and (d) deepening knowledge about progress toward its goals (Elmore and Burney 1998). Not all districts have developed these capabilities.

The roles that districts play in school improvement efforts are quite diverse. Some have a higher capacity to design, to direct, and to coordinate improvement strategies, while others have little reform capacity. Developing distributed leadership capabilities throughout the district was a core capacity-building strategy described in several studies (Chrispeels 2002a; Elmore and Burney 1997, 1998; Hightower 2002a; Massell and Goertz 2002; Snipes et al. 2002; Stein et al. 2002; Togneri and Anderson 2003).

## Leadership

In their study of five U.S. districts that had increased student performance, Togneri and Anderson (2003) described how instructional leadership was distributed across key stakeholders in each district, including board members, superintendents and central office staff, union leaders, principals, teacher leaders, state education leaders, universities, and parents. Each group of stakeholders had clear roles that they performed to support reform implementation. For instance, board members designed policies and supported instruction, while superintendents and central office staff viewed instructional reform as a way to improve student achievement. Union leaders worked actively with district leaders to increase instructional supports for teachers. Principals provided instructional leadership to the school while also transmitting and operationalizing the district vision into the school building. Teacher leaders provided additional onsite instructional support to other teachers. State education leaders provided funding for district-level professional development for teacher leaders, principal training, and other resources. Universities began to partner strategically with districts (Togneri and Anderson 2003, p. 35). Other districts focused their efforts more on choosing strong reform leadership at the superintendent level and then developing principal leadership to direct and implement various dimensions of reform efforts (Elmore and Burney 1997, 1998; Hightower 2002b; Massell and Goertz 2002; Snipes et al. 2002).

### Superintendent Leadership

Superintendents that have the capacity to solve problems, set clear goals, generate clear district norms, rally support, develop and sustain trusting relationships and strong political networks, and secure needed resources help to sustain reform (Christman and Rhodes 2002; Elmore and Burney 1997, 1998; Hamann 2003; Hightower 2002a, 2002b; Marsh 2002; Spillane 2000; Watson, Fullan, and Kilcher 2002). One significant decision that superintendents make relates to the unit of change. Recent research indicates reform is more effectively sustained when the whole district is the focus (McLaughlin and Talbert 2002; Supovitz and Weathers 2004; Togneri and Anderson 2003). This requires on the part of the superintendent sophisticated planning and political skills (Elmore and Burney 1997, 1998; Hightower 2002a, 2002b; Resnick and Glennan 2002; Snipes et al. 2002).

Analyses of reform efforts in New York District 2 (Elmore and Burney 1997, 1998), San Diego (Hightower 2002a, 2002b), Aldine Independent School District, Chula Vista Elementary School District, Kent County, Maryland, Public Schools, Minneapolis, and Providence (Togneri and Anderson 2003) highlight how an articulated theory of education and school reform can direct reform planning. In each of these districts, the superintendents first emphasized improving the quality of systemwide teaching. Some chose literacy frameworks rooted in their theories of education, as in New York District 2 (Elmore and Burney 1997, 1998), San Diego (Hightower 2002a, 2002b), and Providence (Togneri and Anderson 2003). Others developed districtwide curricula closely aligned with state standards (Togneri and Anderson 2003). Typically, superintendents developed systematic processes of differential resource allocation so that the lowest-performing schools received material and human resources to build internal capacity to improve teaching. They also attached importance to variation in teaching strategies (Elmore and Burney 1997, 1998; Hightower 2002a, 2002b; Togneri and Anderson 2003).

Superintendents' beliefs about the nature of learners and the purposes of schooling can determine the normative standards a superintendent sets for a district (McLaughlin and Talbert 2002; Snipes et al. 2002; Stein and D'Amico 2002). In New York District 2, district leadership took a hard stance in setting the normative expectation that all students could learn (Elmore and Burney 1997, 1998). In San Diego, they worked to establish the same normative belief, although with somewhat less success (Stein et al. 2002). At the same time, superintendents can also establish norms of lowered expectations for minority student achievement (Snipes et al. 2002; Spillane 1999). In such districts, superintendents often have a higher standard of achievement for middle- to upper-middle-class students and a lower one for those from poor or minority backgrounds. Superintendents' theories of learning apply also when determining the professional development opportunities they provide for teachers, the curriculum they chose or support for teacher learning, and their beliefs about how best to motivate teachers to learn (Spillane 2000).

A superintendent's lack of knowledge and political biases can also affect whether he or she supports reform efforts (Spillane 1999, 2001). For example, during the early years of the Georgia Project, the first bilingual program in the state, the superintendent of Bulloch County, Georgia, had little in his background to prepare him for the impact of the influx of Latino newcomers into county schools (Hamann 2003). He was also unaware that he lacked the skills to lead a demographically changing district. He knew virtually nothing about either Hispanic culture or bilingual education. He did, however, know the importance of creating alliances with politically powerful locals, especially those who could mobilize resources. Although he did not fully understand what he was backing, he supported a local initiative to develop a bilingual program and created an alliance with the bilingual project leaders as a way to generate more resources for the district, which later cost him the backing of more conservative community members (Hamann 2003).

Superintendents' problem-solving capacities are an understudied, yet important, aspect in reform processes. How superintendents set goals, generate funding for their districts (Snipes et al. 2002), develop resource allocation strategies, and establish data-based feedback loops (Elmore and Burney 1997) can have far-reaching consequences for how reforms are enacted. In studying Philadelphia reform efforts, Foley (1998, 2001) identified district leadership's lack of problem-solving capacity in the areas of coordinating restructuring, aligning resource allocation, changing normative practices, and building partnerships as a primary factor that hindered successful reform implementation.

*District Efforts to Improve School Leadership*
Partnerships between district leaders and school principals are a key
linking and capacity-building strategy used in several districts that
were focused on improving student learning (Hightower 2002a; Stein
et al. 2002; Togneri and Anderson 2003). Several districts have focused
both human and material resources to increase principal capacity to
direct, to manage, and to coordinate reform implementation. In these
districts, principals received systematic and extensive professional
development to help them develop an array of skills district leaders believed were central to ensuring that reforms extended into the
classroom (D'Amico et al. 2001; Elmore and Burney 1998; Foley 2001;
Hightower 2002a, 2002b; Togneri and Anderson 2003).

As with superintendents, principals' roles in systemic reform are
demanding and require a diverse array of skills that include (a) managing their schools' external resources; (b) obtaining the human, intellectual, and material resources needed to support their schools' development activities; (c) establishing strong, productive relationships
with external partners and with central administration; (d) providing instructional leadership while making norms and expectations
clear; and (e) protecting their schools from external distractions and
interference (Elmore and Burney 1998; D'Amico et al. 2001; Foley
2001; Hightower 2002a, 2002b; Togneri and Anderson 2003). Principals are also among the first in the school community to feel the
sparks of external pressure and opportunities for change. They are
thus in a unique position to initiate change that is context sensitive
(Wenzel et al. 2001, p. 58). Reform leaders in New York District 2
found that creating opportunities for bilateral negotiation between
district administrators and school principals was a particularly effective way to meet each school's unique set of needs while also creating
a way for officials in the central office to stay more informed about
reform conditions, challenges, and successes in schools (Elmore and
Burney 1997).

When principals actively promote, support, and assume responsibility for reform implementation, a school is more likely to be successful in its efforts (Datnow, Hubbard, and Mehan 2002; Togneri
and Anderson 2003; Elmore and Burney 1997). Yet beyond the essential role the principal plays, reform progress is facilitated by the distribution of leadership among others in the school community. By

expanding leadership, schools are able to bring in additional expertise and energy while broadening agency and responsibility for reform progress (Wenzel et al. 2001, p. 57).

McDonald and Keedy (2002) examined the ways three Kentucky elementary principals created the conditions for shared leadership in their schools and met the Kentucky Education Reform Act policy framework. In all three schools, principals accomplished these by (1) setting the norm that shared leadership was a "core value" of the school culture; (2) using the consolidated plan as a tool for managing partnerships, collective accountability, and shared decision making; and (3) playing the role of "analytical guides" providing appropriate internal and external resources and supporting teachers as leaders (p. 221). Shared leadership in these schools was a core element of continuous improvement, meeting state annual yearly progress targets, and creating shared responsibility for accountability outcomes.

### District Efforts to Foster Teacher Leadership
Developing teacher leadership, along with teacher content and process knowledge, is one of the key capacity-building and linking strategies used by principals in schools that are focused on improving student learning. There is evidence to suggest that teacher leadership in schools can also help facilitate reform implementation. As with professional development for principals, teacher leaders receive professional development designed to prepare them for the demands they will face as site-level agents responsible for reform initiatives to affect classroom teaching (Hightower 2002a; Massell and Goertz 2002; Snyder 2002; Stein, Hubbard, and Mehan 2002). When working to implement districtwide school improvement, teacher leaders can extend instructional support provided to other teachers, serve as bridges between administration and the classroom, and assist principals by overseeing administrative roles related to instruction, such as data analyses and professional development planning (Togneri and Anderson 2003, p. 35). At the school site, they can also be key negotiators in efforts to build school-level capacity, in part by creating linkages between teacher beliefs and capabilities and reform goals (Stein, Hubbard, and Mehan 2002).

On the leadership chain within the district context, teacher leaders are closest to the actual classroom conditions and teacher factors that affect how or whether reforms are implemented. Teacher leaders have the potential to provide the most developmentally appropriate, directly meaningful, and sustainable professional development opportunities for teachers. These more personal relationships can provide valuable opportunities for creating ideological linkages, while also developing schoolwide capacity for increased teaching (Hightower 2002a; Stein, Hubbard, and Mehan 2002).

In sum, evidence suggests that increasing leadership capacity at the board, district, and school levels in a coordinated way seems to enhance the likelihood of improved teaching and student learning. We hope that we have presented the findings on leadership in such a way that the interconnectedness of leadership capacity building throughout a district is readily apparent. In many reform efforts, district and school leaders are being asked to adopt practices, put structures in place, and solve problems they have not faced before. The skills needed to meet these new job demands are not innate, nor are they often taught in professional schools. Studies reviewed in this chapter clearly indicate that more successful districts have developed leadership capacity throughout the system and have provided opportunities for principals and teachers to learn skills to drive improvement efforts down to classroom practice.

## Coordinating, Developing, and Managing Accountability Systems

Standards-based reforms have required districts to take an active role in developing, coordinating, or choosing accountability systems. There is little actual research on how districts build their internal capacity to develop coordinated, fair, and sound accountability systems. There is, however, a growing body of work explaining the features of various district-level accountability systems.

Key features of these accountability systems include (a) measures of student achievement (Finnigan, O'Day, and Wakelyn 2003; Porter and Chester 2001); (b) developing and/or interpreting clear standards (Snipes et al. 2002; Supovitz and Weathers 2004; Togneri and Anderson 2003); (c) support or professional development systems (Elmore and Burney 1997; Stein et al. 2002); (d) systems for using data for planning, problem solving, and decision making

(Elmore and Burney 1998; Snipes et al. 2002; Togneri and Anderson 2003); and (e) systems of rewards and sanctions (Porter and Chester 2001).

Aligning district standards, curriculum, and accountability systems internally and with state standards is a key linkage that can increase collective district capacity because it helps to focus reform activities (Regional Educational Lab Network 2000). Some districts have developed standards and accountability systems that go beyond state systems (Hightower 2002b). Along with creating a buffer between schools and political vicissitudes at the state level, this kind of proactive stance can become another strategy for focusing goals. Rather than vaguely trying to "improve student achievement," districts have specific, measurable long-term goals associated with deadlines and specific intermediate goals for each year of reform (i.e., school-identified targets) (Snipes et al. 2002).

Several districts have developed greater capacity to use and interpret data to guide decision making, to ascertain whether reform efforts are leading to increased student achievement, and to inform adapting reform strategies. In these districts, leadership keeps aware of conditions in their districts. They base decisions on up-to-date information by gathering data, creating feedback and reflection loops. These facilitate well-informed problem solving, decision making, and planning (Elmore and Burney 1997, 1998; Stein et al. 2002; Togneri and Anderson 2003).

A (now former) superintendent in Duval County, Florida, took a unique approach and drew from his past experience as an Air Force tactical fighter wing commander in developing an accountability system called the "Standards Implementation Snapshot System." The system has clear indicators and used multilevel data to inform both district and school decision making. Strategic goals were set annually by the superintendent and leadership team (e.g., high-performance management teams, academic performance, accountability, safe schools, and learning communities). School-level data concerning target implementation were collected annually, entered into a secured Web site, and then aggregated to provide a "snapshot" of districtwide standard implementation. These data were used by district and school leaders to ascertain levels of implementation and to inform subsequent steps in the implementation of state and district standards. These collective and focused efforts of district and school personnel have led to sustained increased test performance, particularly in comparison to other similar Florida counties (Supovitz and Weathers 2004).

## Curriculum and Standards Development

In their review of district involvement in school reform that spans almost two decades, Mac Iver and Farley (2003) identified an almost ubiquitous need for districts to develop decision-making skills about curriculum and instruction that are linked to standards and to develop their capacity to help teachers achieve state standards. In a context of standards-based reforms, schools increasingly need assistance to build their internal capacity to interpret state frameworks and student performance standards and to change their classroom practices in ways that are consistent with state or district expectations for more rigorous instruction. Several districts have taken the lead in this area (D'Amico et al. 2001; Elmore and Burney 1997, 1998; Snipes et al. 2002; Stein, Hubbard, and Mehan 2002; Togneri and Anderson 2003).

The role of districts in adapting curricula to meet more rigorous state standards is virtually an unstudied area. A study conducted by Spillane (1999) is informative because it explored the relationship between LEAs and state government in Michigan mathematics and science reform implementation. One of his key findings was that LEAs' "will to" and "capacity for" reform are interdependent. Almost all of the district personnel in his study were willing to reform classroom mathematics instruction, but lacking a threshold of capacity (in this instance, mathematical knowledge), few of them could imagine reforming instruction in ways that reflected the more substantive changes in content and pedagogy put forth in state standards.

Although some district personnel acknowledged that they did not have a good grasp of the reforms, most were not aware of a gap in their mathematical and scientific knowledge. In fact, most local policy makers, whose understandings of the more substantive reform ideas were erroneous, were convinced that they were revising local policies in ways that were consistent with the standards. This example highlights the importance of linking local policy makers with outside experts so that they can capably develop curricula for the schools under their jurisdictions.

## Allocating Resources for Reform

Districts vary in their existing levels of material capacity and in their abilities to create linkages with outside stakeholders to bring in more material resources. Some district leaders are more effective at doing this. In these instances, district leaders first had a clear vision or set of goals, then they sought resources that would most directly help them achieve their goals (Snipes et al. 2002; Togneri and Anderson 2003). District leaders used an array of strategies to bring resources into their districts, including (a) grant writing (Hatch 2000); (b) creating business partnerships (Longoria 1998); (c) working with external partners (Datnow and Kemper 2002) and universities (Bryk et al. 1998); and (d) passing bonds (Stein, Hubbard, and Mehan 2002). The ways that districts allocate resources within their districts also varies.

Differential resource allocation within districts can be an important means of increasing school capacity in poor districts. In some districts, extra human and material resources are provided to supplement lack of resources commonly due to poverty as a way to improve the teaching in low-performing schools (McLaughlin and Talbert 2002; Snipes et al. 2002). One of the central tenets of standards-based reform is the notion that instruction will become more equitable and uniform. This tenet has become one of the core tensions in standards-based reform implementation and was a fundamental feature of the New York and San Diego reforms. District leaders' reform strategy dealt with this tension by allocating resources according to school capacity. Those with the greatest need received more resources for improvement (Elmore and Burney 1997; Hightower 2002a).

Differential resource allocation to District 2 schools was rooted in the district leaders' theory of change and was based on what was needed at the school site to build instructional capacity. In deciding how schools would receive resources, district administrators grouped schools according to those that were the ideal model of instructional improvement and professional development; those with strong leadership, but were in early or middle stages of the district defined developmental path; schools with generally strong leadership on the district developmental plan but singled out for special attention and surveillance, typically because of low student performance and high variability in the quality of student work; and schools for whom there was no district instructional strategy to fit their context. Schools that were closest to the ideal received the most freedom and the least amount of surveillance. Schools that had the greatest challenges raising student achievement scores received extra human and material resources but were also monitored much more closely (Elmore and Burney 1998).

Low-capacity districts and schools often need outside expertise and other kinds of assistance to develop the skills necessary for supporting school improvement efforts (Bascia 1996; Hatch 2000). As the findings of Chapter 2 suggest, such schools may need assistance in developing basic organizational and leadership capabilities, reducing nonproductive teacher turnover, creating an orderly school climate, developing teacher pedagogic and content knowledge, and developing self-monitoring and continual learning capabilities. In some instances, improvement efforts also need to include repairing the actual physical plant or building safe, new schools with enough basic equipment for students to learn and teachers to teach (Cotton 1995; Mac Iver and Farley 2003; Reynolds and Teddlie 2000; Reynolds et al. 2002; Snipes et al. 2002; Taylor 1990). Districts that do not have the internal resources and do not have the capacity to develop resource partnerships to improve conditions in high-poverty or low-performing schools have little likelihood of improving the quality of teaching in their schools and thus increasing student learning.

## Type of Reform or Reform Foci

Reform leaders, whether superintendents or external partners, choose different kinds of reform approaches and focus on different core elements to improve schools. For instance, in Chicago, reform efforts initially focused on developing strong site-based management (Smylie and Wenzel 2003; Wenzel et al. 2001); Philadelphia had a multipronged approach (Christman 2001; Christman and Rhodes 2002). Other districts have focused primarily on improving teacher content knowledge and pedagogy and leadership capacity to guide and coordinate reform (Anderson 2003; Massell and Goertz 2002; Snipes et al. 2002; Togneri and Anderson 2003). Increasingly, districts are choosing "research-based" reforms. Some of these models are based primarily on principles for good teaching, some offer guidelines for districtwide reform, and others offer both.

In some districts, organizing principles were imported from university-school partnerships or developed internally. For instance, Providence built its reforms around the Principles of Learning developed by The Institute for Learning (IFL) at the University of Pittsburgh (Togneri and Anderson 2003). The Zuni Public School District in New Mexico embedded districtwide reform efforts in the Standards for Effective Pedagogy developed by the Center for Research, Excellence and Diversity in Education (CREDE) at University of California, Santa Cruz (Tharp et al. 2000). New York District 2 developed its theory of action internally, under the leadership of former superintendent Anthony Alvarado. When Alvarado moved to San Diego, he tried transferring these principles to his efforts at reforming San Diego (Elmore and Burney 1998; Hightower 2002a; Stein, Hubbard, and Mehan 2002). The Principles of Learning from the IFL and the CREDE standards both focus primarily on levers to improve classroom practice. The District 2 reform principles are somewhat broader and address systemwide elements (Elmore and Burney 1998; Hightower 2002a).

The Oxnard Elementary School District in southern California offers another example of a district using principles to guide reform efforts. Similar to District 2's and San Diego's approaches, the principle's guiding reform focused at least as much on districtwide strategies for change as on standards for classroom pedagogy. District leadership created a partnership with a university effective-schools center in California (Chrispeels 2002a, 2002b) to achieve its goal of improving teaching and learning. The university-based systemic effective-schools model was implemented at both the district level (e.g., district leadership team meetings, curriculum alignment) and the school level (e.g., leadership team training, facilitated grade-level meetings). The model is based on the notion that systemwide reform can build the social and human capital (e.g., Bourdieu 1986; Coleman 1988; Lareau 1989) of a district and its schools, thereby making it particularly relevant to institutions serving economically disadvantaged students.

Chrispeels (2002b) reported that although the Oxnard Elementary School District (California) systemic reform program was still in the early implementation stages, there was evidence for two types of positive change. First, survey and interview data from teachers indicate changes are being made in professional practice areas such as knowledge of content standards, comfort in helping students master the standards, and sharing of knowledge and instructional strategies. Second, there was evidence of increased academic achievement in the schools involved in the project when compared with the schools' past performance and to the achievement of similar nonproject schools.

The IFL, CREDE, District 2, San Diego, and Oxnard improvement strategies all attempted districtwide reform. The IFL and CREDE models had less systematic plans for developing district capacity, although as we shall describe in Chapter 4, the CREDE effort on the Zuni reservation placed greater emphasis on generating community involvement in establishing reform goals. These examples highlight the importance of having different research-based reform models for districts to choose from when pursuing their improvement efforts. Research consistently indicates that the most successful efforts adapt to local conditions. They work with the existing skill levels, political systems, and normative cultures in each district. Regardless of the capacity-building strategy, teachers need to understand how district initiatives apply to their daily work (Massell and Goertz 2002).

There is increasing evidence to suggest that that breadth and depth of districtwide reform implementation is more likely when several core elements are in place. These include clear goals and focus, particularly, a primary focus on improving classroom teaching and student learning, a quality accountability system, including standards and curricula, both material and human resources that improve basic school conditions, and high-quality, time-intensive professional development. Establishing these conditions may be only a first step toward improving student learning, however.

## Challenges to Developing Capacity

Several of the studies we included in this section identified challenges districts face in developing systemwide reform capacity. The points we include represent the themes that were consistent across the district literature. Snipes and colleagues (2002) identified several challenges that districts face in trying to develop reform capacity:

- Changing the role, attitudes, and perceptions of the central office.
- Facing controversy when staff were removed or demoted.
- Building the infrastructures to meet the data needs of new approaches.
- Building support from experienced teachers for uniform and pre-scriptive approaches to teaching in the early grades.
- Confronting the charge of a narrow educational focus.
- Confronting the charge that reforms undercut efforts to achieve academic excellence.
- Fighting the fatigue and stress of the constant push for improvement.

Building on this study, Togneri and Anderson (2003) identified three challenges to districtwide instructional reform. These were

- Old system structures that do not easily support new approaches to professional development.
- Developing reform strategies that work in high schools to improve achievement.
- Finding funding to support new approaches to instructional improvement remains difficult.

Mac Iver and Farley (2003) added another set of challenges facing districts including recruiting and retaining high-quality principals and teachers.

In summary, district leaders need to create structures to support improved teaching and learning. This requires a high degree of imagination and problem-solving capacity, as well as an environment that allows experimentation. Systemwide capacity for generating funding for reform also needs to be increased. Lastly, secondary schools pose a unique set of challenges that elementary schools do not. Much of the work in school improvement has been done in elementary and middle schools: What works in these settings is unlikely to transfer easily to high schools, primarily because of their more complex departmental structures. Understanding the linkages necessary to overcome these challenges is a much-needed area of research.

In conducting secondary analyses of the studies and reviews included in this chapter, we have identified several linkages between districts and other stakeholders that appear to be important for facilitating reform efforts. These are (a) professional development and learning partnerships (Elmore and Burney 1997, 1998; McLaughlin and Talbert 2002); (b) creating systems to use data to inform district and school decision making (Massell and Goertz 2002); (c) aligning accountability systems (Finnigan, O'Day, and Wakelyn 2003; Hightower 2002a, 2002b); (d) resource partnerships across school, district, and state levels (Datnow and Kemper 2003; Elmore and Burney 1997; Hightower 2002b; McLaughlin and Talbert 2002; Snipes et al. 2002; Togneri and Anderson 2003); (e) problem-solving partnerships (Resnick and Glennan 2002); and (f) creating ideological linkages (Spillane 1999). Less commonly discussed is the development of trusting and robust relational linkages (Finnigan, O'Day, and Wakelyn 2003; Stein, Hubbard, and Mehan 2002).

## Professional Development and Learning Partnerships

Professional development and learning partnerships both appear to be core areas in which districts need to develop internal capacity to support improved teaching and learning. They are also linkages that help to increase capacity. Virtually all of the studies and reviews included in this section had a component that addressed district efforts to develop professional development or learning partnerships. Very few analyzed learning or professional development at the district level (McLaughlin and Talbert 2002; Snipes et al. 2002), while several addressed professional development and learning partnerships organized at the district level that were designed to improve classroom teaching and increase student learning at the school level (Chrispeels 2002a; Cohen and Ball 2001; D'Amico et al. 2001; Elmore and Burney 1997; Finnigan, O'Day, and Wakelyn 2003; Hightower 2002a; Mac Iver and Farley 2003; Massell and Goertz 2002; Snipes et al. 2002; Spillane and Jennings 1997; Stein et al. 2002; Tharp et al. 1999; Togneri and Anderson 2003; Watson et al. 2002). These studies, taken together, consistently indicate that districts have much to learn about developing, choosing, and coordinating professional development opportunities at both the district and school levels.

Professional development is needed both at the central office and at the school level. In investigating district reform in San Francisco and San Diego, McLaughlin and Talbert (2002) found that these districts fostered norms of inquiry within the central office that brought about systemic commitment and capacity for change. This research identified the substantive and multifaceted nature of the learning agenda for the central office. Reculturing and restructuring the central office to facilitate new reform demands effectively were core components of these reform efforts. District administrators learned how to track schools' progress, then to define specialized support needs, incorporate stakeholders' input on reform goals and engage their support, employ resources strategically and broker educators' access to knowledge resources, and respond to state policies in ways that preserved the district's strategic focus. In this way, the central office modeled the risk taking and learning that are essential for sustained reform for the district workforce (McLaughlin and Talbert 2002).

Districts take three primary approaches to providing professional development to principals and teachers in schools. They either design their own internal districtwide networks, hire external partners to provide professional development to schools, or some combination of the two (Datnow and Kemper 2002; Elmore and Burney 1997; Finnigan, O'Day, and Wakelyn 2003; Hightower 2002a, 2002b; Snipes et al. 2002; Stein, Hubbard, and Mehan 2002; Togneri and Anderson 2003).

The types of professional development and their quality vary widely (Massell and Goertz 2002; Watson et al. 2002). New York District 2's reform is probably the earliest well-documented case of systematic, districtwide teacher and principal professional development. Professional development in this reform effort was a general management strategy rather than a specialized administrative function: "It permeated the work of the organization and the organization of the work" (Elmore and Burney 1997, p. 6). Five different professional development models were available to teachers and principals that ranged from very intensive longer sessions to more informal school-based mentor and buddy systems, including the professional development laboratory, instructional consulting services, intervisitation and peer networks, off-site training, and principal site visits. They all reflected the reform's organizing principles, which included a single-minded focus on improving classroom instruction and a recognition that "instructional change is a long, multi-stage process" that was best fostered in a collegial environment guided by a clear set of expectations (Elmore and Burney 1997).

Since these early reform efforts, several other districts have begun to offer systematic, focused professional development to teachers and principals. In the five districts studied by Togneri and Anderson (2003), district leaders used several strategies, including developing principles for professional development, creating networks of instructional experts, providing support systems for new teachers, strategically allocating financial resources, and providing assistance in using data. They went beyond reliance on traditional workshops or sending teachers to conferences by doing such things as offering professional development that focused on only a few key topics related directly to reform goals. They also created opportunities for job-embedded professional development and shifted teacher release days back to schools so that there was more site-level flexibility in creating professional development time.

Snipes et al. (2002) found that all of their case study districts engaged in focused, substantive, and intensive professional development. The approaches they used varied. For instance, Sacramento received a Packard Foundation grant to hire twenty-eight teacher coaches. These coaches went to school sites, modeled lessons, and observed teachers teaching, and then gave specific feedback about what teachers needed to improve. The district provided slightly over a week of professional development that focused only on instruction and implementation of the new district curriculum. They also initiated common time for teacher planning. Charlotte-Mecklenburg did not hire outside teacher coaches; rather, they trained lead teachers and relied on them to provide site-level assistance in implementing the district curriculum. They also provided three days of instruction in implementing the new district reading curriculum and allocated time for shared teacher planning. The chancellor's district in New York City is an example of a district that initially relied on external curriculum vendors until it developed its own internal capacity to provide professional development.

Massell and Goertz (2002) in their twenty-three district study found that district leaders in virtually all of their research sites expressed the belief that professional development was an important part of any reform process; yet, only a few of them demonstrated a deep commitment to professional learning as the cornerstone of sustained reform. Districts in this study used a mix of professional development formats whose type and number appeared to depend primarily on the availability of resources inside and outside of the district. These researchers were particularly struck by the commitment a few of the districts showed to allocating time and human and material resources to providing nontraditional, more in-depth kinds of professional development. This professional development was extended in time, with follow-up throughout the academic year. The most frequent strategy was to deploy district staff in schools for continuous professional development designed to meet individual school needs. They also identified teacher leaders who then received focused training with the idea they would subsequently provide professional development to their colleagues. District support providers also engaged teachers in policy development such as creating assessments or standards (Massell and Goertz 2002).

In analyzing the Chicago accountability system, Finnigan, O'Day, and Wakelyn (2003) found that reform leaders needed to develop their own capacity to choose effective vendors to provide professional development to teachers. Vendors who were hired to increase teaching capacity in sanctioned schools fell short of their charge for several reasons. First, virtually none of the external providers had a systematic approach to literacy development. Second, the professional development methods used were not deep or intensive enough to affect changes in teaching practices. Most external partners relied on either one-day workshops or train-the-trainer models. Neither of these approaches was successful in changing classroom teaching. A more promising approach involved onsite literacy coordinators. This intervention involved experts working one-on-one with teachers, observing their classroom teaching, and providing specific feedback about how to improve their literacy instruction.

Third, because of the emphasis on increasing test scores, professional developers tended to focus on low-level test preparation activities. At that time in Chicago, the Iowa Tests of Basic Skills (ITBS), not state or district standards, drove the curriculum. External partners focused their professional development efforts on skills that would be tested and helped teachers map curriculum on to the test specifications. Focusing professional development on the test rather than on state standards proved problematic (Finnigan, O'Day, and Wakelyn 2003).

In general, evidence suggests that the time needed to improve classroom teaching is typically more than reform leaders initially imagine. Supovitz and Turner (2000), for instance, proposed that it takes from 80 to 160 hours of professional development in a content area to see significant changes in teaching practices. Improving teaching and, subsequently, student learning are proving to be a more complex undertaking than policy makers, reformers, and many educational researchers might have thought. There is also evidence suggesting that professional development is not enough to increase student learning. In analyzing District 2 reform efforts, D'Amico and colleagues (2001) examined what aspects of the District 2 literacy program and accompanying district support led to improved student learning for all grade 3 to 5 students, as measured on standardized assessments. What mattered most, they found, was providing professional development in conjunction with choosing curriculum frameworks that develop basic and higher-level thinking skills. In their research, it was the combination of the Balanced Literacy program, the Investigations curriculum for math, and high-quality professional development that provided the support so that teachers improved student learning overall, and began to close the achievement gap between poor minority students and their middle- to upper-middle-class counterparts. More recent research has also found that both depth of reform model implementation and the kind of reform model chosen affected achievement outcomes for linguistically diverse students as measured by standardized student assessments (Datnow et al. 2003).

## Problem-Solving Partnerships

There is virtually no research at the district level on district leaders' efforts to create problem-solving partnerships. Snipes and colleagues (2002) found that in the districts they studied, one of the preconditions for reform was district initiation of partnerships with outside experts. External partners were enlisted to help board members and district superintendents identify the problem areas in their district, develop a reform vision, use data, and create infrastructures for using data to guide planning and decision making. Resnick and Glennan (2002) have identified problem-solving research and development as a necessary component in building collective district capacity. This kind of work brings together researchers and practitioners to develop theories and tools of change, as well as a pool of leaders to facilitate change to spread through a district.

Porter and Chester (2001) analyzed the efforts they made as partners with Philadelphia reform leadership in developing the district's accountability system. Together they tackled many substantive issues in developing a symmetrical accountability system that attempted to hold all key reform stakeholders accountable for student learning. One of the external partners brought to the table a framework grounded in the test standards developed jointly by the American Educational Research Association, the National Council on Measurement in Education, and the American Educational Research Association's position statement on high-stakes testing (Porter and Chester 2001, p. 5). The framework had three parts: (1) setting coherent and good targets for instruction; (2) creating an assessment system that held students and schools accountable; and (3) developing an assessment and accountability system that is fair. Another core component of the process in developing the accountability system was using multiple sources of data to guide development of and adaptations of the system. For instance, after initial targets for improvement were instituted and incoming student data, along with teacher, principal, and district input, indicated that the targets were unreasonable, reform leaders and external partners struggled for months with how to make the targets rigorous yet attainable.

## Resource Partnerships

What we call "resource partnerships" refer to a linkage that focuses on bringing some form of human or material resources to states, districts, or schools in need of additional resources to support improvement efforts. Improving teaching and learning in schools requires

(a) financial resources to hire external partners capable of increasing leadership capacity and teacher content and pedagogical skill and knowledge and (b) technological resources, books, teaching guides, and other material resources (Finnigan, O'Day, and Wakelyn 2002; Hamann and Lane 2002; Horn 2000a; Longoria 1998).

States, districts, and schools that have been more successful in sustaining improved teaching and learning generated extra financial resources by realigning funding sources and/or finding new sources of money that supported their improvement efforts (Clune 1998; Lusi 1997; Togneri and Anderson 2003). These can be partnerships with external partners such as reform design teams, philanthropic organizations, businesses or other community organizations, and universities (Bodilly 2001; Datnow et al. 2003; Henig et al. 1999; Stone et al. 2001). This kind of linkage is particularly important for high-poverty districts or schools simply to bring financial and human resources up to a level closer to what middle-class and wealthy districts and schools enjoy by virtue of their locale and tax base (Horn 2000b; Snipes et al. 2002).

## Ideological Linkages

When reform leaders initiate improvement efforts that challenge individuals' existing belief systems, one of the most important linkages that people need to make is ideological. Creating shared vision is one of the most commonly cited linkages across reform stakeholders – both within schools and more broadly (Elmore and Burney 1997; Snipes et al. 2002; Teddlie and Stringfield 1993; Togneri and Anderson 2003). Creating a shared vision or sense of purpose can mean that ideological chasms need to be bridged, particularly when working with a broad spectrum of reform stakeholders. If the ideological chasms cannot be bridged, productive change is unlikely to occur.

A district or school's ability to respond to any form of external performance-based accountability is determined by the degree to which individuals share common values and understandings about such matters as what they expect of students academically, what constitutes good instructional practice, who is responsible for student learning, and how individual students and teachers account for their own work and learning (Elmore and Fuhrman 2001). Educators in school sites do not simply react to mandates. They are active agents when responding to policy (Datnow, Hubbard, and Mehan 2002). Belief systems are critical in understanding how teachers exercise their agency when responding to district or state policy mandates. Beliefs about students' race and socioeconomic status are particularly important in the ways they shape community, district, and teacher willingness to implement equity-based reforms, as well as state mandates requiring teaching rigorous curriculum to all students. In short, the politics of racism and division are an unacknowledged and potent part of mainstream American ideology, thought, and action (Beck and Allexsaht-Snider 2001) that have direct consequences for district reform implementation and classroom teaching.

Parents in San Diego City schools fought core aspects of the district reforms dealing with differential resource allocation. The affluent parents in the district did not agree with the strategy of putting more resources into poor schools. They saw this as taking resources away from high-achieving students. They vigorously challenged reforms and have tried to separate the schools their students attend from the rest of the district. Members of the Latino community who were once supporters of the reform withdrew their support in part because they believed the reforms were not meeting the needs of English language learners. Several community groups have also been very vocal in their complaints about the removal of Title 1 aides from classrooms without parent or community consultation (Stein, Hubbard, and Mehan 2002). These examples point to the importance of creating ideological linkages when reform stakeholders have divergent ideas about reform, its implementation, and access and equity issues.

## Accountability Systems

The standards and accountability systems that have been developed over the past decade are perhaps the most prominent linkages between the federal, state, district, and school levels that we now see. While designed for school improvement, state or district accountability systems can both facilitate and interfere with school improvement efforts (Elmore and Burney 1998; Finnigan, O'Day, and Wakelyn 2003; Hannaway 2003; Porter and Chester 2001; Spillane 1996; Stein, Hubbard, and Mehan 2002). Linkages that sustain well-coordinated and well-financed accountability systems are emerging as critical factors in facilitating improved teaching and student achievement. Linkages within accountability systems also need to exist so that there is coherence in standards, curriculum, assessment, and professional development (Snyder 2002). As discussed earlier in this chapter, learning to develop, coordinate, and provide support for accountability systems is a key area of capacity building for districts.

With increasing frequency, districts impose sanctions on schools that cannot improve student achievement and give rewards to schools that do (Goertz, Duffy, and Le Floch 2001; Snipes et al. 2002). Elmore (2002) asked whether it is ethical to hold educators and students accountable for student learning outcomes that require considerable teaching knowledge and skill when teachers have not had the opportunity to develop the skills it takes to teach more rigorous academic content. He proposed that the school system as a whole, rather than the school itself or the student, should be held accountable for student learning. He also built a strong case for systemwide capacity building to support increased student learning. Simply creating more tightly linked policy domains, or imposing sanctions on low-performing schools, does not develop capacity for improved teaching and learning.

Using data to inform decision making is another important linkage between central office staff and schools, particularly when central office staff use data to understand barriers to teaching and learning, improve instruction, and target where resources are most needed (Anderson 2003; Snipes et al. 2002; Togneri and Anderson 2003). Massell and Goertz (2002) found that school and district staff also used data to identify and network with schools and districts that had demographics similar to their own but had higher student achievement as a way to challenge long-held ideas that students' family backgrounds predetermined student achievement. They also found that some districts were using student achievement data for professional development.

A recent evaluation of Chicago's efforts to provide support to schools that had been identified as low-performing by Finnigan, O'Day, and Wakelyn (2003) is also instructive. We cite extensively from the study, as it is the most comprehensive evaluation we have found to date that analyzes a district-led effort to provide support for

schools under its jurisdiction that were put on probation as a result
of low performance. We first describe core elements of Chicago's
accountability system, then provide key findings from the study.

Chicago's accountability system identified schools as being on probation if fewer than 20 percent of their students score at grade-level
norms on the ITBS in reading. Once identified, schools faced the consequences of decreased autonomy and sanctions. They also received
direct assistance from several sources through the district's external
support system. The support system included five school-level support providers: an external partner, a probation manager who is an
experienced administrator, a regional education officer, a business
manager or intern, and a facilitator from Chicago Public School's
Office of Accountability. Schools chose their own external partners.

The Chicago accountability system had a clear logic and probation
theory of action. The external support system it designed had one
objective in mind – to improve student assessment as measured by
the ITBS. Chicago invested millions of dollars between 1997 and 2001
into their districtwide capacity-building efforts; yet, within a two-
year period, student test scores had not significantly increased. There
were several areas in the intervention strategy and its implementation
that impeded more successful results, including:

1. Coordination and communication across support experts was
   lacking. Particularly, communication among external partners
   and probation partners was low. Because of this, half of the
   schools studied had multiple partners with overlapping strategies. As a result, improvement efforts were duplicated, contra-
   dicted, or lost.
2. Time constraints and demands for immediate improvement
   on test scores created impatience among some external consultants which led to "capacity building" becoming "capacity sub-
   stitution." For example, rather than teaching school leadership
   to monitor classrooms or provide feedback to teachers about
   lessons they had observed, the external partner did the work
   him or herself (Finnigan, O'Day, and Wakelyn 2003, pp. 38–39).
3. Because external partners did not deliver what they had
   promised, teacher and administrator trust decreased in the
   partners' abilities to assist their schools. Because there was
   such a clear trend that external partners could not deliver

what they promised, researchers hypothesized that in some instances external experts or support providers overstated what they could accomplish to ensure they won the service contract.

4. There was no feedback system to help the program monitor or the external partner to learn from their mistakes. The intervention strategy suffered from a relative lack of emphasis on training for support providers and a built-in mechanism for learning, either for the district or the service providers (Finnigan, O'Day, and Wakelyn 2003, p. vi).

These findings led Finnigan, O'Day, and Wakelyn (2003) to make several recommendations including:

- Clarify the roles of support providers, probation managers, regional office staff, and Office of Accountability facilitators. Create a single and clear line of authority in schools and have this authority work closely with external partners to help the school develop and implement a coherent instructional plan.
- Develop opportunities for learning/sharing among partners and probation managers to allow for reflection about their work.
- Discourage schools from developing multiple and fragmented partnerships.
- Develop in-depth, content-based professional development.
- Connect assistance to the standards, not just the test. Promote better use of data in schools by fostering the development of multiple diagnostic tools. (pp. 49–50)

Empirically linking district action to student achievement is difficult to do. There are numerous factors simultaneously affecting both policy implementation and student learning. The empirical linkages between district-level reform efforts and tangible changes in teaching practices and learning outcomes at the classroom level are thus more logically than empirically demonstrated. They are also largely tentative (Anderson 2003; Mac Iver and Farley 2003). When reporting increased student achievement, researchers largely attribute district effects on the basis of temporal correlations between student results on state/district standardized tests and district reform efforts over time. Generally speaking, if test results show significant widespread gains in student results associated with the initiation of district reform plans, and (2) these trends are generalized across all or most schools, and (3) the performance gaps between previous groups of low- and high-performing students and schools seem to be diminishing over time, a case is made that district reform efforts are having a positive effect on student learning. The empirical links between district policies and district leadership reform strategies and gains in student learning at the classroom and school levels (Anderson 2003, pp. 13–14) are not direct or well understood and are thus areas rich for further study. One important area will be the combinations of linking and capacity-building strategies that enhance reform implementation and under what conditions. It is possible that local conditions and capacity might affect the first steps that need to be taken in any district, so having a way to systematically analyze a district's capacity to begin implementing reform becomes important.

Elmore and Burney (1997) reported that District 2 had gone from being ranked sixteenth out of thirty-two districts to second after almost ten years of focused, district-led reform. There is also evidence that Philadelphia achieved modest gains in student achievement in reading, mathematics, and science, decreased dropout rates, and increased attendance between the years 1996 and 2000 of the Children Achieving reform efforts. During this time new leadership took responsibility for the district (Porter and Chester 2001) and the state moved to privatization (Gewertz 2002) rather than a capacity-building strategy for low-performing public schools. Studies by Resnick and Harwell (2000) and (Harwell et al. 2000) found increases in student achievement in both New York District 2 and San Diego, which they related to reform efforts, while analyses attempting to show a relationship between reform-based professional development and increased student achievement conducted in both studies did not yield positive results (Mac Iver and Farley 2003). Snipes and colleagues (2002) and Togneri and Anderson (2003) used purposive sampling when choosing districts for their respective case study research into district-led reforms. Both sets of researchers sought districts that had increased student achievement scores and had begun to close achievement gaps. This suggests that with the increasing availability of district-level student data, more studies can be designed that examine the linkages between district reform efforts and student achievement.

CONCLUSION

The empirical research and reviews we analyzed in this chapter indicate that districts can take a proactive role in directing school reform while also mediating policy mandates from organizations higher in the policy system. As a midlevel policy domain, districts have a key role to play in coordinating communication and resources to and from federal, state, and school policy domains. We have presented evidence suggesting that school boards can play a role in creating the preconditions for reform to take hold in the districts under their jurisdiction. There is also evidence suggesting that inroads can be made into increasing student learning when school boards, superintendents, and district office personnel all agree that teaching and learning need to improve; provide human and material resources to accomplish this goal; and develop a fair and well-coordinated accountability system that uses an array of data to inform decision making. In short, a high degree of consistency at the district and school-board level appears to help focus reform.

We have identified several areas where districts can develop reform capacity. These include distributed leadership; coordinating, developing, and managing accountability systems; developing curriculum and standards; allocating resources for reform; and reform focus. We have also identified several challenges to districts developing capacity to support reform. One of the most important points to make here is that it takes existing capacity to build more capacity.

We have also identified several linkages between the district and other organizations, individuals, or policy domains that appear to be important for reform. These include professional development and learning partnerships, problem-solving partnerships, resource partnerships, and accountability systems. Along with being connections between otherwise disconnected points in the policy system, linkages are an expression of both existing capacity as well as an expression of where capacity for reform may need to be developed.

In much of the district-level research we reviewed, empirical connections between district-level reform efforts and student achievement are largely tentative. We suggest this may be a function of two primary factors. First, such research is difficult to design. Empirically proving such causal relationships would require research models that can analyze the effects of multiple influences simultaneously on student learning. Another factor is that until recently longitudinal district-level student data were not widely available.

Lastly, there are several directions for future research. One would be to systematically analyze linkages and how the flow and quality of resources and communication across these linkages affect reform implementation. Researching how districts have developed their internal capacity to direct, to coordinate, and to support school reform would be beneficial as a way to provide data and models to districts with less reform capacity. Likewise, analyzing how districts develop capacity to develop quality accountability systems would be beneficial to other districts still struggling with how to develop, fund, and manage such systems. Systematically analyzing how reform models transfer from one district context to another would also prove beneficial.

# 4

# Community-Level Reform Efforts

O'Day and Smith (1993) wrote that it takes a combination of improved social conditions and additional educational resources to close the achievement gap between white and poor minority youth. The research studies discussed in this chapter return to the relationship between community capacity and student achievement and the role of the community in reform efforts. They expand and complicate the discussion of urban and rural school reform by bringing to the forefront elements of (a) language (Hamann 2002; Tharp et al. 2000); (b) race (Henig et al. 1999; Horn 2000a; Rich 1996; Stone 1998a); (c) economic (Horn 2000b; Rich 1996) and civic capacity (Stone et al. 2001); and (d) the politics inherent in education reform (Hess 1999; Hill et al. 2000). In this section, the authors we cite stress the importance of considering different dimensions of a locale's political context and the linkages between various governmental agencies and community businesses, organizations, and groups when studying school reform. For several of these researchers, school reform cannot be separated from the social reconstruction of urban centers (Anyon 1997; Henig et al. 1999; Rich 1996; Stone 1998b), or from the economic challenges that poor, isolated rural communities face (Horn 2000a, 2000b).

Figure 4 helps to orient the role of the community in our framework.

In this chapter, we separately address the issues faced by educators in high-poverty rural contexts and high-poverty urban contexts.

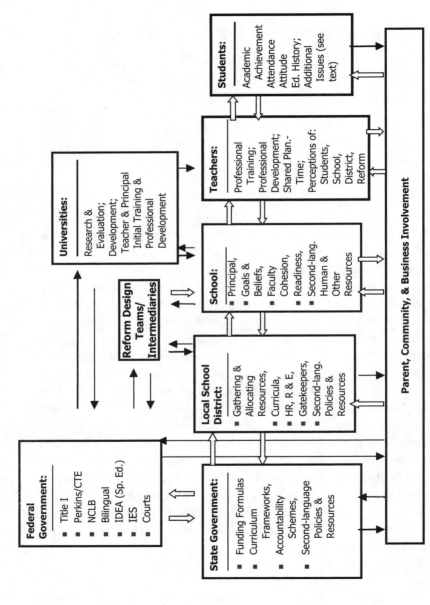

FIGURE 4. A Representation of the Relationships between Parents and Community Groups and "the School System"

Although there are commonalities across these contexts, such as high dropout rates, low student achievement, patronage politics, and difficulty attracting highly qualified teachers (Anyon 1997; Datnow and Kemper 2002; Horn 2000b), there are also distinctly different challenges that face these communities. We also include an analysis of research conducted in Native American reservations with the discussion of issues that face rural schools. We begin with an analysis of urban reform efforts.

### URBAN REFORM AND COMMUNITY LINKAGES

In their studies of urban school reform, Henig et al. (1999), Stone (1998a, 1998b), and Stone and colleagues (2001) used the concept of civic capacity. Stone (1998a) defined civic capacity as:

the degree to which a cross-sector coalition comes together in support of a task of community-wide importance. As an ideal, civic capacity entails not simply bringing a coalition together around the issue of educational improvement, but beyond that engaging the members in activities and promoting discourse. . . . The term civic capacity is thus intended to bring attention to the importance of a broad base of *active* involvement. . . . From this understanding of urban regimes, it follows that it takes a broad mobilization of civic capacity to bring about a thoroughgoing effort at educational improvement. The means by which this happens is not by coalition *pressure* on the school system, but by coalition contributions to critical policy tasks. (p. 254)

Henig and colleagues (1999) defined civic capacity as the extent to which various sectors of a community have developed formal and informal means to define common objectives and pursue common goals. They continued by stressing the importance of civic obligation and alliances in coalition building:

The notion of civic capacity implies a shift from the status quo state of affairs in which participants are focused only on their immediate connections and their particular occupational roles toward embracing a community role and accepting civic obligation. Using the concept of civic capacity facilitates both assessing the web of alliances and interactions that potentially support human capital alliances and interactions that potentially support human capital initiatives, and identifying the obstacles to such alliances where they do not exist, rather than thinking about education as solely the province of a discrete school bureaucracy. (p. 14)

Using the lens of civic capacity, these authors found three primary reasons for urban reform failure in the districts they studied: (1) School districts lacked an array of resources. (2) Specific reforms did not bring about the measurable effects predicted by their more ardent supporters. Sometimes the perceived failure was a function of unrealistic expectations from the beginning. (3) The reform efforts lacked civic capacity. The studies covered in this section of the volume confirm these findings.

The notion of civic capacity is important for analyzing community involvement in school reform because it puts relationships, common goals, coalition building, and political alliances – core elements of creating linkages between individuals, organizations, and institutions – in the forefront. The discussion in this section focuses almost exclusively on linkages between various community members, including mayors, school boards, businesses, churches, other organizations or groups, and schools. When relationships between different individuals and organizations within a community are examined, the links between these elements and the reasons linkages are (and are not) forged, used, or ignored become apparent. Integral to this discussion are (a) the politics of language (Hamann 2002; Tharp et al. 1999); (b) race, suburbanization, or white flight (Henig et al. 1999); (c) corporate and economic divestment (Anyon 1997; Rich 1996); (d) personal and professional relationships (Henig et al. 1999, Stone 1988a, 1998); (e) political alliances, allegiances, and agendas; and (f) shared understanding of reform goals (Christman and Rhodes 2002).

## URBAN REFORM AND COMMUNITY CAPACITY

Urban school reformers are part of a complex web of relationships (Stone et al. 2001). Key stakeholders include mayors, boards of education, district superintendents, teacher associations, local businesses, private foundations, state governments, and federal courts (Stone 1998b). Making educational policy in a multilevel, federated structure involves recognizing the interdependencies of jurisdictions, their separate interests (Elmore 1993), and their different understandings about the purposes of schooling and school reform (Christman and Rhodes 2002; Hess 1999; Stone et al. 2001). Pathways of communication serve as one kind of linkage. An ability to create common goals and shared a sense of purpose, as well as the quality of relationships among the various community stakeholders, are key elements in the coordinated commitment and action necessary to sustain urban school reform (Henig et al. 2001; Stone 1998b).

Christman and Rhodes's (2002) study of Philadelphia Children Achieving explored different dimensions of civic engagement in reform efforts that both facilitated linkages and prevented their creation. The Children Achieving ten-point action design left significant room for different interpretations of the reform. Key stakeholders from differing organizations and political positions had divergent theories of action and could not agree on the reform or its primary objectives. The superintendent who spearheaded the reforms espoused the need to do it all now; yet, he did not develop a clear plan of action, nor did he work to develop a shared sense of purpose across differing community sectors. Thus, reform efforts from the beginning went in several directions. Business and political leaders tended to support more managerial and market-based models of implementation for Children Achieving; they stressed a theory of action based on developing standards and accountability systems. District employees, grassroots leaders, and civic leaders saw economic inequity and racial discrimination as the primary issues needing to be addressed; thus, they promoted redistribution of resources as the primary course of action. Civic, foundation, and some grassroots leaders stressed the importance of democratic revitalization and viewed centralized bureaucracy as one of the key obstacles to improving Philadelphia schools. They argued for increased public debate on the purposes of schooling and stressed an increased role of school councils as a way to change power relationships between schools, parents, and other community members. Higher-education leaders, some civic leaders, and foundation staff believed that professional development opportunities needed to be the reform's highest priority and worked to create an infrastructure of support and expert resources outside of the district that could work with school staff to improve teaching and learning opportunities. In analyzing the broad array of understandings about Philadelphia reform and the divergent courses of action that different community stakeholders took, it becomes clear that Children Achieving reformers lost opportunities to create ideological linkages and to coordinate resources across these different groups that were focused on a single goal (Christman and Rhodes 2002).

Differences in political agendas between state and reform leaders can inhibit linkages between state governments and urban districts. Two very important factors prevented linkages between Philadelphia reform leaders and the governor: one factor was the Republican governor's wish to pass legislation for school vouchers, privatization, and charter schools. His values and beliefs about how to reform the state's schools contrasted with Children Achieving's emphasis on improving public schools. The second factor had to do with an increasingly hostile and personalized fight between Children Achieving leadership and the governor for financial resources.

The state legislature had frozen the state school funding formula in 1993, which led to cuts in state funding to its districts. The battle for state funding became increasingly personal, with Children Achieving leadership taking an increasingly confrontational and vocal stance against the governor and state legislature. District leaders, including the mayor and the city council president, distributed a white paper in 1997 that made school funding a moral issue and explicitly blamed the state for inadequately funding Philadelphia schools. The situation was exacerbated when the district superintendent publicly stated that the state funding policy was racist. The governor continued to hold his position by consistently asserting that the district was using its funds inefficiently and that they needed to provide more financial support for public education. He declared that he would not funnel more money to Philadelphia schools without a state takeover of them (Christman and Rhodes 2002).

In this case, both the ideological differences between Children Achieving reform leaders and the governor and the personalized nature of the struggle for financial support for Philadelphia schools created the conditions in which a critical linkage in the form of coordinated resource allocation from the state to the district did not happen. The ideological differences between key players were so great that bridges could not be built across them. Immense amounts of time and energy were devoted to the struggle with the state for needed financial resources, a struggle that was ultimately fruitless.

One of the early goals in Children Achieving was to involve a broad array of community members in reform efforts. A core strategy was to involve business elites as a way to meet the Annenberg Foundation's condition of raising matching funds. This strategy was never fully achieved, in part because of unexpected economic changes in Philadelphia and in part because of leadership inconsistencies. In the early years of Children Achieving reform, Philadelphia saw a significant shift in its economy. By 2000, only four of the reform's founding CEOs were still in the city. This shift meant that there were fewer businesses led or owned by Philadelphia community members, and fewer business elites who had a vested interest in the city or who understood its history. It also meant the loss of important linkages to channel both human and material resources into the district.

In the initial phase of the reform, seven working groups were created to align the Annenberg Challenge funding with district priorities. Work groups were composed of people from the central office, the union, school clusters, businesses, and the community at large. Each work group was responsible for developing implementation plans for specific areas of the district's reform efforts, such as standards and assessment. These groups were, however, disbanded shortly after their creation for a centralized structure composed of the superintendent and a few select close advisors. This change brought about a centralization of decision making and decreased opportunities for broad-based community leadership to participate in reform implementation. It also represented a significant change in the early reform strategy of civic engagement in the reform.

What started as a reform effort designed to create robust community linkages became a reform centered around and identified with a charismatic leader. Leadership's stance that "you're either for me or against me" did not serve to generate enduring community linkages. Children Achieving never became a shared community theory but remained the theory of a charismatic leader that was perceived differently by community leaders. Without broad public discussions and consensus on a reform strategy, there is little likelihood for deep public involvement in a reform's success (Christman and Rhodes 2002, p. 31).

In examining the role of superintendents in urban reform, Hess (1999) proposed that the motivations compelling superintendents to engage in the politics of reform are often rooted in notions of professional success and the need to gain the support of the local community. Professional and institutional incentives discourage policy makers from proposing those reforms most likely to improve teaching and learning significantly, while encouraging them to pursue more symbolic measures. The decisions superintendents make are shaped in part by whether they will be judged as effective. Superintendents perceived as successful with reform are offered increasingly prestigious positions in larger districts; they find doors into government, consulting, and academia opened to them. Aware of their expected short tenure, superintendents learn to think of their present positions as short-term postings and to keep their eyes open to the job market. When selecting policy options, they choose reforms that maximize political impact and minimize potential reverse reaction – not necessarily the reforms that would be most likely to improve school performance (Hess 1999, p. 123).

In the case of Philadelphia, the district superintendent chose a very risky and ambitious endeavor when he undertook and rallied support for the Children Achieving reforms, as did the superintendents in both New York District 2 (Elmore and Burney 1998, 1999) and San Diego (Hightower 2002a, 2002b). In these instances, superintendents may have been looking for career advancement; yet, they were not unwilling to take risky and controversial action. There were, however, significant differences in their leadership styles. Although both leaders used public relations campaigns to build public and community support as a key strategy early in their reforms, they took different directions in how they worked to institutionalize reforms. The District 2 superintendent set his focus on building school capacity and had one central goal in the beginning of the reform: improving teaching (Elmore and Burney 1998).

Mayors can also be key stakeholders in urban school reform. Rich (1996) proposed that mayors must meet at least six preconditions if they want to exercise leadership in school policy: (1) control over the appointment process or considerable influence in choosing board candidates; (2) credentials as a professional educator; (3) substantial involvement in school budget processes; (4) legal authority to mediate racial integration disputes and union/board conflicts; (5) clear media support during school crises; and (6) the political respect of school activists. Without these essential prerequisites, mayors will be less than effective in leading or lending support for school reform efforts.

## URBAN REFORM, LOCAL ECONOMIES, AND RACE

The role that schools play in the local economy is a core element of urban reform politics and how and why certain community linkages are built or ignored. Along with being a service that students receive, education and education systems create jobs, contracts, and career tracks – all things that represent financial security for people working in the system. The protection of jobs is often at the heart of how education politics is organized (Stone 1998b).

School systems hold an important place in the local political economy, especially in communities that have experienced corporate divestment and white flight (e.g., Detroit and Baltimore). The emergence of school systems as major employers was tied to the decline of manufacturing and heavy industry (Henig et al. 1999; Rich 1996; Stone 1998b; Stone et al. 2001). School districts generate millions of dollars for their local economies (Rich 1996). They serve a core function in the local political economy as sources of citywide economic development, community development, stability, and upward mobility for many people. African Americans in Atlanta, Baltimore, Detroit, and Washington, D.C., have historically depended on public-sector employment, including public schools, for economic opportunity and mobility; they represent a high percentage of the districts' workforces, including administrative positions (Henig et al. 1999; Stone 1998b).

Racial turnover has been closely linked to economic changes that have had long-term consequences for school governance and for urban school reform (Henig et al. 1999; Rich 1996). By the early 1970s, as white flight left both economic and power vacuums, the public school systems in Atlanta, Baltimore, and Washington, D.C., became the "black" agency of local government. Similar trends were also true in the Rust Belt cities of Detroit, Gary, and Newark (Henig et al. 1999; Rich 1996; Stone 1998b).

The African American communities in Atlanta, Baltimore, and Washington, D.C., were closely knit while also being economically divided. As the black population in these cities rose to a majority or near majority, they experienced increased influence and power in city politics. Strong informal networks existed between ministers, teachers, school administrators, and other school personnel. Many of them attended the same universities, had worked in the same school systems for years, and were often members of the same social and religious organizations. With the ascendancy of black leadership in these communities and the divestment of white businesses, more businesses owned by local African Americans obtained contracts with school districts, ranging from supplying food, legal services, data processing, and school security (Henig et al. 1999). These interpersonal bonds created unity and a common sense of purpose across different groups of middle-class and upper-middle-class African Americans, especially because public education holds a symbolic central place as the policy area that brought expansion of opportunity (Stone 1998b).

The hope that racial transition into positions of power would bring an era of progressive urban policy oriented around redistribution and development did not materialize. White flight has left a structural legacy of high need in areas with the weakest tax bases. A serious consequence of middle-class and corporate exodus from city centers is that urban school districts have a disproportionate share of poor and minority students.

When trying to implement reform in urban schools, formal structures can be rearranged, such as mandating new funding formulas. Changing status quo practices, however, cannot occur without transforming the basic relationships and linkages that support coalitions built around personalism and distributive benefits. What matters is how various players relate to one another, whether their emphasis is on improving teaching and learning in schools, and whether they channel resources into reform efforts. In short, policy change comes about only if reformers establish a new set of political arrangements commensurate with the advocated policy (Stone 1998b, p. 11).

Wilbur Rich (1996) attributed failed urban reform efforts in three Rust Belt cities to two primary factors: a lack of solid tax bases caused by industrial divestment and socialization of black leaders into the norms and values of a previously white educational cartel:

An education cartel is not a cartel in a pure economic sense, but its behavior is cartel-like. It is a coalition of professional school administrators, school activists, and union leaders who maintain control of school policy to promote the interest of its members. Membership in the cartel confers income, status, and perks. Members are socialized into and agree to follow cartel norms and rules. (p. 5)

Rich's analysis makes clear that well-planned local action to address urban school reform is difficult to initiate in communities where conditions of concentrated poverty exist. Exit options, such as suburbanization or white flight, also exacerbate problems while diminishing urban resources. Issues of race are undeniable in these contexts. Racial issues intensify some of the structural problems faced by cities, while also presenting a powerful perceptual filter rooted in personal and historical experiences that affect the bonds of trust and loyalty on which political endeavors depend (Rich 1996). So, along with buying into the norms of the previous educational cartel and wanting to protect their positions of status within their communities (as their white predecessors had), African American civic and reform leaders were faced with problems associated with poverty. These cities did not have vibrant, growing economies, and this meant that the opportunity to create linkages with local businesses did not exist. These communities also lacked another important linkage – the political alliances with influential state and political leaders to channel material and human resources into their reform efforts.

Similarly, in her historical analysis of municipal and educational turmoil that plagued Newark, New Jersey, in the 1960s, Jean Anyon (1997) described how patronage politics were pervasive. In the case of Newark, "the control of school policy to promote the interest of its members" went beyond just people directly within the school system. By 1963, a majority of appointments to the board of education had been made by the mayor, thus securing his control over many aspects of the public school system. Throughout the 1960s, money that was to go to schools was largely mismanaged. People "friendly" with the mayor or who would go along with his illegal activities were continually appointed to positions of status or given no-show jobs (p. 116). For example, a person who had been one of the mayor's campaign workers was given the position of supervisor for school accounts, while another was appointed budget analyst. By the early 1970s, a study by the federal Department of Health, Education, and Welfare had ordered Newark to return $1.1 million because it had been spent on schools not eligible for federal funding. In 1970, thirteen schools in predominantly white, higher-income areas of the city were classified as eligible for funding. In the words of a local official, "they were spreading the money around to their friends" (Anyon 1997).

In 1970, when Newark's first black mayor was elected, he inherited a city that was bankrupt and in organizational disaster. Rapid economic divestment of the city in the 1960s, the limited reach of federal educational reforms, federally subsidized suburbanization of white families, a history of local political corruption, and race riots left systemic problems that were virtually insurmountable; their repercussions were felt well into the 1990s (Anyon 1997).

Although this is an extreme case, it does show how an educational cartel can be self-serving. It also points to the importance of community context and systemic linkages as they affect school improvement efforts. The federal Title I and II dollars necessary for providing extra money for a vastly underfunded school system were both underused and misused. City leadership, particularly during the 1960s, gave little evidence of caring for students, the condition of schools, and the qualifications of either school leadership or teachers. Little was done during this period to use existing linkages to improve the city's failing economy or local schools. In short, civic capacity to change the status quo was nonexistent.

Civic capacity is an important concept in understanding the reasons urban reforms fail or succeed because it moves beyond formal authority to determine education expenditures and directs attention to political capacity to reallocate existing resources and to generate new ones (Henig et al. 1999). Longoria (1998) explored the important role that civic capacity played in improving student achievement scores in Houston, Texas, during the mid- to late 1990s. After a new district superintendent was appointed to Houston Independent School District in 1994, district administrators created linkages with elected officials and the business community in several areas, including management issues, strategic planning, accounting practices, and outcomes measurement. This approach to developing and coordinating reform efforts was supported by a broad range of community

members, including the mayor, business, and other community organizations. Education and social programs were seen as human investment policies and were linked to gang prevention, crime reduction,
and economic development.

The empirical data presented by Rich (1996) and Longoria (1998)
poignantly illuminated the significance of the linkage between local
economic conditions, the conditions of urban schools, and the availability of both human and material resources in communities experiencing high poverty. They also point to an important policy implication – private and government seed money for school reform is not
enough to sustain reform efforts in cities that do not have a strong
tax base or vibrant local economies.

The Philadelphia school reforms, albeit fragmented, did bring
about gains in achievement for poor and minority students, especially in elementary schools. Interestingly, schools with higher concentrations of low-performing and poor students made greater gains
than other schools. Improved test scores were especially noteworthy
because Philadelphia had one of the most inclusive testing policies
in the country (Christman and Rhodes 2002).

Where quality private-sector jobs are increasingly scarce and racial
discrimination is a reality, the employment opportunities available to
blacks in public schools are vital to the stability of the African American community. If jobs are leaving and employment opportunities
are bleak, then the perception that reform initiatives could threaten
wages and fringe benefits in the public sector are heightened and
likely to engender greater resistance from black teachers, principals,
and other school employees. School reformers cannot ignore that in
many black-led cities, the public school systems form an important
source of jobs, economic opportunity, and social status for African
Americans (Henig et al. 1999, p. 153).

Key questions need to be asked about the role of state and federal governments in urban school reform and inner-city revitalization. The reports of state takeovers of school systems are mixed.
Rich (1996) asserted that such actions are a "tourniquet for rapidly
flowing red ink." In short, they are no substitute for a weak tax
base. Anyon (1997), however, maintained that although there are
problems with state takeovers, especially when they take a punitive
stance toward districts, they can facilitate the removal of unqualified

patronage appointments and poorly performing or underqualified teachers and principals. She also proposed that urban educational and social reform are symbiotic. Successful educational reform that leads to improved student achievement is not only dependent on a revitalizing city but is also a crucial component of more comprehensive change (Anyon 1997).

A shift toward state authority also has important, if indirect, effects on local school districts. Shifting the decision-making venue can destabilize local-level coalitions (Rich 1996). The racial implications of white-dominated legislatures and appointed boards making political decisions about minority districts such as Atlanta, Baltimore, Detroit, and Washington, D.C., are widely understood by those involved in the process, although external state actors almost never use racial language to justify their intervention. The shift in state authority facing these cities mirrors a long-term decline in the influence they have had on state political institutions. Beyond simple numbers, however, there is a strong sense that state-level institutions have embraced an explicitly antiurban ideology. Large cities are seen as costly liabilities, rather than as centers of wealth and opportunity (Henig et al. 1999).

The studies reviewed in this section point to important, yet often not researched dimensions of urban school reform. Although there is little descriptive or empirical work that focuses on the linkages between local economic conditions and urban school reform, the data presented in this section point to the need to direct more research in this area.

## RURAL COMMUNITIES AND REFORM

Problems common to rural districts include (a) geographic and cultural isolation; (b) high poverty; low levels of adult education (Horn 2000a, 2000b; Russon, Horn, and Oliver 2000; Tharp et al. 1999); (c) a scarcity of resources; (d) few if any opportunities for business partnerships (Horn 2000a, 2000b); (e) nepotism and petty politics; (f) difficulties with teacher and administrator recruitment; (g) high student dropout rates; (h) resistance to change (Datnow and Kemper 2002); and (i) a paucity of stable or high-paying jobs (Horn 2000a, 2000b). Although common issues exist across rural contexts, the research we present also indicates that challenges exist that are also unique to individual communities. For instance, the persistent and enduring segregation and race issues present in the Mississippi Delta community studied by Horn (2000a) were not present in the Appalachian community also studied by Horn (2000b). In presenting the research on high-poverty rural communities that we have included in this chapter, we hope to stress the significance of developing an array of intervention strategies that are sensitive to the diverse contextual factors that affect high-poverty rural schools and communities.

In 2000, the Evaluation Center at the University of Michigan published several different research reports analyzing the implementation of several National Science Foundation Rural Systemic Reform Initiatives. We include three of these that represent examples of the diverse and unique challenges in rural communities that constrain school improvement efforts. One of these communities in the NSF study was Native American, one was in the Deep South, and a third was an Appalachian community in rural Kentucky (Horn 2000a, 2000b; Russon, Horn, and Oliver 2000).

In all three contexts, the NSF resources from the federal government were an important linkage for these geographically isolated, high-poverty communities. The reform grants brought both financial and material assistance, including technological and human resources. They also brought professional development opportunities in the areas of math, science, and technology.

The problems facing the Appalachian community were in part attitudinal and in part pedagogical. The community was predominantly poor and white, with families rooted in place. The adult level of education was generally low, and high school dropout rates were high. Many jobs in the county required only a high school diploma or its equivalency.

The curriculum of the home and the community was typically in conflict with that of the school. It was also common for teachers to hold negative beliefs about their students because of biases or prejudices against their family backgrounds. Cultural and geographical isolation were also a fact of life for many Appalachian families. At the time of the study, roughly 75 percent of households had phones, 15 percent had computers, and only 5 percent had Internet access.

The Appalachian Rural Systemic Initiative (ARSI) had three strategic goals: to strengthen the knowledge and skills of K–12 teachers so that they could teach math and science more effectively; to establish a timely and coordinated system for helping schools enhance their capacity to deliver sustainable, active, standards-based teaching and learning environments; and to build regional partnerships, local leadership, and local community involvement for enduring educational improvement (Horn 2000b).

The role of the state was also important in these reform efforts. With the passage of KERA, the Kentucky Education Reform Act, the influence of "politics as usual" was reduced, organized planning efforts were begun, and schools were expected to teach all students to an acceptable standard of learning. Another significant change was the equalization of resources for schools across the state. This meant that more money was available to schools in the community, although locals were paying higher taxes.

The district was committed to improving the teaching in its schools but had to rely on ARSI staff for professional development, as many administrators and teachers did not know what good science and math programs looked like. ARSI staff also worked with district and school staff to build local capacity to understand and develop standards. Developing community partnerships was limited because of the lack of businesses or organizations with which the district could partner. The district did, however, develop partnerships with a local migrant program, the Parent Teacher Association, a local family and youth resource service, and a local college. Even with stable district leadership, one of the biggest challenges to instituting change in the schools was long-standing beliefs. Schooling and high academic achievement quite simply have not been a relevant factor in many community members' lives for generations (Horn 2000b).

The Mississippi Delta community also experienced many of the challenges described in the Appalachian context, including a high dropout rate, poorly trained teachers, and enduring intergenerational poverty. The low level of adult education was exacerbated in part because the primary local employer was the catfish industry, which relied on a large pool of underskilled, minimum-wage workers (Horn 2000a).

Unlike the Appalachian setting, the Mississippi Delta community experienced enduring racial segregation. When integration was mandated in the 1960s, local white families fled the public school system. In 1999, approximately 60 percent of the twelve thousand residents were African American and 40 percent were white. The student population of the local public school system was 100 percent African American, while the only private school in the area, with an enrollment of about 300 students, was 100 percent white. Hiring well-educated teachers in the public schools was difficult, in part because of the geographic and cultural isolation, low pay, poor condition of schools, and lack of opportunities for educated people (Horn 2000a).

The NSF researchers found capacity throughout the district to be low and found no opportunities for local partnerships, although there were a few district administrators who valued and hoped for improved learning conditions in their schools. They and the evaluation team felt, however, that the deeply rooted segregation and long-standing political arrangements and values, along with little hope of the local economic conditions changing, severely constrained school improvement efforts. There was a very large population in the county for whom education in general, let alone math and science, was totally irrelevant. The concept of schooling for a better life was not understood or internalized. The rags-to-riches stories that many Americans were raised on never filtered down to the poorest in this county (Horn 2000a, p. 21).

We now turn our analysis to three different Native American communities, two in the American Southwest and one in Alaska. In terms of sustaining school improvement efforts in these three communities, two components were consistent across all three settings and considered absolutely necessary by locals and the partnering improvement teams: robust community involvement and culturally relevant curricula (Lipka 1991; Russon, Horn, and Oliver 2000; Tharp et al. 1999). How these evolved and the forms they took differed in each community. In two of these communities, university-based research teams were the primary linkage that brought extra financial and human resources to the community and district. In the third, the NSF and local business were the primary link to added resources.

Teachers in Alaska experienced some of the most extreme geographical and cultural isolation. Villages were small. Their populations in the early 1990s ranged from a few hundred to a few thousand people. They were scattered over vast geographic distances, often accessible only by dogsled or small aircraft. Teachers often taught in a derivation of a one-room schoolhouse and were thus isolated from their colleagues in a way most teachers on the mainland were not. In these isolated areas, the community was often very involved in core aspects of school life (Lipka 1991).

The Gila River Indian community, located in the Southwest, was unique in that it was a sovereign nation and thus the tribal council was not responsible to state or federal governments on matters of education. At the time of the study, all of the schools in the community were part of the Arizona Tribal Coalition (ATC) and the New Mexico Rural Systemic Initiative (UCAN RSI). UCAN's goal was to provide support to selected schools for comprehensive programs that increased the effectiveness of standards-based science, math, and appropriate applications of technology (Russon, Horn, and Oliver 2000).

One of ATC's significant impacts was the creation of a coalition of all-tribal community schools. This lessened teacher isolation and created new linking opportunities. As a result of the alliance and increased teacher collaboration, a culturally relevant math and science curriculum was under development. Some of the community schools adopted a community-based educational model. For instance, one school developed a science curricula rooted in the Pima tribe's historical vocation of farming. In addition to the curriculum being culturally relevant, it was also standards-based. Principals in several of the community schools chose to use the state standards as a way to prepare students for the state-run high schools.

In one school, cultural relevance was achieved by bringing tribal elders into classrooms to aid in teaching science lessons. Creating culturally relevant science lessons necessitated that the curriculum be developed so that the timing of the lessons corresponded to seasonal cycles as prescribed by the elders' knowledge of the local environment. For instance, to study hibernation as a facet of life science, this instruction took place during the time of year that desert animals hibernate. The expert knowledge of the local elders was important in placing these events in a cultural context (Russon, Horn, and Oliver 2000).

The community schools also had various partnerships with local industry. In particular, Intel Corporation and the schools involved in the Intel Partnership Project developed a local education network. Their efforts brought together six technology education centers in 1996, which networked the entire reservation and provided the tribe with access to the Internet. As of 1996, Intel had donated approximately $1.2 million in money, equipment, in-kind grants, and volunteer time to the partner network.

Even with these coordinated efforts to create networks and innovative standards-based math and science curricula, the schools still faced considerable challenges. With the additional resources from the multiple partnerships, state, and Bureau of Indian Affairs funds, tribal community schools were just at the median funding level of the state. Few people in the community had the skills to facilitate school reform. Professional development was offered primarily through UCAN, and it was questionable whether this support would be sustained after the grant ran its course (Russon, Horn, and Oliver 2000).

Another well-documented partnership in reservation schools was undertaken by a team of professors and graduate students from the University of California, Santa Cruz, the Zuni tribal council in New Mexico, the district, and two of the schools under its jurisdiction. A primary goal of the research was to assist the Zuni Public School District in achieving appropriate and effective school reform that would be responsive to the goals and values of the Zuni community, while also increasing student achievement. At the core of the reform efforts were the CREDE Standards for Effective Pedagogy.[1]

Along with offering onsite professional development, conducting classroom observations, and evaluations of teacher implementation of the five standards, another core component of the intervention was facilitating broad-based community involvement in the school improvement process. Although there was strong support and sustained involvement by the community in developing culturally appropriate and sensitive curricula, along with support for the implementation of the five standards, there were significant factors

---

[1] See Chapter 2 for a list of the standards by Dalton (1998) and Tharp et al. (2000).

that constrained reform efforts. These included stubborn resistance from predominantly non-Native, white teachers who typically held deficit views of their students; inertia from a predominantly non-Native school bureaucracy; and many years of enmity between the Zuni tribe and the public school system (Tharp et al. 1999).

Interestingly, state accountability measures and policies both helped and threatened school improvement efforts. On the positive side, after close to ten years of resistance, when it became clear that the state, district, and school imposed accountability measures would not go away, teachers expressed interest in receiving project assistance. The middle school was put on state-imposed probation because of its consistently low student achievement scores, and teachers faced losing their jobs if their teaching did not improve. On the negative side, standardized achievement tests, not constructed with norms for English-language learners, disadvantaged Zuni students, most of whom speak English as a second language (Tharp et al. 1999). Yet, preservation of the Zuni language is absolutely essential for the Zuni to maintain their cultural heritage and religious practices (Tharp et al. 1999). Developing a bilingual program that can develop high levels of functioning in English academic discourse and Zuni is a challenge that is yet to be surmounted.

## CONCLUSION

In this chapter, we reviewed the research literature on community involvement in urban and rural school improvement efforts. We found that the concept of civic capacity was useful in understanding how community linkages are created, sustained, or dissolved in urban reform efforts for several reasons. The concept of civic capacity facilitated analyzing relational linkages as a web of personal and political alliances across a broad spectrum of reform stakeholders. It also provided a framework for analyzing local economic conditions that affected school improvement efforts, as well as the role of school systems in local economies that have experienced enduring poverty.

The notion of civic capacity informs analyses of community involvement in school reform because it puts in the forefront the notions of developing common goals, coalition building, and political alliances – all core elements of creating linkages between individuals, organizations, and institutions. It facilitates understanding systemic reasons why urban reforms fail or succeed because it moves beyond the boundaries of the school or district itself and directs attention to political capacity for affecting school improvement, reallocating existing resources or generating new ones. We found the following to have powerful influences on efforts to improve teaching in urban schools: politics of race; suburbanization, or white flight; corporate and economic divestment; personal and professional relationships based on personalism and nepotism; political alliances, allegiances, and agendas; and economic cartels.

Our analysis clearly showed that along with being a service that students receive, educational systems create jobs, contracts, and career tracks – all things that represent financial security for people working in the system. School systems hold an important place in the local political economy, especially in communities that have experienced corporate divestment and white flight. School districts generate millions of dollars for their local economies. They serve a core function in the local political economy as sources of citywide economic development, community development, stability, and upward mobility for many people. Attempts to reform urban schools ultimately affect much more than the school system itself. In areas where few other job options exist, preserving the status quo can mean preserving financial security for millions of urban dwellers.

Well-planned local action to address urban school reform is difficult to initiate in communities where conditions of concentrated poverty exist. Exit options, such as suburbanization or white flight, exacerbate problems while diminishing urban resources. Racial issues intensify some of the structural problems faced by cities, while also presenting a powerful perceptual filter rooted in personal and historical experiences that affect the bonds of trust and loyalty on which political endeavors depend.

We analyzed rural reform efforts separately with the logic that there are challenges that are unique to rural contexts. Problems common to rural districts include geographic and cultural isolation; high poverty; low levels of adult education; a scarcity of resources; few if any opportunities for business partnerships; nepotism and petty politics; difficulties with teacher and administrator recruitment; high student dropout rates; resistance to change; and paucity of stable or high-paying jobs. While there are common issues that exist across rural contexts, the research we presented also indicates that there are challenges that are also unique to individual communities.

Overall, the role of communities in educational reform for culturally and linguistically diverse students is critical yet complicated because of several factors, including the politics of language and race. One key area for future research is in understanding how to better use both relational linkages and political alliances at the community level to facilitate improved teaching and learning in schools. Relational linkages and political alliances seem to hold a particularly salient role in whether reform efforts within various communities support the status quo or work to improve the conditions for student learning. Further research is also needed to understand how reform efforts connect (or do not connect) with local community contexts, and how much-needed resources can be more permanently sustained in high-poverty communities. This will be especially necessary to inform reform efforts in areas that have endured intergenerational poverty, whether because of sustained corporate divestment or geographic isolation.

# 5

# State-Level Reform Efforts

This chapter focuses on the role of the state in developing, implementing, and supporting school improvement efforts. Central to this analysis is how political and organizational contexts at the state level shape, direct, and support improvement policies and accountability systems. At the core of our analysis is the notion of capacity – or the skillful coordination of individual capacity, collective capacity, and material capacity to achieve the goals of providing improved learning opportunities for all individuals within the policy system (this includes policy makers, state department of education employees, district personnel, administrators, teachers, and students) and of improving teaching, equity, and excellence in classrooms. There is little descriptive or empirical research that examines how states build internal capacity to meet new reform demands or how they create linkages to facilitate standards-based reform implementation successfully. Much more research attention has focused on how to develop school-level capacity for reform and, more recently, on efforts at developing district reform capacity.

Figure 5 locates the role of the state in our conceptual framework.

We first discuss political context as it shapes state policy development and implementation. The different dimensions of capacity at the levels of the state, district, reform team, school, and teacher follow. We then analyze linkages between the different policy domains. We close the chapter with an analysis of state accountability systems

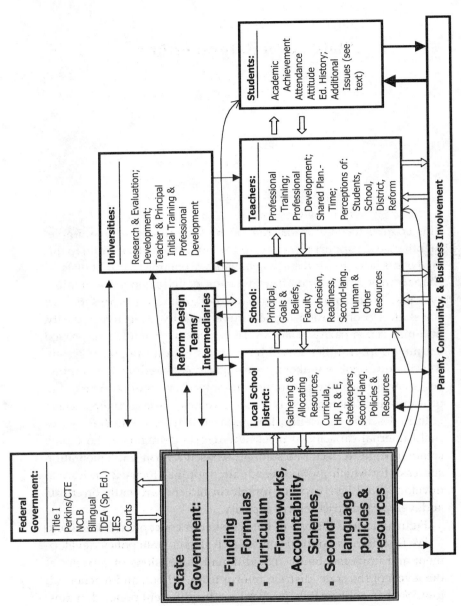

FIGURE 5. State Involvement in and Connections to School Reform

and implications for the academic achievement of culturally and linguistically diverse students.

Politics and political struggles cannot be separated from urban school-reform efforts (Beck and Allexsaht-Snider 2001; Cibulka and Derlin 1998; Hamann 2002; Oakes et al. 2000; Spillane 1999). Educational change mandates represent a coalition of interests brought together under a common name at a particular point in time (Goodson 2000). Educational policies are generated when people representing multiple interests and roles interact as they aim specific actions at a problem for announced purposes (Placier, Hall, McKendall, and Cockrell 2000). Ultimately, they are an expression of people's values, beliefs, and political or moral purposes, which are embedded in contexts of power, relationship, institutional, and societal norms, as well as the economic or political movements unique to the time in which policies are generated (Lasky 2001). Policies are intertwined with politics, leadership, state political cultures and traditions, the institutional capacity of state departments of education, and local demands (Massell 1998).

State political context and capacity shape how urban school-reform efforts are developed, implemented, or circumvented (Erlichson and Goertz 2001; Fairman and Firestone 2001; Lusi 1997; Oakes et al. 2000). Although they share common political structures and processes, all states have their own norms and ways of doing things that significantly shape implementation processes. They also differ in their capacity to design, direct, coordinate, and support accountability systems and improvement efforts. These elements, combined with changes of people in key political offices (both appointed and elected), are significant contributing factors in the life spans of policy initiatives.

Sustainability of state policies is difficult. This is partly because many state policies get rejected by a new governor, chief state school officer, state board, or legislature before they are either adopted or implemented (Cibulka and Derlin 1998). In examining the adoption of state accountability policies in Colorado and Maryland, Cibulka and Derlin (1998) found that the key component to the sustainability of accountability policy implementation in both states was sustained political support that included increasing the institutional capability of the school system. Lack of state-level coordination and leadership is also a major problem, resulting in confusion and bureaucratic obstacles (Erlichson and Goertz 2001).

Continuity in political will and climate are essential for effective and sustained capacity-building efforts to improve teaching and learning (Clune 1998; Massell 1998). In examining nine NSF statewide systemic initiatives, Clune (1998) found that the states that were most successful in creating both depth and breadth of reform implementation built on previous reforms that went back to the 1980s. In these instances, there was continuity, rather than discontinuity, between the earlier reform efforts and the current systemic reform efforts. California provides an example of where changing political will and climate significantly changed the direction and content of improvement efforts. From the early to mid-1980s until the early to mid-1990s, California had been in the forefront of standards-based reform and innovative ideas for teaching and learning. However, the state began to experience sharp reversals in the mid-1990s. Poor state showings on the National Assessment of Educational Progress (NAEP) exam led to several substantive changes in the direction California had taken over the last decade, including the governor's veto of funding for the state's newly developed performance-based assessment program; a questioning of the state's progressive language arts and mathematics frameworks; and an examination of the existing structure for creating standards and tests by state policy makers. Legislation that was enacted shortly after the governor vetoed the state's assessment system specified major revisions in state academic content and testing policies. A complicated range of curriculum guidance initiatives was subsequently issued from numerous agencies as state officials began designing a new system. The state department of education also began organizing task forces on mathematics and language arts, and the work of creating standards, curricula materials, and state assessments began anew (Massell 1998).

In describing the efforts of sixteen schools implementing ambitious equity-minded middle-school reforms, part of Carnegie's Middle Grades Schools State Policy Initiative called Turning Points, Oakes and colleagues (2000) documented how the reform efforts were vulnerable to the changing political climates in California, New Jersey, Texas, Vermont, Massachusetts, and Illinois. Over the five years of their study, the researchers observed how changes in political leadership in each of these states first supported, then hampered, the reform efforts. Along with changes in governorships and in key appointed or elected political positions, came changes in state education policies and the creation of alliances that shifted both material and human resources first toward supporting the Turning Points reforms, then away from them.

## CAPACITY

State officials who oversee and direct standards-based reforms have been asked to create new systems and ways of working. They are also being asked to solve problems in areas that are new to them. State departments of education engaged in standards-based reforms and trying to implement mandates required by the federal No Child Left Behind Act are taking on a charge very different from their traditional roles for licensing teachers and accrediting schools. They are now faced with leading and managing complex, knowledge-intensive, and uncertain reforms. Little is known by state department of education staff or others at the state level about how to establish a coherent policy system promoting and supporting the redesign of teaching and learning in schools. Some states are also working on designing new assessment systems, standards, and curricula to meet the more rigorous accountability requirements (Lusi 1997).

This requires capacity building at the state level. Although there is little empirical research in this area, we have identified the domains for capacity building that are often addressed inferentially in the work that does exist. Capacity building needs to occur in several areas at the state level, including: (a) development of clear and effective standards (Mintrop 2004); (b) coordination of or alignment of federal, state, and district accountability systems (O'Day and Gross 1999); (c) reform leaders learning how to develop contextually sensitive reform implementation plans (Oakes et al. 2000); (d) restructuring of state departments of education or other state agencies to meet accountability and new federal policy demands (Lusi 1997); (e) restructuring of state finance systems to meet accountability and new federal

policy demands (Odden 1999; Odden and Clune 1998); (f) developing partnerships with outside experts or partners (Hamann and
Lane 2002; May, Supovitz, and Lesnick 2004); (g) providing professional development at the state level (Cohen and Hill 2001; Oakes
et al. 2000; Spillane 2001); (h) facilitating capacity building at the district and school level and providing appropriate professional development at the district and school levels (Darling-Hammond and Ball
1998), especially for schools states have taken over or reconstituted
(Desimone et al. 2002; Finnigan et al. 2003); and (i) creating effective
linkages between different policy domains and among reform stakeholders (Beck and Allexsaht-Snider 2001; Darling-Hammond et al.
2002; Hamann 2002; Lusi 1997; Oakes et al. 2000).

Massell (1998) identified four organizational-level capacities necessary at state, district, and school levels to enhance the improvement
of teaching and learning:

- Number and kinds of people supporting the classroom.
- Number and quality of social relationships.
- Material (non–human resources).
- Organization and allocation of school and district resources. (p. 3)

In the discussion that follows, we explore how differing levels of
state capacities in these areas affected state agency abilities to design,
direct, and support school-level improvement efforts and accountability systems successfully.

In investigating the role of state departments of education in complex school reform between 1991 and 1993 in Kentucky and Vermont,
Lusi (1997) identified several contextual factors that greatly influenced each state's department of education's effort at reform implementation. These included the role of the state department of education in designing the reform; the role of key external policy players,
the legislatures, and state boards of education; the state policy history
and regulatory environment; agency leadership; and scale. She also
found that capacity and normative practices were significant factors
in reform implementation. In both states, there was solid evidence of
reform implementation in all districts. The processes of implementation, although sharing some similar aspects, were unique to each
state's context and varied significantly. Each state's efforts at capacity

building exemplify Hatch's (2000) notion that it takes capacity to build capacity.

Kentucky is often viewed as a positive example of a state developing its capacity to more effectively direct reform efforts. It moved from a system of primarily sanctions and rewards to one of statewide capacity building for improved classroom teaching Mintrop (2004). The state developed tests that measure more than basic skill development in students. Kentucky also created a relatively well-aligned and consistent accountability system and allocated funding and experts to provide professional development with the goal of reaching all teachers. Consequently, the state had some success in improving student learning in some districts, not simply increasing student scores on tests that assess only basic skills (McIntyre and Kyle 2002; O'Day and Gross 1999).

## State Capacity to Support Professional Learning in State Agencies

There are several areas where states can develop capacity to better support the learning of state-level employees to better design, direct, and coordinate reform efforts. Billig, Perry, and Pokorny (1999) asked state education agency staff to describe models, strengths, challenges, and lessons learned as they implemented the school support provisions of the Improving America's School Act (IASA). They identified several areas where state agencies need assistance in building internal capacity to meet their new responsibilities.

Researchers found that states were slow in responding to legislative requirements. State education agency (SEA) respondents reported this was largely because the IASA changed so many of their operating procedures and roles. Three years after the act was in place, all but ten states had one of three kinds of school support models. States used three strategies to provide assistance to their schools: using a cadre of distinguished educators, using intermediary agencies, or creating unique models. The ten states that did not have support systems in place had either experienced SEA downsizing and thus lost the person in charge of system design or lost SEA leaders due to retirement. In each of these instances, there was no one in place to direct the development of the support system.

All SEA representatives faced challenges in designing systems that had not previously been in place. These challenges included coordinating work assignments and reports of support teams; providing quality training of sufficient frequency, depth, and breadth to be useful; and issues of quality control (Billig, Perry, and Pokorny 1999). Many of them discussed the need to provide in-depth professional development on a multitude of issues, including what a good state plan looks like; how to collect and analyze data; how to access information and resources; the need to experiment and evolve; and what it means to be responsive to local needs. The authors concluded their analysis by saying that SEAs need to share information about their models, develop more consistent training and management systems, and promote the use of support structures if they are to be viable systems. They would also benefit from direct guidance on how to establish these systems.

## State Capacity to Support Professional Development in Districts and Schools

Numerous states have developed their capacity to better design, direct, and coordinate district- and school-level professional development. Massell (1998) explored the strategies that eight states – California, Colorado, Florida, Kentucky, Maryland, Michigan, Minnesota, and Texas – used to build capacity for improving teaching and learning. All eight state departments of education attempted to reorganize so that they could meet the new demands to provide professional development and technical assistance for improved teaching and learning. Some of them introduced new managerial strategies based on a more client-oriented approach. States such as Florida, Kentucky, and Texas reduced or eliminated compliance monitoring and school evaluations based on site inspections (except in the cases of chronically low-performing schools). California had a particularly unique approach called Program Quality Review, an extended process of self-review and feedback from outside consultants. Among other things, it emphasized analyzing student work through multiple measures, focused on their results, and used content and performance standards as core features of the review; these elements in concert directed the improvement plan (Massell 1998).

In Massell's (1998) study, all eight state departments of education made the decision not to directly offer technical assistance and professional development. The most prevalent strategy they used to provide professional development to schools was to build or support an external infrastructure of assistance. They relied on preexisting groups or institutions to fulfill these needs. This was done in part because of a belief that higher levels of government should decentralize decision-making authority to local levels to improve the quality of service. State department of education staff also had been reduced 25 percent or more in several states, meaning they did not have the personnel to offer assistance directly to schools. Most of the states in the study developed networks of teachers, other educational experts, schools, or districts to build professional capacity to implement reform efforts. There were three kinds of networks: One focused primarily on improving the knowledge and skills of the individuals in organizations. Another network deployed cadres of teachers or other experts who could offer knowledge or skills to others. The third kind was used to develop and disseminate specific products (Massell 1998).

Massell's (1998) study found that many state support systems did not provide enough professional development to affect student test scores. This led Massell to propose that state departments of education need greater understanding about the extent to which the external groups hired to provide professional development can actually meet the needs that districts and schools have for improving classroom teaching and leadership capabilities. In many instances, these groups provided shallow assistance or traditional workshops; these were not effective for changing classroom teaching. This led researchers to ask whether support providers themselves have the knowledge, skills, or time needed to provide high-quality and appropriate professional development. Service providers both lacked the expertise and numbers of professional developers to reach the numbers of teachers who needed assistance (Massell 1998).

In examining why only 10 percent of the teachers in California were able to implement new state mathematics standards successfully, Cohen and Hill (2001) found that appropriate professional development offered by the state was the key factor. For instructional policy to improve student achievement, it must do so directly through changes in teacher practice. The content and amount of professional development mattered when creating consistency between state instructional policy and classroom instruction. Teachers who took workshops that were extended in time, and which focused on teacher study, discussion of tasks students would do, and assessment had deeper understanding of mathematical topics and concepts. They also reported more classroom practices similar to those in the state reforms. In contrast, teachers who took workshops more focused on other tangential topics, such as gender and cooperative learning, were less likely to report pedagogic practices consistent with state reforms (Cohen and Hill 2002; Finnigan, O'Day, and Wakelyn 2003; Stein et al. 2002).

If the 80 to 160 hours of professional development in a content area that Supovitz and Turner (2000) proposed is an accurate figure to see significant changes in teaching practices, then most support provided to schools is too fragmentary and not time intensive enough to have the deep effect needed to change instruction. External providers simply cannot provide the intensity of professional development needed to change classroom practice within the current resource constraints (Finnigan, O'Day, and Wakelyn 2003) that states face.

Massell (1998) proposed several questions that policy makers and other state representatives directing and overseeing school improvement efforts need to ask themselves about their own internal capacity to facilitate standards-based reforms, including:

- Does the state's infrastructure for technical assistance and professional development have adequate resources, knowledge, and people power to carry out its assigned responsibilities? Do they use high-quality models of professional development and technical assistance?
- Does the state have a strategy for helping schools and teachers translate into practice the data generated by the accountability and testing program?
- Do the state's capacity-building initiatives meet the following research-supported criteria: Are the initiatives well suited to individual school settings? Are the initiatives extended over time, providing opportunities for feedback and reflection? Are the initiatives reform-linked and curriculum-specific?

- Can the state play a role in encouraging and brokering research on curriculum and instructional practices that improves the performance of all students?
- Do the state's initiatives provide adequate incentives for students, teachers, schools, districts, institutions of higher education, and other external organizations to build capacity?
- Does the state policy system send coherent and consistent signals to schools and teachers about building needed knowledge and skills? (p. 42)

We now move to an analysis of linkages. The areas identified as important linkages in many instances are areas where states also need to develop capacity to better support school-improvement efforts.

## LINKAGES

Although none of the work incorporated into this section of the report had as one of its research goals the identification of linkages between states and other policy domains, several authors did described linkages and reform processes similarly. These were informal communications between key reform stakeholders (Hamann 2002); creating political alliances (Beck and Allexsaht-Snider 2001; Oakes et al. 2000) and partnerships (Lusi 1997; Oakes et al. 2000); realigning funding or finding new sources of funding (Darling-Hammond et al. 2002; Lusi 1997; Oakes et al. 2000); and policy mandates, memoranda, and accountability systems (Beck and Allexsaht-Snider 2001; Darling-Hammond et al. 2003; Lusi 1997; Oakes et al. 2000).

## Policy Alignment

The one linkage common to all research cited in this chapter is state policy. State policies, memoranda, accountability systems, curriculum frameworks, and resource allocation can be important linkages between states, districts, schools, and classrooms. For instance, curriculum frameworks can provide guidelines to district and school personnel so that classroom teaching can be brought into closer alignment with state standards and accountability measures (Cohen and Hill 2001). These linkages do not, however, guarantee coordinated resource allocation or expectations, especially when schools are subject to more than one accountability system (O'Day and Gross 1999), as we discussed in our analysis of state capacity building. We have also provided several examples of ways in which change in policies can shift resource allocation away from reform efforts (Oakes et al. 2000).

In his work to identify reform efforts that achieved both breadth and depth of implementation, Clune (1998) found that the combination of state assessment as the lead policy instrument and professional support networking as a delivery structure operated as a universal link between the higher and lower levels in the policy system. This held true regardless of whether state policy was developed based on central or local control. States with strong centralized policies needed a way to bridge the gap between state agencies and schools, while states that emphasized local control found that the assessment and support network was a politically amenable way to provide strong instructional guidance. In both kinds of states, assessments and support networking bridged the gap between the large "grain size" of the standards and the more specific tasks demanded by teaching and learning.

### State Funding and Funding Infrastructures

Financial support from states is a fundamental and structural condition for schools to function. The presence of financial support is also a condition for implementing reform and improving teaching and learning. Little is known, however, about how much financial support is actually needed for schools to meet the challenge of providing all students with a high-quality education (Guthrie and Rothstein 1999; Massell 1998).

States are an important source for allocating material resources to schools. In the United States, each state is responsible for K–12 education within its borders. The school finance system is established in state law and frequently supplemented by state department of education regulations. Revenues to fund K–12 education come almost equally from state and local resources (about 93 percent of the total), while the remaining 7 percent or so come from federal sources. State revenue comes from each state's general tax and other revenues in most states. Other revenues come from sales and income taxes (Bernie and Stiefel 1999).

The ways these resources are organized and structured can facilitate or hinder capacity-building efforts (Massell 1998). There are three primary areas of funding that are relevant to this discussion: (1) the actual dollars that go to schools to support basic day-to-day operating procedures; (2) the money that is needed to improve the conditions of the physical plant in rundown schools; (3) the financial support to provide professional development and material resources to build internal capacity in the areas of leadership, subject-area knowledge, and teaching technique.

Odden and Clune (1998) proposed that state school financing systems are "aging structures in need of renovation" (p. xi). State school finance systems are under attack, not only because they have failed to do the job for which they were produced but because these dated systems are also inadequate both for current finance problems and for the finance challenges that standards-based reforms place on school systems (Odden 1999). Odden argued that, in several states, school finance formulas in the present reform context actually exacerbate fiscal disparities (Odden 1999). Odden and Clune maintained that the infrastructures and formulas states have in place have proven to be ineffective in providing schools with adequate funding, particularly in the current standards-based climate where all students are to be provided a high-quality education. They and others (Duncombe and Yinger 1999; Guthrie and Rothstein 1999; Minorini and Sugarman 1999) built a case that rather than using models based on equity, which focus on providing equal funding to all schools, a model based on adequacy is better suited to provide financial resources to all schools, particularly to those schools in the poorest areas, schools with at-risk students, or those identified as needing improvement.

The logic behind an adequacy model of state school financing proposes that an adequate level of school financing enabling students to learn to higher standards needs to be developed. Such a model would identify inputs necessary to support high-quality teaching and learning for all students, as well as outputs, primarily in the form of student learning outcomes as measured by multiple measures, which identify more than basic competencies. Once a basic level of adequacy is established, formulas need to be established to provide extra financial resources to those schools that are in poor areas, schools identified as low performing, and schools with high numbers of poor, minority, new immigrant, second language, and special-needs students (Guthrie and Rothstein 1999; Odden 1999).

State departments of education, state legislatures, and state supreme courts have been trying to develop definitions for adequacy since the late 1970s. This has proven to be no small task. Basic questions these people have wrestled with are, Adequate to do what? Adequate how? Adequate for what purpose? At a minimum, answering these questions requires policy judgments about (1) learning or performance levels to be attained by students and (2) resource levels likely to facilitate schools accomplishing newly established performance levels (Guthrie and Rothstein 1999).

Establishing what adequacy means is not an easy task and is inherently value-bound. People who value a democratic threshold principle for education are likely to ask for more resources for schools to ensure that all students leave school better prepared to be fully participating members of a democratic society. Others, who hold more functional or market-based approaches to educational funding, are more likely to argue for fewer resources being allocated to schools, as they tend to hold a more narrow interpretation of the role of schooling in society, one that may focus primarily on preparation for the job market, rather than including civic participation as a goal of education (Ladd and Hansen 1999).

The optimal mix and level of resources needed to improve teaching and learning in low-performing schools is unknown, and several researchers have proposed that further research needs to be conducted to identify what different states will need to provide high-quality education to all students (Duncombe and Yinger 1999; Guthrie and Rothstein 1999).

### Funding Reform

Creating new pathways for funding and realigning existing funding structures have been key components in several reform efforts in which states have been involved. For example, in trying to implement the Carnegie reforms in Texas, the Carnegie state task force leader created an alliance between her office and the Texas Education Agency's Gifted and Talented Office. Along with providing professional development, the collaboration also achieved reallocating state Chapter 2 funding to help support Turning Point efforts. For the first time in Texas, teachers of some of the lowest-achieving, low-income African American and Latino students in the state had access to the intensive, high-quality professional development usually reserved for the state's most privileged students (Oakes et al. 2000, p. 232).

Reform leaders in Vermont also sought external funding partnerships as a way to bring in extra financial resources for their reform efforts. The Vermont Department of Education (VDE) pursued external grants from organizations such as the National Science Foundation and the New American Schools Corporation. The VDE was selective and intentional when it applied for grants. Reform leaders applied to funding organizations that could directly support their statewide capacity-building efforts in the areas of identifying exemplary schools and improving teacher content area and pedagogical expertise (Lusi 1997).

The case of Maine points to how a state with a small population was creative in the way it gained access to and used federal Comprehensive School Reform (CSR) grant funds. In states with small populations, and relatively few Title I–eligible students, receiving CSR funds can be a challenge. To accrue CSR funds for its Promising Futures high school reform strategy, Maine effectively petitioned for a federal waiver to allow it to add parameters to the federal CSR program guidelines. The waiver allowed Maine to integrate elements of Promising Futures into CSR and to confine CSR eligibility only to high schools. By achieving these goals, high schools that agreed to implement Promising Futures gained access to CSR resources to implement the reform (Hamann and Lane, 2002).

On a grander scale, many states across the United States are finding they simply do not have the money they need to help the number of schools that have been identified as in need of improvement. For instance, in 1999–2000, California identified over 3,000 schools as underperforming, yet only included 860 of them in the first two years of its Immediate Intervention/Underperforming Schools Program. Other states limit the schools they identify as needing assistance to match the resources they have available. Maryland and Connecticut are two of several states that identify only their lowest-performing schools for state assistance. Many states rely primarily on federal funds – particularly Title I funds – to support program improvement initiatives (Goertz, Duffy, and LaFloch 2003, p. 37). Even with the additional federal dollars, they still do not have enough to provide extra human and financial resources to all schools identified as needing improvement.

### Political Allegiances, Partnerships, and Relational Linkages

Inseparable from resource allocation at the state level are political allegiances or alliances. Beck and Allexsaht-Snider (2001) described how the English-only preference of the Georgia Superintendent of Education influenced the ways she directed the state's bilingual program, whom she chose as the state's Title I director, and how funds were allocated. To assure consistency in action, the Superintendent of Education chose a Title I director who shared her beliefs about bilingual education. In 1999, the state's Title I director, in support of the state Superintendent of Education's political agenda and acting in accordance with her plan for bilingual education, eliminated migrant education curriculum coordinators positions by cutting funding. In this instance, it becomes apparent how political agendas and alliances created certain kinds of linkages while eliminating others.

Partnerships were another important linkage between states, professional development providers, outside experts, districts, and schools. Creating partnerships and alliances between a broad array of stakeholders was a core element of several state-led reform efforts (Clune 1998; Hamann and Lane 2002; Lusi 1997; Oakes et al. 2000). These partnerships served multiple purposes, primarily building the internal capacity of state agencies to direct and support improvement efforts and bringing in financial or material resources. In each of the cases we describe, state reform efforts would not have made the inroads they did without the partnerships.

For example, the Vermont Department of Education established strong linkages and networks with outside groups, such as practitioners and groups representing them; state universities; the business community; the State Board of Education; and the state legislature. They developed the Vermont Restructuring Corps, a group of close to one hundred people throughout the state from differing professional backgrounds who were trained to develop capacity for restructuring districts and schools.

As we have said before, coordinating the movement of human and material resources across the linkage is very important. In the early phases of implementing the Kentucky Education Reform Act, the Kentucky Department of Education (KDE) created several policy documents and official notices that were sent to districts and schools. Both district and school personnel reported that these documents from the KDE contained mixed messages concerning the reform and its implementation, thus making difficult the coordinated and clear action necessary to support reform efforts (Lusi 1997). In this instance, the KDE created a linkage; yet, reform implementation was not facilitated because of uncoordinated movement across the linkage.

However, the Carnegie strategy for implementation of its Middle Grades Schools State Policy Initiative is an interesting example of an outside agency developing strong relational linkages with state agencies to develop an equity-based, democratic reform. To build reform capacity at the state level, the Carnegie Corporation provided an array of material and human resources to all participating states. They helped states assemble task forces composed of people across agencies and organizations, such as governors, state school officials, heads of health and social service agencies, legislators, middle-grade educators, leaders in other reforms, and teacher licensers and testers. Central project staff carried out task force work by doing such things as fostering collaboration among and between agencies and establishing networks of reforming schools. In each state, strategies to create linkages, such as promoting reform, creating networks, aligning state infrastructures and policies with Carnegie goals, and realigning and creating funding pathways, were designed to coincide with state normative practices and capacity. Reform efforts in Illinois and Vermont took more bottom-up approaches, given their long-standing traditions of local broad-based, grassroots political involvement. In Massachusetts, Turning Points' project directors grappled with how to promote democratic, equity-based reform in an increasingly centralized policy context, while simultaneously respecting local communities' deep-rooted preferences for local control. California and Texas both had much more top-down-driven reform efforts (Oakes et al. 2000).

Partnerships can be developed through formal structures such as those described in the Carnegie case, or they can come about as a result of more informal communications between colleagues, community members, business owners, and university personnel. The Georgia Project, a bilingual education program, began when a prominent member of a small Georgia town was invited into his granddaughter's elementary classroom. The young woman was struggling with how to teach increasing numbers of Spanish-only-speaking students in her classroom. Her grandfather's visit led him to contact a local business owner who contacted a friend at the Universidad de Monterey in Mexico, and a chain of events began that marked the inception of the first large-scale bilingual education effort in Georgia (Hamann 2002).

### Ideological Linkages

Ideological linkages, or shared values, vision, and goals among reform stakeholders, are another salient factor in school reform. For example, the Carnegie Foundation's efforts to promote detracking practices met with resistance from upper-middle-class or wealthy, predominantly white parents who were motivated by racial fears, academic anxieties, and issues of status and access (Oakes et al. 2000). In all of the racially mixed schools with significant numbers of middle-class or more affluent families, parents battled heterogeneous grouping. In these cases, community values and the politics of race and social class were inextricably intertwined with beliefs of intelligence. Little in states' strategies prepared them to deal explicitly with the cultural and political contradictions that the Turning Points reform often brought to light. Several key elements necessary for change were not present: social supports, technical knowledge, a tradition of intellectual rigor, or firm mandates to sustain attempts for equity. Nor could people "stay ahead of their own countervailing inclinations" toward exclusion (Oakes et al. 2000, p. 118). In this case, several ideological chasms could not be bridged. This lack of ideological bridge building was a primary factor explaining why reforms were not successful at the local level.

In his study of the implementation of the Early Childhood and Academic Assistance Act of 1993, Spillane (2001) found that a "web of interdependent and mutually self-supporting beliefs undergird" educators' responses to state policies that push for a more intellectually rigorous curriculum for all American students.

> Simply telling teachers that all children can and should do intellectually challenging work is unlikely to bring about such substantive instructional change. Understanding local educators' implementation of policies that challenge conventional wisdom about educating poor students, necessitates considering their knowledge and convictions about students *in relation* to their beliefs about teaching, learning and classroom practice. (p. 217, emphasis in original text)

District and school personnel in the South Carolina schools Spillane studied chose not to implement new state standards because they believed that their students were not capable of performing to the more rigorous standards. Because the teachers and principals in his study understood learning from a behaviorist perspective and saw disadvantaged students chiefly in terms of their deficiency in basic language and behavioral skills, they shelved proposals for more intellectually challenging content and pedagogy. Believing that teaching the basics was a prerequisite to any instruction in more intellectually demanding content, teachers focused on getting disadvantaged students up-to-speed on basic skills and never managed to get to the more intellectually challenging content.

Receiving professional development and seeing their students perform to the new standards were critical to changing the beliefs and practices for two teachers in this study. As these teachers developed new understandings of mathematics and literacy instruction, their practice changed. They began to teach more academically challenging content and tried new instructional approaches. In observing their students' academic successes with the more demanding content, these teachers saw for themselves that poor students of color were capable of learning more demanding intellectual content. They thus created the conditions that changed their own beliefs about poor African American students. In these interactions, teachers' "will to reform their teaching" was fueled by their new understandings and skills that in turn fueled their efforts to further develop their knowledge (Spillane 2001, p. 238).

### State Accountability Systems

Federal and state accountability systems are one of the most salient linkages between the state as a policy domain and districts and schools. They are also an expression of existing state capacity to develop, interpret, and use data gathered from accountability systems to inform decision making. That state accountability systems and NCLB are affecting how and what students learn, how their learning is measured, and what is being measured cannot be denied. Although mechanisms of school accountability vary from jurisdiction to jurisdiction, they tend to share some common components, including establishing performance target levels with consequences, typically at the school level, to ascertain whether schools are meeting state and federal guidelines (Goertz, Duffy, and LeFloch 2001; O'Day 2002).

Although there is a high degree of consistency in how the accountability systems are used, there are notable differences in several areas of accountability system development and administration, including language or content and performance standards. Comparing the results of one state with another can be problematic (Chun and Goertz 1999) in part because the language used in developing, analyzing, and reporting state accountability varies considerably (O'Day 2002). Content standards used by states to develop their accountability systems also vary in specificity and rigor. In short, content standards and state tests are much more rigorous in some states than in others.

State-developed performance standards, which determine the scores used to define proficient performance, also vary widely across states. For example, Linn, Baker, and Betebenner (2002) found that the percentage of students reported on the state department of education Web sites to have scored at the proficient level or higher on state grade 8 mathematics assessments in 2001, was 39 percent in Mississippi, 7 percent in Louisiana, and 92 percent in Texas. Although there may be true differences in mathematics achievement in these three states, they cannot be as large as the differences in these percentages. Proficient or passing clearly mean different things in these three states (Linn, Baker, and Betebenner 2002).

Several states presently are developing or revising high school exit exams (Amrein and Berliner 2002; Goertz et al. 2001) in response to NCLB. In examining which states have implemented high-stakes exit exams, Amrein and Berliner (2002) found that they were more common in states that spent less than the national average per pupil per schooling as compared with the nation; had more centralized governments; were highly populated states or states with the largest population growth compared with the nation, in the South, and the southwest; and in schools with high numbers of African American and Hispanic students. Although there is variability in these data (for instance, all states with high numbers of high-poverty students have not adopted high-stakes testing policies), high-performing schools were not the targets for these policies; rather it was poor, urban schools with high numbers of low-achieving students (Amrein and Berliner 2002).

It is highly contested whether implementation of high-stakes accountability systems actually improves student learning, are valid, or are used ethically (Elmore 2002; O'Day 2002). While some research shows real gains in learning (Carnoy, Loeb, and Smith 2000; Grissmer and Flanagan 1998; Grissmer et al. 2000), there is a growing body of empirical research that questions various aspects of the implementation and consequences of states' high-stakes accountability systems (Amrein and Berliner 2002; Elmore 2002; O'Day 2002) as well as NCLB. Even with the dissenting evidence, it is also clear that state accountability policies are powerful linkages between the federal government, states, districts, and schools.

## Alignment between Accountability Systems at Different Policy Levels

Alignment between state and other policy domains appears to be important for successful reform. We propose that alignment is an important linkage across states, districts, and schools. Research, however, finds that such alignment is not present.

In their analysis of Title I accountability in two states – California and Kentucky – and three districts – San Francisco, Chicago, and New York City – O'Day and Gross (1999) examined both the congruence among the policies governing Title I accountability and those governing accountability for all schools in each jurisdiction. They also examined whether there was congruency in how schools were identified across state and district domains. They found that Title I lists and state/local lists were not kept together in any jurisdiction except Kentucky. Different offices kept records of Title I schools and low-performing schools identified as needing intervention. Once offices were identified, finding employees who could provide researchers the data they needed was not easy or direct, particularly with Title I school records. Once these individuals were found, they were frequently unable to provide information on policy processes or support systems.

O'Day and Gross (1999) also found that the majority of state-identified, low-performing schools were Title I schools. These different accountability systems often were not in accord with each other. This led the authors to propose that Title I schools were sometimes subject to at least two accountability systems that measured student performance – one required by the Title I provisions of the Elementary and Secondary Education Act (ESEA) and the state or local jurisdiction in which the school was located. These different accountability systems sent information to low-performing Title I schools that at times were not coordinated and were not aligned with the other. When state and Title I accountability systems have discrepancies in the ways schools are identified as needing improvement, the inconsistency is often found in the criteria used for detection. Researchers proposed these inconsistencies in criteria occur because of three inter-related factors: differences in the purposes of the accountability systems, differences in who identifies the schools, and general problems in implementation and administrative coordination.

The most commonly identified factor accounting for the differing criteria among systems was the level of governance that identified schools as needing intervention because of poor student performance. Kentucky had removed local units from the decision-making process, while Maryland had different levels in the education system conducting analyses and had differing criteria at the local level. In Maryland, these factors resulted in a relatively small number of schools being consistently identified by the state and local accountability systems as needing assistance because Title I identification of schools differed from county to county, while no such variation occurred in the state accountability system (O'Day and Gross 1999). Their analysis points to several areas where states need to develop linking capacity, including establishing basic communication between personnel working in different agencies responsible for Title I and low-performing schools; linking or coordinating databases, filing systems, and basic record keeping; coordinating or aligning how Title I schools are identified across jurisdictions; and coordinating intervention plans and resource allocation to schools. The issue of states providing assistance to schools identified as low performing under NCLB is turning out to be more complex than many policy makers and school reformers realized.

## State Support and Sanctions That Accompany Accountability Systems

States provide both pressure and support for improved student achievement scores (Goertz, Duffy, and LaFloch 2003; O'Day 2002). Incentives are often financial rewards for increased achievement scores (Amrein and Berliner 2002). Pressure can be manifested by publicly displaying student test results, public ranking of schools (Acker-Hocevar and Touchton 2001), and school probations (Lindle 1999) or reconstitutions (O'Day 2002). Some states are leaning toward developing teaching capacity; for example, North Carolina and Kentucky have developed detailed structures for statewide capacity building in schools that do not meet annual yearly progress (Mintrop 2004).

Acker-Hocevar and Touchton (2001) investigated the perceptions of principals from high-poverty, minority, failing schools in Florida toward state accountability measures. Principals in their study were not against using the Florida Comprehensive Assessment Test as a measure of student success. They did, however, feel pressure from the state to improve student test scores, and spoke about being in a "Catch-22" situation in which they found themselves focusing on the short-term goal of increasing student test scores to improve their schools' "D" or "F" grades. In doing this, principals reported they were creating the conditions in their schools in which student learning was compromised because of the "drill and kill" environment and the narrowed curriculum as schools focused primarily on subjects and skills that were tested. There is mounting evidence to suggest that when the pressure from the state to improve student achievement scores is too great, schools and teachers narrow the curriculum and teach to the test (Klein et al. 2000; Madaus and Clarke 2001) or replace regular curriculum with test-preparation materials, in essence teaching with predominantly test-preparation materials (McNeil 2000; McNeil and Valenzuela 2001) even when schools are attempting to build internal capacity by adopting reform models (Datnow and Kemper 2002).

There is little research on state reconstitution or takeover efforts, as they are a relatively new state intervention strategy. They are, in short, an area that needs much more research attention because there is much to be learned about their effectiveness or how such intervention efforts can be improved. The little research that does exist indicates that the results of state takeovers and reconstitution efforts for schools that have been sanctioned are mixed (Mintrop 2004). On the positive side, they can help to eliminate nepotism within a school district's decision-making processes; improve a school district's administrative and financial management practices; and upgrade the condition of rundown school buildings (Rudo 2001). There is virtually no evidence, however, that state takeovers or reconstitutions actually improve teaching and learning in schools (Desimone et al. 2002; Rudo 2001).

Desimone et al. (2002) studied three theories of action that guided reconstitution efforts in six schools from one large urban district, which give a sense of what we might expect with state school reconstitutions. First, in examining the premise that requiring all staff to reapply for their positions would rid schools of weak staff while also replenishing the school with strong staff, the authors found that the larger social context characterized by chronic teacher shortages did not bring more highly certified staff to schools. Second, in examining the premise that reconstitution would encourage fundamental redesigning of schools, data indicated that the redesigning reformists had hoped for (e.g., inclusive governance structures) did not happen. High teacher and administrator turnover, confusion, and pressure interfered with the more complex endeavors reconstitution efforts were meant to generate. These schools were not able to develop the capacity to include school staff, parents, and community stakeholders systematically in designing new organizational repertoires and instructional practices that might facilitate increased opportunities for student learning in their schools. Finally, during the three years under study, none of the six schools being reconstituted was able to meet their ultimate goal of consistently increasing student achievement. Again, high student, teacher, and administrator turnover severely hampered each school's ability to build the internal capacity needed to improve the conditions for learning. Taken together, these findings led the researchers to conclude that the theories of action nested in reconstitution efforts are untenable because they fail to address the broader contextual factors that mediate school capacity, especially in altering their performance. They proposed that more empirical studies are needed to develop a knowledge base on the substantive viability of this approach to improving student achievement.

## Test Validity and Other Questions

Increasing numbers of educational researchers are questioning the validity of high-stakes student assessments and how they are being used (Elmore 2002; O'Day 2002) and calling for more systematic testing and developing of student assessments (Shavelson, Baxter, and Pine 1992), including those in science (Ruiz-Primo, Li, and Shavelson 2002), for English-language learners (ELLs), and poor or minority students (Fuller and Johnson 2001; Padron, Waxman, and Rivera 2002; Solano-Flores and Trumbull 2003). Testing practices for ELL students are often driven by politics rather than by theory (August and Hakuta 1998).

For instance, student performance on state accountability tests is sensitive to the wording of test questions. When testing includes linguistically diverse populations, wording issues become even more pronounced, both when developing the tests, as in translating questions so that they measure the same construct across languages, and when students read and translate the questions in a way they can understand (Solano-Flores and Trumbull 2003). These researchers conducted a microanalysis of one mathematics test item for fourth- and fifth-graders on three dimensions: formal properties, empirical properties, and differential properties. They asked students to calculate the amount of money they would need to buy lunch for one week. The sentence read, "His mother has only $1.00 bills." Researchers found that 56 percent of American Indian and 52 percent of African American students read this sentence in the word problem incorrectly, while 84 percent of White students read this sentence correctly. The African American and American Indian students, overwhelmingly, interpreted the sentence to mean that their mothers had only one dollar for the week. This led researchers to conclude that when trying to understand and reply to the test question, students drew from their personal experiences of living in households with little money.

In examining the scores of Mandarin and Spanish speakers, Solano-Flores and Trumbull (2003) also found that these ELLs performed better on some items in one language and better on other items in the other language. These findings led the authors to conclude that culture-free tests cannot be developed. For this reason, they proposed that issues of test validity and translation be incorporated into the reasoning that guides development of accountability systems, particularly tests that measure student content and process knowledge.

In short, state accountability systems need more rigorous study (Fuller and Johnson 2001). Padron, Waxman, and Rivera (2002) stated that there is a need to move beyond the debates about state accountability systems and examine ways to improve high-stakes testing practices so that they can better assess Hispanic students' abilities. Valenzuela (1999) maintained that because the Texas Assessment of Academic Skills in Texas was given in English only, there was no way to discern whether students who were transitioning Spanish-English speakers were being tested on their English-speaking skills or their subject-area content knowledge. Another study found that in addition to content knowledge affecting student achievement scores, ELL students have unique sets of weaknesses and strengths in English, along with unique sets of weaknesses and strengths in their primary language. These factors together affect second-language learners' achievement scores; yet, tests do not have a way to separate the effects of these influences on ELLs' achievement scores (Solano-Flores and Trumbull 2003).

Last, using multiple sources of student data is important in determining the generalizability and validity of the findings of any one source of data. Especially when the stakes are high, it is imperative to use multiple indicators of student achievement (Fuhrman, Goertz, and Duffy 2002). In investigating claims that Texas achievement gaps were narrowing, as measured on TAAS, Haney (2000) used data from several different sources, including NAEP and national and state student retention and dropout data. In comparing TAAS with NAEP data, he found an inconsistency in the TAAS and NAEP findings pertaining to the achievement gap. NAEP student data did not indicate that the achievement gap was closing. By examining multiple sources of student data, he also found that by the end of the 1990s, 25–30 percent of Black and Hispanic students repeated grade 9, compared with only 10 percent of white students. This supports the finding by McNeil (2000) that grade 9 classes in some of the minority urban high schools in Texas were becoming numerically half of the student population. She also found that, to improve the numbers of Latino tenth-grade students passing the TAAS, some schools counseled students to leave school after ninth grade (or did not discourage those who might want to leave) because the schools' scores would be higher if these students left before taking the grade 10 TAAS.

Research indicates with increasing consistency that accountability systems will not necessarily improve student learning, nor will they inherently close the achievement gaps between poor, minority, and more affluent students. In comparison to student social class, which is still the overwhelming predictor of school test performance, policy instruments appear to be weak interventions. While student social-status measures encapsulate a lifetime of inequities and their effects over the years, measures of curriculum and teacher learning address only a single year in students' school lives. It is logical to propose that the benefits of strong instructional interventions might also accumulate over the years of schooling (Hill, Cohen, and Moffitt 1999) and that such benefits could be effectively measured. How this accumulated learning can be thoroughly and ethically measured in students is an area that is hotly contested and ripe for further empirical study.

## CONCLUSION

At the current time, especially with the advent of NCLB, state officials are being asked to create systems many of them have never before been asked to design, and they are being asked to solve problems in areas that are new to them. This requires capacity building at the state level. Few studies actually look within state departments of education or other state agencies to examine what states have done to restructure, why they chose the restructuring strategies they have, or what learning opportunities they provided to officials and employees at the state level. In our examples in which state officials and policy makers have sought problem-solving or capacity-building partnerships with outside experts, there is virtually no research conducted that follows the processes or steps that were used so that other states could learn from such processes.

State political context and capacity shape how urban and rural school-improvement efforts are developed, implemented, or circumvented (Oakes et al. 2000). All states have their own norms and political climates that shape implementation processes; this combined with changes of people in key political positions significantly affects the life spans of policy initiatives designed to improve teaching and learning in schools. Another key factor is the capacity of people in state agencies to interpret federal guidelines or policies and to design, direct, coordinate, and support improvement efforts and accountability systems.

From the studies reviewed in this chapter, it is evident that states need assistance in many areas to design, direct, coordinate, and support improvement efforts in schools and accountability systems. Capacity building needs to occur in several areas at the state level, primarily in:

- Administrative coordination of federal, district, and state systems (O'Day and Gross 1999).
- Coordinating or aligning federal, state, and district accountability systems (O'Day and Gross 1999).
- Reform leaders learning how to develop context sensitive reform implementation plans (Oakes et al. 2000).
- Learning how to restructure state departments of education or other state agencies to meet accountability and new federal policy demands (Billig, Perry, and Pokorny 1999; Lusi 1997).
- Learning how to restructure state finance systems to meet accountability and new federal policy demands (Odden 1999; Odden and Clune 1998).

- Providing professional development at the state level (Cohen and Hill 2001; Oakes et al. 2000; Spillane 2001).
- Facilitating capacity building at the district and school level and providing appropriate professional development at the district and school levels (Darling-Hammond and Ball 1998), especially for sanctioned schools states have taken over or reconstituted (Desimone et al. 2002; Finnigan, O'Day, and Wakelyn 2003).
- Creating effective linkages between different policy domains and among reform stakeholders (Beck and Allexsaht-Snider 2001; Darling-Hammond et al. 2002; Hamann 2002; Lusi 1997; Oakes et al. 2000).
- Developing accountability systems that include both standards and tests that teach and measure higher-level-thinking skills, including for students who have English as a second language (Amrein and Berliner 2002; Linn, Baker, and Betebanner 2002; Ruiz-Primo, Li, and Shavelson 2002; Solano-Flores and Trumbull 2003).
- Learning how to design, direct, and support improvement plans for sanctioned schools, particularly those that are either reconstituted or taken over by a state (Desimone et al. 2002; Malen, Croninger, and Muncey 2002).

Although none of the work incorporated into this chapter had identifying linkages between states and other policy domains as one of its research goals, several authors did describe linkages as they described reform processes. These were as follows:

- State policies, memoranda, other formal communications, including state accountability systems (Amrein and Berliner 2002; Beck and Allexsaht-Snider 2001; Chun and Goertz 1999; Goertz, Duffy, and Le Floch 2001; Hightower, 2002a and b; Lusi 1997; McNeil 2000; O'Day 2002; Oakes et al. 2000; Solano-Flores and Trumbull 2003).
- Continuity over time with reform goals and focus (Clune 1998).
- Continuity over time with political will and climate to support improvement efforts (Clune 1998; Massell 1998).
- Creating political alliances and partnerships (Beck and Allexsaht-Snider 2001; Lusi 1997; Oakes et al. 2000).

- Informal communications between key reform stakeholders (Hamann 2002).
- State funding formulas (Ladd and Hansen 1999; Odden 1999; Odden and Clune 1998).
- Realigning funding or finding new sources of funding (Darling-Hammond et al. 2002; Lusi 1997; Oakes et al. 2000).
- There are several areas where states can develop linking capacity. These include establishing basic communication between personnel working in different agencies responsible for Title I and low-performing schools; linking or coordinating databases and basic record keeping; coordinating or aligning how Title I schools are identified across jurisdictions; and coordinating intervention and then resource allocation to schools (O'Day and Gross 1999).

We suggest that more research attention should be given to state efforts at building internal capacity, robust linkages, and coordinated flow of resources across linkages. There are few studies that actually focus on what state agencies have done to restructure internally to accommodate the new requirements of standards-based reforms and of NCLB, how they have facilitated learning at the state level to increase their internal capacity to more effectively develop, direct, and support school and district improvement policy, and coordinated accountability systems.

# 6

# The Role of Reform Design Teams

INTRODUCTION

This chapter focuses on research on the impact of reform design teams in school improvement or, more specifically, the contributions of comprehensive school reform (CSR) models developed by reform design teams. Design teams are often also referred to as "intermediary organizations." Intermediary organizations recently have emerged as important units of analysis for research on school reform and change (Coburn 2004; Honig 2004; McLaughlin in press). As noted by McLaughlin, "intermediaries comprise a 'strategic middle,' operating between the top and bottom of the implementing system" (p. 220). Their positions provide them access to a diverse array of knowledge and tools which might help schools they work with to develop new capacities or to efficiently utilize existing capacities.

For the purposes of this review, we discuss the intermediaries, or in this case, design teams, that work with schools in the implementation of CSR models. The design team is the group that conceives of the reform model; engineers the principles, implementation strategy, and materials that accompany the reform; and often provides support to local schools and districts in the form of training, consulting, follow-up checks, or other types of professional development.

Figure 6 locates the design team in our conceptual framework.

Design teams, or intermediary organizations, come different forms and serve different functions. Our focus here is on design teams that

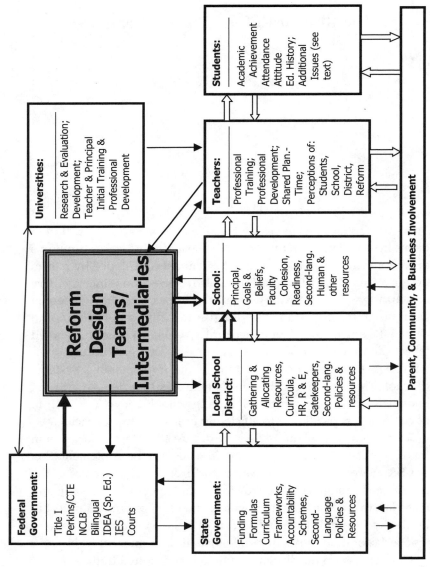

FIGURE 6. Comprehensive School Reform Design Team Involvement and Connections to School Reform

**Federal Government:**

Title I
Perkins/CTE
NCLB
Bilingual
IDEA (Sp. Ed.)
IES
Courts

**State Government:**

Funding
Formulas
Curriculum
Frameworks,
Accountability
Schemes,
Second-
Language
Policies &
Resources

**Universities:**

Research & Evaluation;
Development;
Teacher & Principal
Initial Training &
Professional
Development

**Reform Design Teams/ Intermediaries**

**Local School District:**

Gathering &
Allocating
Resources,
Curricula,
HR, R & E,
Gatekeepers,
Second-lang.
Policies &
resources

**School:**

Principal,
Goals &
Beliefs,
Faculty
Cohesion,
Readiness,
Second-lang.
Human &
other
resources

**Teachers:**

Professional
Training;
Professional
Development;
Shared Plan.-
Time;
Perceptions of:
Students,
School,
District,
Reform

**Students:**

Academic
Achievement
Attendance
Attitude
Ed. History;
Additional
Issues (see
text)

**Parent, Community, & Business Involvement**

124

assist primarily with school-level reform, rather than district level reform (such as the IFL, discussed in Chapter 3). Some design teams, such as the Coalition of Essential Schools at Brown, Success for All at Johns Hopkins, and the Comer School Development Program at Yale, originated in or still exist within universities. There are also many other university-based school reform groups that work with smaller numbers of schools in communities across the country, some of these functioning as process facilitators in school change efforts. Private, nonprofit organizations – such as the New American School Corporation, Advancement Via Individual Determination Center (AVID), the Modern Red Schoolhouse Institute, and the Core Knowledge Foundation – have also developed and disseminated school reform models. For-profit organizations, such as the Edison Project, are also part of the design team ecology (Rowan 2001), as are federally funded regional educational development labs.

The comprehensive school reform movement which began in the 1990s marked a shift away from the notion that school improvement should proceed organically, one school at a time. Instead, there was the extension of a particular reform model from one school or a handful of schools to many schools in diverse locales. In the mid-1990s, several urban districts, including Memphis, Miami, and San Antonio, provided a menu of various CSR models for their schools to choose from and hence used CSR as part of a systemwide reform approach (Bodilly 1998). In other cases, single schools from across the country have adopted particular reform models and joined in a network of sometimes more than a thousand schools undertaking a particular reform.

Although CSR models differ in their approaches to change, common to many of them is an interest in whole-school change, strong commitments to improving student achievement, new conceptions about what students should be expected to learn, and an emphasis on prevention rather than remediation (Oakes 1993). As we will explain, numerous whole-school reform models have also been associated with gains in student achievement (see Borman et al. 2000; Herman et al. 1999; Slavin and Fashola 1998; Stringfield et al. 1997).

The reforms range on a continuum from those that are highly specified and provide curriculum, lesson plans, school organizational models, implementation plans, and professional development, to those that are much less specified, asking schools to commit to a guiding set of principles and engage in an inquiry-guided, locally driven process of self-renewal. In this regard, some reform designs are more nearly "prepackaged," whereas others are much looser and presume local development of the change effort. Reform designs also have different focuses; some focus more directly on pedagogical practices, and others attempt to change the school culture or structure. Accordingly, the design teams, or intermediaries, have different theories of school change and theories of action.

At the less-specified end of the continuum, Accelerated Schools (Levin 1987), the Coalition of Essential Schools (Sizer 1984), and the Comer School Development Program (Comer et al. 1996), for example, provide frameworks for reform and leave particulars to each school. These designs point to the primacy of local development efforts, so long as the process is guided by a set of overarching principles (and school management structures, in the case of the Comer School Development program). Such reform designs operate according to a "concept dissemination" approach, rather than a program dissemination approach.

A bit further along the continuum, the Core Knowledge sequence (Core Knowledge Foundation 1998), for example, provides detailed curricula for half of each day for each elementary grade while leaving issues of how to teach and how to organize the school to the judgment of the principal and faculty. Similarly, with the Modern Red Schoolhouse design, for example, some materials and technical assistance are provided, but typically, teachers in local schools develop lesson plans.

At the most "highly specified" end of the continuum is Success for All, a design that provides detailed descriptions of how to organize schools and classrooms with respect to reading (Slavin, Madden, and Wasik 1996). Success for All is known as a fairly prescriptive school reform design. Importantly, however, it is only prescriptive in the area of reading, not in all school subjects.

Numerous comprehensive school reform models have existed for quite a few years. For example, the Comer School Development Program originated in the late 1960s, the Coalition of Essential Schools dates to the early 1980s, Success for All started in 1987, and the Accelerated Schools movement began in the late 1980s. Although the number of schools implementing these and other models has grown steadily over the past two decades, rapid growth in the adoption and number of CSR models did not occur until the mid-to-late 1990s.

The scale-up of CSR models was bolstered by the founding of the New American Schools (NAS) in 1991. Created as part of Goals 2000, NAS was charged with securing financial support from foundations and corporations to fund new designs for "break-the-mold" schools (Kearns and Anderson 1996). NAS funded the development and scale-up of nine reform designs in the early to mid-1990s. NAS continues to exist as a "business-led, nonprofit organization," and it plays a key role in the reform movement. In addition to showcasing eleven reform designs, NAS funds research and serves as a networking source and a policy advocate in the comprehensive reform movement. NAS was influential in the creation of the federal CSR legislation, which is discussed in more detail below (New American Schools 1997).

The growth of CSR adoption in is the 1990s was due in large part to two key policy changes. First, in 1988, there were changes in Title I regulations that greatly expanded the option to use federal funds to support schoolwide rather than targeted programs in schools enrolling a majority of low-income students. The change in Title I regulations was supported by school effectiveness research (Edmonds 1979).

Most significant for its effect on the growth of CSR, however, was the passage of the Comprehensive School Reform Demonstration Program (CSRD, now known as CSR) by the U.S. Congress in 1997. CSR, also known as the Obey-Porter initiative, was based on research documenting the advantages of schoolwide improvement efforts over pull-out programs (see Borman et al. 1998; Stringfield et al. 1997). Consequently, in the past decade, many schools have used Title I funds to pay for the costs associated with implementing comprehensive school reform models. Obey-Porter legislation allocated $145 million initially (and additional funds in subsequent years, e.g., $310 million in 2003) to schools for the adoption of "research-based" school reform models. The "purpose [of CSRD] is to stimulate schools to revamp their overall educational operation by implementing a comprehensive reform program" (U.S. Department of Education 2000). Typically, schools apply to their state departments of education for CSR funds, which are at least $50,000 and range to over

$100,000 annually for three years. Most CSRD funding is allocated for Title I schools. Thousands of schools have received CSRD funding since the program's inception in 1998.

CSR has led not only to an increase in the number of schools adopting CSR models, but it also led to the emergence of many new CSR model providers since 1997 (New American Schools 1997). Consequently, the options of CSR models have increased, as has the competition among model providers. Most funds for CSR are targeted to schools serving large numbers of low-income students. Borman and colleagues (2002) cited recent data from the Southwest Education Development Laboratory that shows that schools receiving CSRD funding have an average poverty rate of 70 percent. Moreover, Menken (2000) notes that the bulk of federal CSR funds are targeted for Title I schools and one in every five Title I students is an English language learner (ELL), and "it is therefore important that the needs of these students be addressed through comprehensive school reform" (p. 1).

In the next section, we will first discuss the findings on student achievement and CSR models. We will then discuss issues of CSR implementation at the school, district, state, and design team levels, paying particular attention to the adaptability of reforms for racially and linguistically diverse student populations.

### ACHIEVEMENT

In this section, we review five significant reviews of the achievement effects associated with CSR models.[1] We chose to examine "reviews of research" rather than the studies themselves, as the latter task would be beyond the scope and resources of this project. The research reviews we review here include: *What Do We Know?* (Wang, Haertel, and Walberg 1997); *A Catalogue of School Reform Models* (Northwest Regional Educational Laboratory 1998); *Show Me the Evidence!* (Slavin and Fashola 1998); *An Educator's Guide to Schoolwide Reform* (Herman et al. 1999); and *Comprehensive School Reform and Student Achievement: A Meta-Analysis* (Borman et al. 2002). The reviews will be discussed in the order of their release.

[1] Portions of this section draw from Stringfield (2000).

A note of caution and explanation must precede the actual discussion. Three of the five sets of review authors are themselves involved in one or more of the reforms they have reviewed. For more than fifteen years, Dr. Margaret Wang developed, refined, and disseminated the Community for Learning program.[2] Over that same period, Northwest Regional Educational Laboratory has developed and disseminated Onward to Excellence (Blum and Butler 1987; Kushman and Yap 1999). Although Slavin has been associated with a wide range of scholarly activities (e.g., Slavin 1998), he currently is most associated with Success for All (SFA) (Slavin et al. 1996), one of the most widely researched CSR models. The Herman and colleagues review was commissioned by several groups with no ties to specific reforms, and the Borman and colleagues review also has no specific ties to reforms, except that the study arose out of Johns Hopkins University, where SFA was developed; however, Borman and his colleagues have no formal associations with SFA.

Wang directed the federally funded research and development center focused on urban school reform and then directed a federally funded educational development and dissemination laboratory for the mid-Atlantic states (New Jersey, Pennsylvania, Maryland, Delaware, and Washington, D.C.). The Wang, Haertel, and Walberg (1997) review could be thought of as providing practical information to educators in that region, and it has been disseminated widely. The report has spawned a Web page that is substantially more detailed than the report in the current review.[3] Wang, Haertel, and Walberg provide virtually no text descriptions of each of the reforms. The core of the Wang, Haertel, and Walberg review is a series of three very large tables, each providing the core list of twelve school reforms crossed by over eighty dimensions the authors deemed significant. For example, all twelve programs were deemed to include the goal of "improve student learning," and seven are deemed to involve cooperative learning.

A limitation of the Wang, Haertel, and Walberg review is that the authors specifically chose not to report on outcome data. Indeed, they reported, "finally, we note a lack of information on perhaps the most

[2] Formerly known as the *Adaptive Learning Environments Model* (Wang 1992).
[3] Available at http://www.reformhandbook-lss.org/home.htm.

important feature of the programs achievement results. [E]vidence of whether the programs actually yield better learning is sorely lacking." Given that academic achievement is one of the primary purposes of schooling, and given that the other reviewers found achievement data they deemed sufficient for discussion, this becomes a significant limitation of the Wang, Haertel, and Walberg piece.

Wang, Haertel, and Walberg provide a useful initial introduction and reference guide to the breadth and components of U.S. whole-school reforms. That the review is readily obtained and has been updated are both obvious pluses. The omissions of detailed program descriptions and effects data in the written document are limitations. The more recent Web page at least partially addresses this problem.

Northwest Regional Education Laboratory (NWREL) is another federally-funded regional dissemination center. NWREL is located in Portland, Oregon, and serves the Pacific-Northwest states of Alaska, Washington, Oregon, Idaho, and Montana. NWREL's review is available in paper form directly from the laboratory, or from the lab's Web site.[4] It provides one-to-three page descriptions of twenty-seven whole-school reforms and their specific characteristics (plus twenty-one non-whole-school programs). In place of the rather convenient check-off tables of Wang, Haertel, and Walberg, NWREL provided text descriptions of the reforms. In clearest contrast to Wang, Haertel, and Walberg, NWREL provided detailed descriptions of research on each of the reform efforts. This includes research on challenges to implementation and, importantly, research on effects.

NWREL's authors presented all of the available studies of research data. The brief presentation for each study may imply that each study of each reform is of equal value and implicitly invites a simple count of studies per reform. Clearly, the studies are not of equal value. Some are single-school implementation case studies. Others summarize multiyear data across multiple schools and districts. Some have control groups; others do not. Some use nationally recognized and/or normed tests; others do not. Very few summary statements are made as to the overall strength of findings regarding the potential for implementation or possible effectiveness of each reform.

4 Available at http://www.nwrel.org/scpd/catalog/index.shtml.

Slavin and Fashola's (1998) *Show Me the Evidence!* is a continuation of Slavin's work on reviewing "what works" over the previous two decades (e.g., Slavin, Leavey, and Madden 1982; Slavin, Karweit, and Madden 1989; Slavin, Karweit, and Wasik 1994). Given that Slavin coined the term and technique for "best evidence syntheses," it is no surprise that he and Fashola declared clear and demanding criteria for considering research on the diverse programs reviewed in their volume. In the case of *Show Me the Evidence!*, the authors placed great weight on full, quasi-experimental methods (Cook and Campbell 1979). The limitations of this rigorous test is obvious. The authors initially present data from a limited number of whole-school and other reforms and then would have had to end their analyses rather abruptly, as few reforms have produced studies that meet the matched-control criterion. The authors apparently felt compelled, however, to lower their standards, without explanation, to discuss other reforms. For example, Slavin and Fashola discussed all of the NAS designs, although several clearly had not produced any studies that meet the matched-control design criteria.

Slavin and Fashola included sixteen whole-school reforms in their discussion of Comprehensive School Reform. According to the authors, the reforms showing the most promise, based on extensive research on student achievement and replicability, were Success for All and Direct Instruction. While Roots and Wings met the criteria for evaluation and replicability, research was cited for only one study in four Title I schools in rural southern Maryland. While the other reforms did not meet the evaluation criteria for student achievement or criteria for replicability, preliminary data suggested positive effects for Core Knowledge, Modern Red Schoolhouse, Expeditionary Learning/Outward Bound, ATLAS Communities, and Co-Nect. Mixed results were found for Accelerated Schools and the Comer School Development Program. Based on scant research, no significant differences were found for Paideia and a potentially negative effect in math achievement was found for Coalition of Essential Schools.

Herman and colleagues (1999) produced a volume that is fourth in the chronology. The research that went into *An Educators' Guide to Schoolwide Reform* was funded by five of the most important independent groups in U.S. education: the National Education Association, the American Federation of Teachers, the National Association of Elementary School Principals, the National Association of Secondary School Principals, and the American Association of School Administrators.

Herman and colleagues provided descriptions of the reforms, reviewed research, frankly discussed studies that did not produce positive effects across multiple studies, summarized strength of findings within and among reforms, and provided hundreds of references. Although the report is available on the Internet, the paperback version is even more useful because it includes responses to the review by various reform developers, some of which dispute the reported results.

Herman and colleagues (1999) reviewed over 130 studies of achievement effects of twenty-four schoolwide reforms and found only three models with strong evidence of raising student achievement levels: Direct Instruction, High Schools That Work, and Success for All. They state that "in general, evidence of positive effects on student achievement – arguably the most important feature of any reform approach – is extremely limited. . . . As a result, educators often are considering schoolwide reform without vital information on which to make decisions" (pp. 2–3).

Borman and colleagues' (2002) more recent, very comprehensive meta-analysis is geared more for a researcher audience than any of the reports previously described and, as such, it is far more careful in detailing its methodology and reporting results. Borman and colleagues' (2002) systematic meta-analysis includes 232 studies on twenty-nine models. The studies were chosen according to rigorous inclusion criteria. After analysis, they grouped the models into four categories depending on the quality of evidence (i.e., research evidence from control-group studies or third-party control-group studies), the quantity of their evidence (i.e., the number of studies and their generalizability), and the statistical significance of their results. They found only three models that they considered *proven models* based on the above criteria. These included Direct Instruction, the Comer School Development Program, and Success for All. *Highly promising models*, those that had positive and statistically significant results but did not have research bases that were as generalizable as the proven models, included Accelerated Schools, Expeditionary Learning, Outward Bound, Modern Red Schoolhouse, and Roots and

Wings. *Promising models* had too few studies to generalize with confidence but did have statistically significant results. These included ATLAS, Montessori, Paideia, and the Learning Network. Seventeen of the twenty-nine models were placed into the *more research needed* category, as they either had too few studies to establish statistically reliable or generalizable results, or Borman and colleagues judged the extant studies as lacking in rigor.

Borman and colleagues concluded that CSR programs, in general, have positive effects on student achievement. They stated that "the average student who participated in a CSR program outperformed about 56% of similar children who did not attend a CSR school" (p. 47). However, the effects for individual models were much more variable, as noted in the four categories.

Borman and colleagues also found that the characteristics of the studies predicted more about the effects than the characteristics of the models. That is, studies performed by the developers yielded stronger effects than studies performed by third-party evaluators. They hypothesized that developers were perhaps more actively involved in ensuring high-quality implementations in the schools that they were studying.

What do these reviews tell us about the effects of reforms in schools serving diverse student populations? Borman and colleagues' meta-analysis uses schools' percentage of free lunch as a contextual moderator variable (the average level of poverty of the CSR schools studied was 65.06 percent of students eligible for the free or reduced-price lunch program) but does not tell us whether the socioeconomic, racial, or linguistic diversity of a school's population factored into the achievement results. This is presumably because such data were not available. The newest version of the NWREL catalog includes a section for each reform entitled "student population." The catalog explains that

each model had an opportunity to apply to be highlighted for its efforts in serving selected student populations. The five categories were urban, rural, high poverty, English Language Learners, and special education. To qualify for a category, a model had to demonstrate (a) that it included special training, materials, or components focusing on that student population, and (b) that it had been implemented in a substantial number of schools serving that population.

However, the catalog does not ask developers to describe evidence of effectiveness in varied contexts. Herman and colleagues' *Educators' Guide* does not address context a great deal either.

Numerous authors have noted the absence of research on the effects of CSR models on the achievement and educational experiences of ELLs (Hamann et al. 2002; Menken 2000). Menken (2000) also raised the problem of assessing the effectiveness of CSR models where ELLs are concerned. She stated the well-accepted fact that, "ELLs are at a disadvantage with 'one-size-fits-all' assessments – particularly when English-medium tests that were developed to assess native English-speakers are used to evaluate the content-area knowledge of ELLs" (p. 5). The inadequacy of standardized tests to assess ELLs' achievement properly is certainly an issue (Menken 2000); however, simple inattention to the needs of these students seems to be the major problem.

One recent study that we were involved in assesses the achievement outcomes for ELL students in schools implementing CSR models. Datnow, Stringfield, Borman, and Overman (2002) conducted a study of the achievement outcomes of students in thirteen culturally and linguistically diverse schools that were implementing one of six CSR models: Audrey Cohen College System of Education, Comer School Development Program, Coalition of Essential Schools, Core Knowledge, Modern Red Schoolhouse, and Success for All. The schools that implemented CSR models in the "Sunland County" district under study did not achieve basic-skills and advanced-skills outcomes that were substantially different from the outcomes of the non-CSR comparison schools. However, there are some caveats to these findings. First, there were several CSR models that did appear to make a difference for students in general and for ELL students in particular. Students from the Success for All, Comer School Development Program, and Coalition of Essential Schools models all enjoyed some achievement advantages relative to their counterparts from the matched comparison schools.[5] In addition, Core Knowledge and Success for All schools appeared to show particular benefits for ELL students. Finally, and perhaps most importantly, the studies'

---

[5] However, the authors stated that they could not comfortably attribute these results to the Coalition of Essential Schools reform itself because they found little evidence of its implementation in the two schools they studied.

results on implementation and achievement, taken together, reveal that stronger implementations of the CSR models were in general associated with better outcomes for ELL students.

Apart from the above study (which only assesses outcomes for ELLs in a small number of schools implementing CSR models), there is (only) one reform model whose effects on ELLs have been well documented. Slavin and Madden (1999) reported on two ELL adaptations of Success for All. One is a Spanish-bilingual version, called *Éxito Para Todos*, in which students are taught to read in Spanish and then transitioned to English reading, usually in third or fourth grade. The other integrates English as a second language (ESL) strategies with English reading instruction. Summarizing the results of these programs, they find that the effects of SFA on the achievement of ELLs are, in general, substantially positive.

In all schools implementing *Éxito Para Todos*, effect sizes for first graders on Spanish assessments were very positive, especially when schools were implementing most of the program's elements. Even after transitioning to English-only instruction, *Éxito Para Todos* third graders performed better on English assessments than control students who were primarily taught in English. For students acquiring English receiving ESL instruction, effect sizes for all comparisons were also positive. (p. 1)

Similar studies have not been conducted on other types of reform models.

Overall, a careful reading of the set of reviews on achievement outcomes associated with CSR models reveals a need for additional well-designed, well-controlled studies. Most importantly for this project, we are left with little knowledge about how CSR models affect the education of ELLs and/or students from particular racial or ethnic groups.

In the sections that follow, we review findings about CSR implementation at various levels of the system. We begin with the school level because this is where CSR efforts are typically focused.

### SCHOOL LEVEL

Much of the research that has been conducted on CSR focuses on what needs to happen at the school level for reform to be successful. First, researchers consistently find that it is important for schools to adopt a reform design that is a good fit (Bodilly 1998; Consortium for Policy Research in Education 1998; Desimone 2000; Education Commission of the States 1999; U.S. Department of Education 1999). Yet prior research suggests that educators in schools adopting reforms often feel uninformed and lack sufficient time to make educated choices (Bodilly and Berends 1999; Consortium for Policy Research in Education 1998; Datnow 2000; Stringfield and Ross 1997). Teachers seldom make free, fully informed choices about reform models. Rather, teachers often have had to go along with the reform choices of school or district administrators and in many cases did not report full buy-in to reform efforts at the outset.

Not surprisingly, in any school there is always a range of opinions about a given reform; yet, teacher support has been found to be critical. In a study of the early years of the Memphis City Schools restructuring initiative (where many schools in the district were implementing NAS designs and two other models), Smith et al. (1998) found that teacher support for the school restructuring efforts was an important factor in successful implementation. Berends (2000), in a survey of teachers and principals in 130 schools implementing the NAS designs, found that teacher support for the reforms was related to the level of communication about the designs, as well as the level of resources to support reform efforts. Teachers' knowledge and understanding of the reform designs are also important to implementation, as teachers cannot reliably implement a model that they know little about (Schmidt and Datnow 2002).

Several studies also comment on the need for strong leadership for reform at the school level. In particular, Berends, Bodilly, and Kirby (2003), in reporting findings from a comprehensive study of NAS districts and RAND Corporation schools, concluded that "schools [undertaking comprehensive reform designs] need strong leaders – principals who can bring a unified sense of vision to the school and staff, provide instructional leadership, and organizational leadership in terms of making sure the teachers have the necessary time, resources, and support to fully implement the design" (p. 127). Research also supports the idea that different reform models have different requirements for school leaders. For example, Datnow and Castellano (2001) studied leadership in six schools implementing Success for All and found that it demanded both management and monitoring skills from principals and reform facilitators. On the contrary, Hall and Placier (2003) studied leadership in schools working with the Coalition of Essentials Schools, a principle-driven model, and concluded that "if there is one 'requirement' for CES leadership, it is the ability to cope with uncertainty, ambiguity and one's lack of control over other people" (p. 232).

In addition to teacher and principal support for the reform, numerous other factors influence the implementation of comprehensive school reform designs, including the nature of the reform and the level of support provided by the design team. In a study of schools in Memphis experiencing the most and least implementation success with CSR models, Smith and colleagues (1998) found that adequate professional development from the design team was important to schools that were fast starters with implementation. They also found that more specified models were more likely to reach full implementation early on, whereas process-driven models took more time to evolve. Berends (2000) also found that "individual teachers' support and *reports about design team communication* were significantly related to implementation and the teacher reported effects of NAS designs on teachers and students" (p. 78, emphasis added). He also found that teachers' perceptions of the *adequacy of resources* for the reform were positively related to teacher support of the design and implementation. (We return to these issues later in subsequent sections.) The RAND study also found that schools needed authority over curriculum, instruction and schedules, the budget, personnel, and professional development to implement reform designs well (Bodilly 1998).

### Schools, Comprehensive School Reform, and Linguistic and Cultural Diversity

Although we know that most CSR schools are those serving large numbers of low-income and minority students, we are just beginning to learn about the impact of these variables on reform and the effects of reform on schooling for these students. A study by Kirby, Berends, and Naftel (2001) revealed that NAS schools serving numbers of poor and minority students tended to have lower levels of reform implementation. On the contrary, a study by Datnow (2005) revealed no clear patterns regarding reform implementation according to the characteristics of schools in the Sunland County study, and, in fact, the patterns that do exist favor schools with poor and minority students. In this study, four of the five schools that sustained reforms at moderate to high implementation levels for long periods of time were in fact very large schools with high-minority, significant limited English proficient (LEP), and low-income student populations. Schools serving high- and low-minority, middle- and low-income, and LEP populations and those with varied student achievement levels also dropped reforms at roughly the same rate.

The Sunland County study reveals other findings with regard to the implementation of CSR models in schools serving ELLs. For example, Stringfield and colleagues (1998) described a successful school-level adaptation to accommodate language differences that occurred at a school implementing the Core Knowledge Sequence. The Core Knowledge Sequence is a list of topics and is not accompanied by materials or a teacher's manual. Rather, lesson plans are locally developed by teachers, thus allowing for substantial flexibility in methods of presentation. At this school, bilingual instruction of Core Knowledge topics in Spanish and English enabled students to benefit from this curriculum reform, regardless of English-language proficiency.

While the teachers at this school believed that this bilingual adaptation of Core Knowledge has been successful, they had some difficulty finding age-appropriate materials on Core Knowledge topics in Spanish. Because of the demands required by teaching Core Knowledge in both languages, the teachers have elected to teach teach a selection of topics. Meanwhile, the Core Knowledge Foundation suggests teaching all topics in the sequence. It is notable that this school received a waiver, long before implementing Core Knowledge, to conduct two-way bilingual instruction. Teachers in another Core Knowledge school that conducted instruction in English attempted to use visual aids and peers as interpreters for LEP students to make the content accessible to students.

Other schools in the same study struggled to make programmatic adaptations to serve LEP students effectively (see Datnow, Hubbard, and Mehan 2002). Teachers at an Audrey Cohen College System of Education school felt that the design would be far more adaptable in a context where students were all native speakers of English. A teacher at one school explained that because her first-grade students could not read in English, she read the books to them, explaining the concepts in Spanish at times, and then writing the main points on the board for students to copy. Audrey Cohen College was willing to make some adaptations to accommodate speakers of other languages. For example, they allowed students to write in their "purpose record books" in their native language. However, they did not provide any materials in languages other than English.

Ironically, the schools that had the most difficulty adapting the reform to meet the needs of LEP students were Success for All schools. Although SFA has a Spanish version of the curriculum (hence a significant LEP student accommodation), this was not helpful in the schools that served Haitian Creole students. Furthermore, the district's policies prohibited reading instruction in students' native languages. The SFA design team began working on an ESL adaptation, but it was completed only after some schools had attempted implementation of SFA for three years, which caused frustration at some school sites. Moreover, because the district required that LEP students be taught by ESL-certified teachers, the LEP students could not be placed in reading groups according to level, as SFA specifies. Instead, the LEP students in the primary grades remained in self-contained classes that were not grouped according to reading level, but instead were heterogeneous. The teachers did a number of things in their classrooms to adapt the SFA materials for use with their LEP students, including rewriting some materials and replacing some of the SFA vocabulary words with more familiar ones. Teachers also occasionally dropped the SFA lesson plans in favor of using ESL strategies for oral language development. The curriculum was often significantly diluted for LEP students in terms of time and pacing. These are, of course, just several examples, and it is quite likely that the reform designs have evolved since this period of this study.

Adding to the knowledge of CSR models in LEP contexts, Menken (2000), in a newsletter for the National Clearinghouse on Bilingual Education, briefly described a Philadelphia middle school's efforts to implement the Talent Development program. The school was densely populated by ELLs; yet, the model had never been implemented before with such a population and hence

It did not require the use of literature appropriate to ELL students' language proficiency levels or to their cultures, and did not ensure that these students received necessary language supports. Furthermore, the professional development provided was not geared towards the education of ELLs. In response to teachers currently struggling in the implementation phase, the school district has supported local educators in their quest to account for the educational needs of these students within the model. (p. 3)

Datnow, Hubbard, and Mehan (2002) and Hubbard and Mehan (1999) also found that educators' and policy makers' ideologies about language, race, and social class influenced CSR implementation. In some schools (and entire districts), educators specifically chose reforms on the basis that they had been used in schools serving populations that were demographically similar to their own. In other cases, educators resisted or thwarted the implementation of reforms that they felt were not well suited. For example, a teacher in one school felt that their chosen reform required adaptations for low-income, recent immigrant Hispanic students, who were "culturally" more accustomed to teacher-directed rather than student-centered instruction. The researchers also encountered schools where LEP students did not receive as many benefits of the reform because they were perceived to be unable to understand material, or when policies dictated a different form of instruction for them (Stringfield et al. 1998).

Similarly, in Hubbard and Mehan's study (Datnow, Hubbard, and Mehan 2002; Hubbard and Mehan 1999) of the scale-up of the AVID untracking program in twelve high schools in four U.S. states (Virginia, California, Kentucky, and North Carolina) over a three-year period (Hubbard and Mehan 1999), they, too, found that educators' beliefs about minority students often got in the way of reform. When AVID was implemented in a district in North Carolina, the reform confronted educators' entrenched beliefs about African American students' inability to achieve. In some cases, teachers resisted the placement of African American AVID students in their Advanced Placement classes, arguing they were not qualified. These findings are consistent with those of Oakes and her colleagues (Oakes et al. 1997; Oakes and Wells 1996), who found that implementing a reform designed to detrack racially diverse students requires more than the technical tinkering with the organization of course offerings. It requires changes in belief systems and political arrangements as well.

Overall, these findings point to the ways in which a school's capacity for change, local adaptations, policies, and ideologies influence CSR implementation at the school level. Next, we examine how external entities' capacity also influence implementation.

### DISTRICT LEVEL

Studies specifically point to the need for district-supported CSR implementation but often find that what exists is insufficient. Clear, strong district support positively influenced reform implementation and the lack thereof often negatively affected implementation. In the Special Strategies follow-up study, Yonezawa and Stringfield (2000) found that schools that sustained reforms had district and state allies that protected reform efforts during periods of transition or crisis and secured resources (e.g., money, time, staff, and space) essential to the reforms. On the contrary, schools that failed to sustain reforms were sometimes located in districts that were "infamous for experimenting with new kinds of programs" but did not provide ongoing support for any of them (Yonezawa and Stringfield 2000, p. 48). This finding was consistent in a study of Core Knowledge implementation in twelve schools as well. As one teacher in a Core Knowledge school stated: "Like all regulatory bodies, they want all kinds of change and innovation, and as long as the individual school is willing to bear the cost, they're all for it" (Stringfield et al. 1999, p. 26).

Similarly, reporting on the RAND study of NAS, Berends and collegues (2003) stated: "Many of the NAS districts failed to provide organizational, public, and instructional leadership to the schools implementing the designs. Even where initial support existed, often support for NAS designs was often limited to one individual – the superintendent – rather than to the central office staff" (p. 127). They further added: "In many districts, the failure to protect the NAS reform effort from conflicting regulations and mandates put in place by district leaders anxious to show improvement again caused the reform to be virtually abandoned" (p. 127). Datnow (2005) also found that when district leadership and policy changes occurred, schools engaged in reform often looked on this as an opportunity to drop reform efforts. Only those schools that had well institutionalized reforms were able to sustain them in the absence of district support for the models.

Moreover, the RAND research found that higher levels of implementation of NAS designs were associated with districts:

- Whose leadership teachers perceived as being stable and strongly supportive of the effort and who communicated clearly how the NAS fit with other restructuring efforts.
- That lacked political crisis, such as significant budget reductions, labor-management strife, or redistricting debate.
- That had a relatively stronger culture of history of cooperation and trust between central office and the schools.
- That provided some school-level autonomy, commensurate with that needed to promote the design.
- That provided more resources for professional development and planning. (Bodilly 1998, p. 105)

The role of district superintendents and their years in leadership also proved important to design implementation. The school superintendents in the jurisdictions with higher overall design implementation appeared to transmit clear goals and support for NAS by:

- Making public statements and speeches, with backing from their boards, to commit to NAS initiatives.
- Making specific statements to schools in personal visits and other forums that whole-school reform was the way the district would go and that all schools would eventually adopt designs that were "research based."
- Changing school planning processes and policies to embedded whole-school design approaches.
- Insisting that the schools would be judged on their results, usually within three years. (p. 92)

These efforts were from superintendents who had been in office for several years and who were staying in their positions for a while longer. These factors lent an air of immediacy and commitment to NAS designs in these locales. Staff at the schools in these districts understood that NAS design implementation was central to their districts' improvement efforts. In the jurisdictions with not as much success with design implementation – Miami-Dade, Philadelphia, and Pittsburgh – superintendents were less stable in office (Bodilly 1998).

The level and type of professional development were important and were controlled primarily by district policy (Bodilly 1998). In examining NAS implementation in San Antonio, Berends and colleagues (2001) found conflict between district mandates and design-team requirements in several areas. NAS teachers were obligated to attend as many of the district in-services as their colleagues in non-NAS schools, along with the professional development required for NAS design implementation, so the amount of professional development activities served to heighten teacher frustration in NAS schools. Another exacerbating factor was that the district and design teams did not tend to coordinate their professional development efforts, which meant that teachers had virtually no help integrating the information they received from each. As a result, their workloads increased and they experienced confusion about what needed to be prioritized. Teachers also found it difficult to implement district-level professional development without modifying the essence of the design in their schools. Not knowing how to integrate central office initiatives with design aspects, teachers tended to compromise designs by selecting and modifying only those elements that could coexist with district guidelines.

Although the district expressed support for the philosophy of NAS designs and provided funding for designs in its schools, it unknowingly hindered design implementation in virtually all schools implementing NAS by establishing an increasing presence in the daily activities of classrooms. During year 1 of the NAS study in San Antonio, design elements were clearly visible in NAS classrooms. In year 2, the growing influence of central office policies on classrooms was evident, and teachers were having increasing difficulty integrating district demands with design practices while maintaining design integrity. By the second year, classroom instruction was strikingly similar across the district with almost every teacher following the district's approaches to reading, math, and language arts (e.g., virtually every teacher opened the day with a daily oral language drill, taught the reading process, used "Everyday Math," and taught spelling out of the same district spelling book). Teachers were under great pressure to raise students' scores on the state test at that time, the Texas Assessment of Academic Skills (TAAS), and hence reading and math received the most attention (Berends et al. 2001). This meant that reform-related activities were often pushed aside as teachers taught to the test. (See Chapter 5 for more details.)

Finally, the RAND studies identified clear communication between design teams and the district and school personnel as an important factor in design implementation. Berends and colleagues' (2001) study of San Antonio revealed in some detail the need for this three-way communication or linkage. The San Antonio district attempted to ensure a frequent flow of information by arranging quarterly meetings between design team and district staff, hiring four "instructional stewards" who were responsible for providing instructional guidance to a "learning community" of schools. There were challenges, however, as in some cases design principles conflicted with district initiatives. In other cases, there was overlap and teachers did not know which plan to follow. Hence, this communication was critical.

Sunland County also established a similar plan to improve communication between the district, school, and design teams (Datnow, Hubbard, and Mehan 2002). In 1995–1996, Sunland's superintendent at the time favored promoting the use of externally developed reforms. As one teacher explained, he was "very supportive." Under his tenure, the district created an Office of Instructional Leadership to support design implementation. This office had six regional directors who were responsible for providing the various restructuring schools within their regions with training and support. The purpose of these regional directors was to provide information, practical assistance, and encouragement to the restructuring schools.

The following year, however, the district leadership changed dramatically. First, the district, which had elected its school board members at-large, moved to a subdistrict-specific election format, dramatically altering the makeup of the board. Second, industry leaders in the district and surrounding areas began to make their voices heard, and they published a high-visibility report highlighting industries for which schools should be preparing their students. A culture and value shift had occurred. The focus on student employability intensified with the arrival of a new superintendent whose background was in vocational and secondary education. This superintendent's reform agenda matched the concerns of the new board and local businesses. His priority on school-to-work educational programs shifted the district's focus even further away from the restructuring models toward helping students become "viable products" for industry leaders. He also emphasized, to a lesser extent, reading instruction and community schools (Yonezawa and Datnow 1999).

The new district administration eliminated the Office of Instructional Improvement in early 1997. District officials reasoned that the dismantling was a response to fiscal belt tightening at the district level; however, many educators in the restructuring schools and other local observers saw the move as a priority shift. The director of the office was transferred to another division. Three of the six district regional directors were also transferred to other district offices and two retired. The last regional director was given a new position as the Director of Curriculum Support Services and Special Programs, where she was responsible for doing the same job that six directors had done the previous year. Not surprisingly, district support for many of the restructuring schools decreased dramatically.

### Districts, Comprehensive School Reform, and Linguistic and Cultural Diversity

Although Berends and colleagues' (2001) study of the NAS reforms in San Antonio discussed the challenges of reform as those that might be typical in a high-poverty district, we do not know much about how the racial and linguistic makeup of the student population influenced reform efforts, even though this is a district with a high number of ELLs.

In the Sunland County study (Yonezawa and Datnow 1999), we do find some information on the district and linguistic diversity issues. First, in this district, a consent decree required all non-ESL-endorsed teachers of LEP students to complete ESL training over a six-year period. For many of the teachers, the training was extensive, sometimes demanding up to three hundred hours of district-led inservice. Consequently, this consumed much of the district's energy and resources and significantly affected the implementation of the more curricular-based reforms (all except for Coalition of Essential Schools and the Comer School Development Program).

The district's plan for enhancing its bilingual program had a profound effect on many of the reforming schools. More specifically, the schools found that they had less time for staff development because of the ESL training requirements and less flexibility with their scheduling because of the consent decree mandate that LEP children are taught only by ESL endorsed teachers. For instance, teachers at Modern Red Schoolhouse schools found it difficult to juggle after-school ESL training with the additional planning demands the designs required. Administrators at some schools found themselves correcting student placements much later in the school year than usual. At one school, the principal became so frustrated with the lack of flexibility in her school schedule that she asked her nonendorsed faculty if they would be willing to complete the ESL training in one year, rather than the maximum six years the district allowed (Yonezawa and Datnow 1999). As these findings make clear, frequent and sustained communication and problem solving between district, design team, and school staff are critical to successful implementation and sustainability of reform efforts.

## STATE LEVEL

Several studies have documented how state accountability systems (generally negatively) affect the implementation of CSR efforts. Often, low scores on state tests are what lead schools to take on CSR models in the first place. Ironically, however, some prior studies of CSR have shown that when state testing and accountability demands were high, reform strategies were then later abandoned in favor of test preparation activities (Bodilly and Berends 1999; Datnow, Borman, and Stringfield 2000).

Demands from the state and district levels related to state standards and accountability – specifically, standardized tests – constrained or increased the tension of reform implementation. Many of the schools Datnow and Stringfield (2000) studied, particularly those in Tennessee, Florida, Maryland, and Texas, were located in states with high-stakes accountability systems. Teachers in these states typically felt great pressure to prepare students for the test, separate from implementing reforms. This was especially true in two schools that were deemed by their state departments of education to be "reconstitution eligible." In those schools, externally developed reform efforts went by the wayside almost completely. Across all of their studies, the presence of a high-stakes testing program invariably meant that test-preparation activities, unconnected to any previous or ongoing instructional activities, took precedence over traditional or reform activities.

Similarly, in their study of San Antonio, the RAND researchers found that instead of NAS designs guiding curriculum and instruction, it appeared that the state initiatives directed the educational missions of all schools. In short, TAAS was the driving force behind all of this (Berends et al. 2001). Researchers found that instruction had narrowed to honing tested skills, as teachers questioned whether the instructional approaches promoted by their respective designs alone would bring about increased test scores. The presence of TAAS on classroom instruction was also seen, with all teachers reviewing specific TAAS skills and objectives.

Teachers rarely reported that the external demands for accountability enhanced their implementation of reforms. However, in some cases, teachers and principals hoped and believed that the implementation of reforms would help raise test scores. In Memphis, three-year test score gains on the state testing system did improve in schools implementing most of the NAS and other whole-school reforms generally, and Success for All/Roots and Wings in particular (Ross et al. 1999). Similarly, teachers at two schools clearly attributed scores on Baltimore and Maryland tests to their acquisition of the Calvert School curricular and instructional model (McHugh and Spath 1997; Stringfield 1999).

Bodilly (2001) noted the tighter linkage between design teams and states that evolved over time as a result of state standards and accountability systems:

By 1998, NAS was riding a wave of state-mandated standards, curriculum, assessments, and accountability ... [R]egardless of what their original stance on development of their own standards and of what progress they had made toward that development, all teams agreed to use existing standards and assessments in partner districts and changed the language of their designs to indicate that the design standards and assessments would be accommodated to the districts in which the team worked. (p. 64)

To help students become successful at meeting state standards and district demands, several designs moved away from their original goals of offering rich and varied, project-based curricula. Instead, design teams had to accommodate districtwide textbooks and programs for basic skills acquisition (Bodilly 2001). This was particularly apparent in large, poor urban districts. In schools with high numbers of poor and minority students, basic literacy and numeracy programs were adapted or developed, as were processes to train teachers to develop rubrics for assessing student work against state or district standards. Some designs also moved away from their original goals of teacher-developed curricula toward developing curricular units for teachers, as they found that districts often did not provide the time needed for teachers to engage in such development (Bodilly 2001). Adaptation of reform designs was also obstructed because of a lack of alignment between the reform designs and district- and state-mandated tests and a lack of alignment between the design and district- or state-mandated curriculum requirement (Bodilly 2001; Kirby, Berends, and Naftel 2001). It is here that we see some of the ways in which design teams, districts, and states were not well aligned for improving student achievement.

Aside from influencing school reform efforts through their accountability systems, other actions at the state level have also been instrumental in comprehensive school reform. For example, some states have provided funding and legislation and funding for the AVID reform, which provided a strong inducement for districts to adopt the reform (Datnow, Hubbard, and Mehan 2002). In New Jersey, schools have been forced to adopt whole-school reforms as part of a court mandate resulting from *Abbott v. Burke V* (Erlichson and Goertz 2001).

In these cases, an ample resource base and the ability to use resources flexibly to support implementation have also been found to be important. Erlichson, Goertz, and Turnbull (1999) found that early CSR implementation efforts in New Jersey were thwarted when schools did not receive the resources from the state that they were expecting to pay for materials and training. This was compounded by a lack of capacity for school-based budgeting and insufficient direction from states and districts. Similarly, the AVID reform faltered in states where it was an administrative priority but not a legislated line item in the state budget (Datnow, Hubbard, and Mehan 2002).

States have played an increasingly active role in comprehensive school reform (at least theoretically) since the advent of the federal CSR program in 1998, as states are charged with dispersing federal CSR funds to districts. In a study of CSR implementation in twelve schools in three states (California, Texas, and Florida), Datnow and Kemper (2002) found that there was considerable variability in how states approach CSR and their work with schools. Texas approached CSR mainly as a funding source and itself as the distributor of funds. Florida purported to take a more active role in working with schools, and California appeared to be somewhat in between. While these differences may perhaps have an effect in the coming years, they did not seem to affect the schools in Datnow and Kemper's study, most of which were part of the first cohort of CSR schools. With all states in the developmental stages of their CSR programs, they appeared to have roughly the same amount of interaction – minimal – with individual schools. As CSR matured and states' experience with the program deepened, there may have been further changes.

Second, Datnow and Kemper (2002) found that CSR can certainly motivate school reform and improvement, but this was not a given. Indeed, the federal CSR program has operated as an incentive for some schools to pursue reform, as the legislation and funding is intended to do (U.S. Department of Education 2000). For example, several schools in a Florida district that were funded for reform efforts through CSR appear to have been motivated by the CSR funding; and without it, they perhaps would not have pursued any reform efforts. Yet in these schools, reform seems very unlikely to be sustained beyond the CSR grant period. However, in numerous schools studied, CSR was not the primary motivator for reform; it was a funding source used to support and enhance existing school-improvement efforts. These schools had invested considerable time, energy, and resources into improvement in general, and in some cases, they had already invested in the particular reform they were funded to implement before CSR. Not surprisingly, researchers saw more evidence of change at most of these sites. In sum, what the researchers found was that the original whole-school improvement goals and the components[6] that guided the creation of the CSR project do not seem to have always made the transition from the federal legislation to the state, the district, and the school as envisioned. The authors state: "This is not, however, a call for terminating or downscaling CSR in any way. Quite the contrary. We believe that the important goals and intentions of CSR require more support to improve both the initiation and sustainability of reform efforts" (p. 47).

## States, Comprehensive School Reform, and Linguistic and Cultural Diversity

A particularly useful paper by Hamann et al. (2002), from the regional educational laboratory at Brown University, reviewed all references to ELLs in the proposals of seven states (Vermont, New Hampshire, Maine, Massachusetts, Connecticut, Rhode Island, New York) to the U.S. Department of Education regarding CSRD and in the states' correspondence with schools and districts. This is the only research study we found that deals with comprehensive school reform, states, and language or cultural diversity. The authors found that "an opportunity to remedy some CSRD oversights in reference to ELLs was largely missed when states did not think of them explicitly and in-depth as they were formulating their CSRD strategies. In missing this opportunity, SEAs were no more or less guilty of failing to adequately accommodate ELLs than the long list of other educational stakeholders who have created the status quo, nor were they exceptional" (p. 3).

---

[6] The nine CSRD components include: (1) Effective, research-based methods and strategies; (2) comprehensive design with integrated components including instruction, assessment, classroom management, professional development, parental involvement, and school management; (3) professional development; (4) measurable goals and benchmarks; (5) majority of faculty/staff members support model implementation; (6) parental and community involvement; (7) external technical support and assistance; (8) evaluation strategies; and (9) coordination of resources (http://www.ed.gov/offices/OESE/compreform/csrdgui.html).

However, the results are disappointing, as Hamann and colleagues argued, because state education agencies are in a unique position to influence the market of CSRD models. They posited that perhaps the solution is simply for personnel involved with CSRD at the state level to become more knowledgeable in the education of ELLs and to become "the sources of information regarding how to bridge the unnecessary dichotomy between whole school reform initiatives and the issues of ELL accommodation" (p. 25). However, they worried that the solution is not that simple. First, there are substantial challenges in operationalizing and learning the knowledge, both within the SEAs and between the SEAs and schools and districts. It is here that linkages are important. This quote from Hamann et al., while lengthy, bears noting on this issue:

Why haven't existing effective practices not become more widely known and in use? At a minimum, there needs to be a mechanism for operationalizing such knowledge. As Lusi (1997) advocates, there need to be conscious intents on the part of SEAs to become learning organizations. There need to be means, for example, for CSRD program implementers to learn from Title VII Coordinators, Migrant Education Coordinators, and other SEA staff who do have expertise in ELL education. There need to be means so that successful school site practices with ELLs are captured, and the essential procedural knowledge of those successes is disseminated with sufficient support for necessary customizations in new sites. None of the state plans included a line or paragraph to the effect that "We recognize that ELL students fare particularly poorly in school and, as such, we are going to ensure that when effective practices for ELLs are developed we will incubate them, learn from them, and change our ways as indicated by our new understanding." As noted already in an endnote citing Wong, Fillmore, and Meyer (1992), it is both unfortunate and symptomatic of the educational politics of the last thirty years that viable mechanisms to capture and disseminate ELL-responsive procedural knowledge have been consistently undercut. It is telltale that none of the models and practices implemented with ELLs through Title VII, Migrant Education, and multiple another mechanisms have been sources for CSRD models. It is as if there is an assumption among SEA staffs (and at multiple other tiers of the formal education enterprise) that nothing broadly applicable can be learned from effective instruction of ELLs. (p. 27)

Specifically on the idea of linkages, Hamann and colleagues discussed the importance of "lateral communication" between those involved with CSR, Title I, Title VII, and Migrant Education at the state level.

Datnow and colleagues (2002) and Bodilly (2001) both found that just as schools and districts change, so do reform design teams. Datnow and colleagues claimed that this lends a "building the plane while it's flying" quality to the reform implementation process. Bodilly found that changes in the NAS designs and their strategies for implementation were driven by planned development of the teams, adaptations to teacher and student needs, adaptations to nonsupportive policy environments, and learning from the teams. Similarly, Datnow and colleagues observed that many design teams refined their models based on educators' experiences with them or in response to schools' demands. In some cases, this meant adapting the reform model for use in particular contexts. Design teams also changed aspects of their reforms to suit new policies and political realities affecting education, as well as to stem competition from other design teams. Not surprisingly, these forces sometimes converged when, for example, schools implementing reform models demanded assistance in meeting new state accountability systems or standards.

Bodilly (2001) reported that as NAS design teams moved from being "thinkers of break-the-mold designs" to service providers or assistance organizations, they faced many internal capacity-building challenges. In examining the design and design-team factors that affect implementation of NAS designs in ten jurisdictions across the United States, Bodilly (1998) found that no one or two design or design team factors explained varying degrees of implementation evident in schools. Instead, she identified a complex set of variables that jointly added to strong effects. These were

- A stable team with a capability to serve schools and teachers.
- Design team's ability to communicate the design well to schools.
- Effective marketing to the district and the ability to gain needed resources for implementation.
- Type of design or relative elements emphasized.
- Implementation support to schools. (pp. 63–64)

In general, design teams had differing levels of capacity that affected their ability to work with districts and schools. They were also undergoing learning processes and were simultaneously growing to meet the increased demand for their reform models. During the period of the RAND study, the teams were required to evolve from small, often research-oriented organizations into entrepreneurial enterprises. They were expected to serve more schools as well as deliver quality in sound implementation and student outcomes. All teams suffered growing pains that affected their ability to work with schools (Bodilly 2001). Turnover among staff within design teams also hampered implementation of the reform at the school level (Erlichson and Goertz 2001).

Designs were adapted significantly due to the pressures posed by states, districts, and unions to meet the existing regulatory, organizational, and cultural environment. The reality of working in the scale-up districts caused design teams to make several changes, including gradually lengthening implementation schedules, dropping elements of the design, or changing their thinking from trying to achieve required activities toward principles schools worked toward achieving (Bodilly 2001).

Although most often the changes that occurred in designs took them away from the reformers' original intents, in one respect, there were improvements. That is, over time, NAS design teams began to provide more implementation support, assistance, and specifics regarding the process of reform design selection. These changes were often based on experience working with schools (Bodilly 2001). However, some also became more specified in their training and support packages as a response to new CSR regulations (Datnow et al. 2002).

Overall, Bodilly (2001) found that higher levels of implementation were associated with design teams that

- Had a stable team with the capacity to field qualified personnel to serve growing numbers of schools.
- Effectively communicated their designs to schools and avoided staff confusion.
- Effectively marketed to districts and gained the resource support required for the design.

- Emphasized the core elements of schooling common across the designs: curriculum, instructions, student assignment, assessments, and professional development.
- Supported implementation with whole-school training, facilitators, extensive training days, and materials. (p. 76)

Bodilly (2001) concluded that for successful design implementation, design teams need a base of well-developed materials that explain the design and clarity the teachers commitment in implementation. But materials are not enough. To sustain reform efforts over several years, implementation teams must have strategies or plans that their schools can readily adopt to establish structural changes that allow a common time during the regular school day for teachers to work on lesson planning, for significant and sustained staff development, and for sharing at the school level.

## CONCLUSION

In summary, we have seen that when it comes to implementation of a CSR model, a strong effort is required on the part of multiple actors at multiple levels. Second, in the best-case scenario, schools implement reforms with the assistance and flexibility of design teams, districts, and states. Long-term support and targeted staff development can help schools incorporate new practices and address local realities. This process of support and flexibility, both on the part of the design team and the district, can help schools adapt models to local contextual needs, increases teacher buy-in, and increases the possibility that implementing a reform will actually result in school change. This is not to say that schools must develop reforms themselves but rather that externally developed reforms must allow flexibility for teachers to find them workable in their schools and in classrooms. Educators choosing among reforms should attempt to gauge their own capacity and flexibility in incorporating new models.

In addition to these factors, we have learned about the importance of smooth, thoughtfully planned leadership transitions, as well as the importance of long-term district and state support, or, at the least, the relative absence of district-level implementation interference. All of these features are necessary for an externally developed CSR model to lead to meaningful school improvement.

Overall, the molding of reform models to fit the linguistic diversity of school populations is a significant issue, as the demand for change and the number of LEP students continues to grow, particularly in urban areas. Hamann and colleagues (2002) noted that none of the CSR models had its origins in Title VII, Migrant Education, or any other program created specifically to serve ELLs. However, there are a few resource guides (Wilde, Thompson, and Herrera 1999) that discuss CSR models' responsiveness to ELLs. Menken (2000) presented a set of questions for consideration when ELLs are served through CSR models.

Because reinventing the wheel may not be necessary when it comes to reform models, a certain amount of invention might always be necessary when dealing with the site- and community-specific dimensions of change in schools serving large numbers of LEP students (Goldenberg 1996). What makes these matters all the more tricky are the differences of opinion that surround bilingual education and how best to teach second language learners. Reform models, which bring their own theories about language, can conflict with educators' beliefs. These issues become even more heated when they reach political levels outside the school. Another issue is the transience rates of LEP students. Goldenberg (1996) explained that "A program that is 'effective' under fairly stable conditions might be taxed to the breaking point with a continual stream of new enrollments."

In spite of these challenges of adaptation to local settings, the findings on achievement suggest that more experimentation with CSR models in ELL contexts is needed. Hamann et al. (2002) made an important point when they stated that "it seems possible that some ELL students could gain academically after the introduction of a model, not because the model is necessarily ELL-responsive but because at least a prescriptive model (e.g., Success for All, Direct Instruction) might offer direction to a teacher who is otherwise untrained/ill-prepared to work with ELLs" (p. 6). Further research is needed into the impact of CSR on ELLs and racial minority students.

# 7

## The Role of the Federal Government
## in Reform Efforts

Attempting to discuss "the federal lens" on almost any U.S. topic is a daunting task. The United States spans a continent plus islands near the middle of the Pacific Ocean. Our nation includes over two hundred eighty million people living in fifty states plus the District of Columbia. Several U.S. states are larger in terms of land mass, population, and gross domestic product than the average nation in the rest of the world.

The best available anthropological evidence is that perhaps as recently as fifteen thousand years ago there were no human beings on either the North or South American continents (Diamond 1997). From then to now, the ancestors of today's U.S. citizens have arrived in ever-increasing numbers. Some of today's U.S. citizens descend directly from people who arrived twelve thousand years ago, and much larger numbers of our citizens arrived in the past twelve years. The ancestors of today's U.S. citizens spoke thousands of languages, and several of today's school districts serve students who, collectively, are fluent in over one hundred different languages. Not only is the United States the most diverse nation on earth; America today is the most diverse nation in the history of the earth. Attempts to generalize about such a group do not come easily.

In this chapter, the majority of data presented will be descriptive. There is no random assignment to nations or to national policy. A history of the federal role in U.S. public schooling will be followed by a few summary analyses from the National Assessment of Educational Progress, a descriptive analysis of one program as policies, funds, and accountability move from Washington, D.C., to the local classroom, and brief notes on possible directions for future research. Figure 7 orients the federal role in our conceptual framework.

## A BRIEF HISTORY OF THE FEDERAL ROLE IN U.S. EDUCATION WITH RESPECT TO EQUITY

One cause of complexity in describing the U.S. government's current roles in education relates to the complexity of our history over more than two centuries (Cross 2004). With respect to equity and the education of racially diverse student populations, the Supreme Court's May 17, 1954, decision in the case of *Brown v. Board of Education of Topeka* (Kansas) stands out as an obvious marker. The courts found that the operation of dual systems of education (one for students whose ancestors were of European extraction and one for students whose parents were of African origin) that were operated in several states were inherently inequitable. This ruling has led to a series of subsequent court interventions designed to desegregate schools from Boston to California.

With respect to reform, federal actions in support of education were generally less dramatic than the Supreme Court's 1954 step until October 4, 1957, when the Soviet Union launched the first man-made earth satellite, *Sputnik*. Republican President Dwight Eisenhower decried the shortage of qualified scientists and engineers in the United States, and, in the name of national defense, the president and the Congress began funding a range of programs to increase the numbers of students who were highly proficient in mathematics, science, and foreign language. Most programs focused on universities, but the Congress and administration did offer some funding to local education authorities (LEAs) in support of mathematics and science education.

More dramatic presidential actions occurred under President Lyndon Johnson. Shortly after the death of President Kennedy, Johnson initiated a series of task forces that, collectively, outlined Johnson's Great Society program. A task force chaired by John

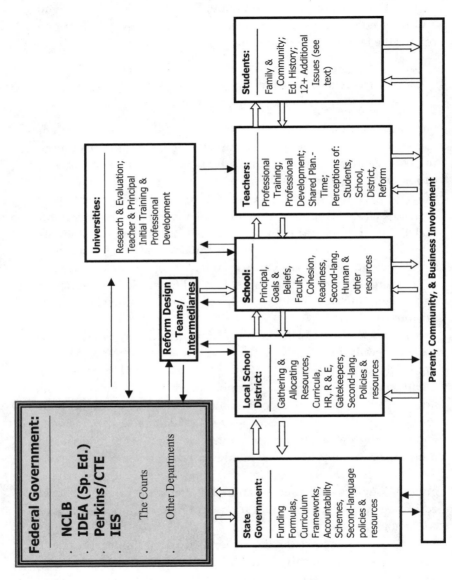

FIGURE 7. Federal Involvement and Connections to School Reform

**Federal Government:**

- **NCLB**
- **IDEA (Sp. Ed.)**
- **Perkins/CTE**
- **IES**

. . . . . .

The Courts

Other Departments

**Universities:**

Research & Evaluation;
Teacher & Principal
Initial Training &
Professional
Development

**Reform Design
Teams/
Intermediaries**

**State
Government:**

Funding
Formulas,
Curriculum
Frameworks,
Accountability
Schemes,
Second-language
policies &
resources

**Local School
District:**

Gathering &
Allocating
Resources,
Curricula,
HR, R & E,
Gatekeepers,
Second-lang.
Policies &
resources

**School:**

Principal,
Goals &
Beliefs,
Faculty
Cohesion,
Readiness,
Second-lang.
Human &
other
resources

**Teachers:**

Professional
Training;
Professional
Development;
Shared Plan.-
Time;
Perceptions of:
Students,
School,
District,
Reform

**Students:**

Family &
Community;
Ed. History;
12+ Additional
Issues (see
text)

**Parent, Community, & Business Involvement**

Gardner, president of the Carnegie Corporation of New York, concluded the following:

Thus in those areas where the [at risk] children need more intensive educational services than other children, they often get less. For too many of the poor, educational experience has been a series of failures, each failure reinforcing the lesson of failure so that education is for them an habituation to despair. (*Report of the President's Task Force on Education* 1964, p. 6)

Johnson used that report to draft the Elementary and Secondary Education Act (ESEA), which he sent to Congress in January of 1965. The bill passed in under three months, and Johnson signed the bill in front of the old one-room Texas schoolhouse in which he had once taught. Title I remains as ESEA's largest funded program.

Because the formula under which Title I funds are distributed is driven by percentages of students living in poverty, "The Title I program . . . is the principal embodiment of the national commitment to help educate economically and educationally disadvantaged children" (Jennings 2000, p. 1). In its first year, Title I was funded at $1 billion ($959 million), and Johnson had imagined that amount doubling annually for several years. However, there was substantial resistance in Congress to the federal government having any role in K–12 education, and total Title I funding did not reach $2 billion for a decade, the 1976–1977 school year. Funding redoubled to $4 billion for school year 1988–1989 (Stringfield 1991), again redoubling to over $8 billion for the 2000–2001 school year. For the 2003–2004 school year, Title I funding was $12.3 billion, and President Bush has proposed adding $1 billion, or 8 percent, to that total for the next fiscal year (http://www.ed.gov, 2004).

Special education is the second large area of direct federal education investment. The Individuals with Disabilities Education ACT (IDEA) provides direct funding to states and districts to assist in the potentially very expensive area of special education. Individuals with Disabilities funding was $10.1 billion for fiscal year 2004.

Over the past several decades, many additional U.S. Department of Education (USDE) investments in education have evolved, including career and technical education, Indian education, education for native Hawaiians, migrant education, and English language acquisition; from support for the education of homeless children to "Troops to

Teachers." However, added together, funding for those programs do not approach funding for Title I or special education.

A final area of major investment by the USDE is in the area of research, development, statistics, and assessment. The USDE and its predecessors have continuously invested in these areas for over forty years, with the current investments largely coordinated through the Institute of Education Sciences (IES). For fiscal year 2004, IES was funded to $430 million. Institute of Education Sciences activities range from the support of various research and development centers (such as the Center for Research on Excellence and Diversity in Education, the funding source of this volume), to a wide range of research for individual projects, often focusing on improving reading and mathematics, to the new What Works Clearinghouse and the ERIC system.

The second area within IES is the National Center for Education Statistics (NCES), which gathers and provides data on general statistical trends in education, statistical analyses, and methodological studies intended to enable more efficient data collection and information production. The third IES investment is in assessment, and specifically in the ongoing work of the National Assessment of Educational Progress, which provides key measures of the status and trends in U.S. student learning over time, by subject area. Additional NAEP information will be provided in the next section. The final IES investment area concerns research and innovation in special education.

Beyond the USDE, every significant department in the U.S. government, from Defense to Agriculture, has programs related to the education of American children. The Department of Agriculture underwrites the free- and reduced-price lunch programs in virtually every public school in the country. The Department of Health and Human Services funds the multibillion-dollar Head Start program and pays for some of the specialized special education services in public schools.

A full description of the many ways in which the USDE attempts to support equity in education would take more than one chapter. Readers interested in a current overview might wish to examine USDE's Web site, at www.ed.gov. In the next section, we will highlight two examples of the federal government's work in U.S. education.

## TWO CURRENT EXAMPLES OF FEDERAL INVOLVEMENT:
### NAEP AND NCLB

*NAEP*

For over thirty years, the National Assessment of Educational Progress (NAEP) has provided the United States with a reasonably objective, longitudinal national educational outcomes picture. Currently, the overall NAEP initiative is funded at $94 million per year.

Guided by a national advisory board, NAEP staff contracts for the gathering of data from large samples of students relative to their academic skills level in reading, mathematics, science, and writing. Data are gathered from nationally randomized samples of students who are ages 9, 13, and 17. Data are presented by NAEP in several forms ranging from large reports to somewhat interactive Web-based analytic engines (http://nces.ed.gov/nationsreportcard). As two examples of longitudinal NAEP data, consider Figures 8 and 9. Figure 8 presents reading scores over time and shows no pattern of raised achievement for ages 13 and 17 but shows that the reading achievement of age 9 students rose between 1999 and 2004. Figure 9 provides data on mathematics scores by age over time and shows that the average fourth- and eight-graders' scores have risen significantly over time, especially over the past thirteen years.

Because the NAEP data sets are so large, additional analyses by subgroup are possible. Table 1 shows NAEP data by racial group: white, black, and Hispanic.[1] Data are presented as white – [minority group] scale score differentials. The education trust interprets a 10-point difference between students as roughly equivalent to one year's worth of learning (http://www2.edtrust.org/edtrust). The frustrating news is that large gaps between majority and minority groups persist. The encouraging news is that the size of the gaps has decreased over the past generation.

National Assessment of Educational Progress data are also made available for a range of secondary data analyses. An excellent example of this "recycling" of a large, expensive data is Flanagan and Grissmer (2001). Working within the CREDE center, the authors reanalyzed a decade's NAEP data, broken down by region of the country (northeast, southeast, midwest, and west) and by three community types

---

[1] Similar tables are provided by the USDE on other ages and content areas.

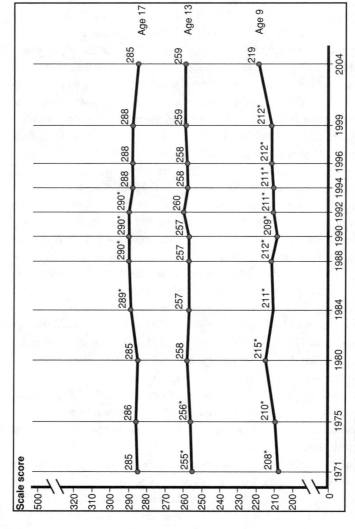

FIGURE 8. NAEP Trends in Average Reading Scale Scores for Students Ages 9, 13, and 17: 1971–2004

*Note:* "*" denotes scores significantly different from 2004 scores.

*Source:* U.S. Department of Education, Institute of Education Sciences, National Center for Education Statistics (2005a).

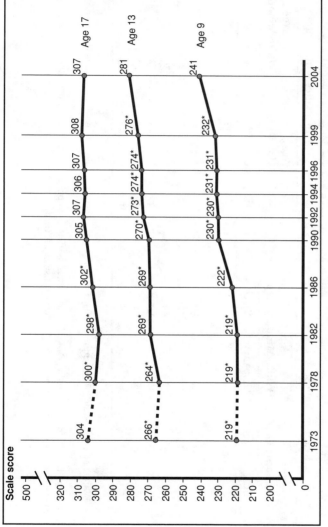

FIGURE 9. NAEP Trends in Average Mathematics Scale Scores for Students Ages 9, 13, and 17: 1973–2004
*Note:* Dashed lines represent extrapolated data. "*" denotes scores significantly different from 2004 scores. *Source:* U.S. Department of Education, Institute of Education Sciences, National Center for Education Statistics (2005a).

163

TABLE 1. *30-Year NAEP Achievement Gap Trends by Race/Ethnicity*

| | Reading Scale Scores | | | | | Mathematics Scale Scores | | | |
|---|---|---|---|---|---|---|---|---|---|
| | Age 9 White-Minority Gap* | | Age 17 White-Minority Gap* | | | Age 9 White-Minority Gap* | | Age 17 White-Minority Gap* | |
| Year | Hispanic | Black | Hispanic | Black | Year | Hispanic | Black | Hispanic | Black |
| 1975 | 34 | 35 | 41 | 52 | 1973 | 23 | 35 | 33 | 40 |
| 1980 | 31 | 32 | 31 | 50 | 1978 | 21 | 32 | 30 | 38 |
| 1984 | 31 | 32 | 27 | 32 | 1982 | 20 | 29 | 27 | 32 |
| 1990 | 28 | 35 | 22 | 29 | 1986 | 21 | 25 | 24 | 29 |
| 1994 | 32 | 33 | 33 | 30 | 1990 | 21 | 27 | 26 | 21 |
| 1999 | 28 | 35 | 24 | 31 | 1994 | 27 | 25 | 22 | 27 |
| 2004 | 21 | 26 | 29 | 29 | 1999 | 26 | 28 | 22 | 31 |
| | | | | | 2004 | 18 | 23 | 24 | 28 |

* Gap equals White average scale score minus Hispanic or Black average scale score. Data from (http://nces.ed.gov/nationsreportcard/).

** A general rule of thumb for interpreting NAEP scale scores is that a 10-point difference between student scores is roughly equivalent to one year's worth of learning (http://www2.edtrust.org/edtrust).

TABLE 2. *Average NAEP Scores and Percent of Student Population by Region and Locality (from Flanagan and Grissmer 2001)*

| Locality | Region | Percent of U.S. Student Population | Average NAEP Test Score (Standard Deviation) |
|---|---|---|---|
| Suburban | Northeast | 11.6 | 0.32 |
| Rural | Northeast | 3.6 | 0.29 |
| Suburban | Midwest | 12.4 | 0.28 |
| Rural | Midwest | 5.4 | 0.26 |
| Rural | West | 3.3 | 0.07 |
| Suburban | West | 11.6 | −0.03 |
| Suburban | Southeast | 14.8 | −0.05 |
| Rural | Southeast | 7.3 | −0.14 |
| Central City | West | 7.0 | −0.15 |
| Central City | Midwest | 6.6 | −0.22 |
| Central City | Southeast | 10.8 | −0.30 |
| Central City | Northeast | 5.5 | −0.46 |

(urban, suburban, rural). Their two most striking examples can be derived from Table 2 below.

On a very positive front, by comparing NAEP data with data from the Third International Math and Science Study (Flanagan and Grissmer 2001), the authors demonstrated that students in the four highest-performing cells (northeast suburban and rural, midwestern suburban and rural) "would likely rank at the top of international distributions" (p. 13).

The more troubling finding was that by far the lowest scores were in the four urban cells (urban northeast, urban southeast, urban west, and urban midwest). Clearly, it is America's large, complex, diverse urban districts that require the greatest improvements.

NAEP provides one example of the uniquely valuable role that the federal government has played in keeping the public, policy makers, and Congress informed as to the current standing of U.S. students' academic achievement. As will be noted in the NCLB section, the government now imagines yet another valuable role for NAEP.

### No Child Left Behind

President Johnson signed the original ESEA legislation in 1967, with Title I funding growing over the subsequent decades from just under $1 billion to the current $12.3 billion. President George W. Bush declared education to be one of his major interests and advocated an expansion of ESEA into the No Child Left Behind Act, or NCLB. An eleven-hundred-page bill based on President Bush's recommendations became law in January 2002, with final regulations supporting the bill published in December 2002.

The purposes of NCLB are to raise all students' achievements to high levels of proficiency and more specifically to eliminate all "gaps" in levels of academic achievement – between persons of poverty and affluence and minority and majority status – and to do so by 2014. Many would argue that the fundamental difference between NCLB and all previous educational legislation was changing the focus from providing equitable access and opportunity to achieving equitable outcomes.

First, NCLB requires the *states* to continue fiscal oversight of LEAs[2] and to develop new student outcome accountability requirements. At present, states are diligently working to declare academic frameworks for various grades and to select and implement tests of most students in grades 3–8 and at least one grade between 10 and 12.

Assuming these requirements are being addressed, the USDE forwards funds for NCLB to the state departments. Each state is allowed to hold back a small percentage of those funds to ensure adequate guidance and administration of NCLB dollars, but 95 percent to 99 percent of the funds flow directly to LEAs. The state departments then monitor the implementation of NCLB within the LEAs and the gathering and reporting of fiscal and student academic outcomes.

States report the academic outcomes to the federal government as well as to the public. Public reporting is typically done through the production of both district- and school-level "league tables," in which schools' outcomes can be examined and rank ordered. One of the more advanced examples of such a public reporting is the Maryland State Department's "Report Card" available at http://msp.msde.state.md.us/. Through the passage of a new law, the federal government pressures both local school districts and individual public schools to raise test scores. School leaders, in turn, pressure teachers and students to improve test scores, attendance, graduation rates, and other measurable outcomes.

---

[2] The auditing is both in terms of the expenditure of NCLB funds, but also involves the "supplement not supplant" provisions of the law, and hence affects a broader accounting function.

In terms of school and district inputs/processes, NCLB requires schools to report the percentages of teachers meeting high qualification standards. In addition, each school must formally notify parents when a student's teacher does not meet those (state-defined) high academic standards. (Note that, as in the previous paragraph, the federal government is able to work through the states and the schools to force LEAs and schools to become more transparent, albeit on somewhat arbitrary measures.)

Most other measures relate to student outcomes. No Child Left Behind moves away from the national trend of exempting increasingly large percentages of students from taking tests because of declared disabilities and directly addresses the widely discussed, though minimally documented, possible trend of having some low-achieving students simply not come to school on testing days. The simple mechanism in NCLB is a requirement that test score data must be reported on at least 95 percent of all registered students.

No Child Left Behind mandates that in all states, test score data in key areas must be analyzed and reported at the whole-school level and then disaggregated by gender, race, free-lunch status, native language, and special education status. The effect of this disaggregation is that an individual school may be accountable for between ten and twenty separate categories of measurable outcomes. The NCLB requirement is not simply that the overall school, or the initially low-achieving students, make annual academic progress but that the whole school and each of the ten to twenty of the subgroups all make annual progress.

Once a baseline has been established for each school, subgroup, and district via an initial administration of tests, the NCLB requires that each state establish annual measurable objectives (AMOs), which are a quantitative method for demonstrating progress from a school's/district's/state's current achievement levels to meet the NCLB standard of 100 percent of students achieving levels of academic proficiency at each measured grade by 2014. Some states elected to set AMOs for the first few years that essentially require no progress on the measured outcomes, followed by years in which the schools have to make extremely and unprecedented gains on student outcomes.

Once theoretical State 1 has selected a specific set of tests, and School A has administered the test once, it will have a prescore. For

TABLE 3. *Theoretical Achievement Gain (AYP) Requirements for Students in Two States That Have Made Differing AMO Decisions*

| Year | '03 | '04 | '05 | '06 | '07 | '08 | '09 | '10 | '11 | '12 | '13 | '14 |
|---|---|---|---|---|---|---|---|---|---|---|---|---|
| State 1 | | | | | | | | | | | | |
| School A | 50% | 50% | 50% | 50% | 50% | 50% | 50% | 50% | 62% | 75% | 87% | 100% |
| State 2 | | | | | | | | | | | | |
| School B | 50% | 55% | 59% | 64% | 68% | 73% | 77% | 82% | 86% | 91% | 96% | 100% |

discussion's sake, let us assume that the school has 50 percent of its fourth-grade free-lunch students score at or above the level deemed by the state to represent "proficient." Under NCLB and State 1 rules, that 50 percent level can suffice for several years, but then in the last few years between 2010 and 2014, the school's free-lunch population must raise its scores on the state test such that all (100 percent) of School A's free-lunch students score at the proficient level by 2014.

By contrast, State 2 elected to declare that progress must begin immediately and reflect at least a straight line of progress from current status to 100 percent of all students achieving at proficient levels by 2014. School B, which is demographically identical to School A in State 1, also had 50 percent of its fourth-grade free-lunch students initially score at or above the proficient level. However, because State 2's AMO required continuous progress on the state test, School B must find ways to get an annually growing percentage of students to perform at a higher level each year. The difference can be seen in Table 3.

Assuming that the two states' tests are of similar difficulty levels, one can question whether School A can make the dramatic jump between 2010 and 2014 required in State 1's AMOs. One could equally question whether school B can make the continuous improvement required in State 2.

Whatever the AMO trajectories selected by a given state, schools and districts are then required to report measures of the extent to which they have made annual yearly progress (AYP). To the extent that a school and its various subgroups are able to demonstrate AYP (e.g., produce attendance, graduation, and test score gains that meet or exceed each year's AMO), those schools are deemed to have made

AYP. However, it is not just the overall school scores that are counted; it is the gains made by each of the previously mentioned ten to twenty subpopulations within each school.

Should a school, or one or more of the ten to twenty subgroups within a school not make AYP for two consecutive years, NCLB requires that the school be formally identified as needing improvement, and the district must offer to all parents the option of transferring their child to another school in the district, regardless of the individual student's or his/her subgroup's scores or gains. Should the school not meet AYP for a third year, the year 2 sanctions remain in effect, and the school and district must offer supplemental services (e.g., after-school tutoring services provided by an external vendor) to students attending that school.

Should a school fail to meet AYP for four consecutive years, then all year 3 sanctions remain in place, plus the district must adopt one or more of the following additional steps:

1. Locally reconstitute the school.
2. Allow the state to reconstitute the school.
3. Hire an external management group to run the school.
4. Offer to allow the school to become a charter school.
5. Engage in "significant" staff restructuring.
6. Offer public school choice and additional supplemental services. (Yakimowski 2004)

As the years of education under the federal NCLB law move forward, these provisions will produce a large numbers of complexities and conundrums, such that federal guidelines will inevitably be modified to deal with what are often unavoidable realities. The first of those modifications occurred in the winter of 2003–2004, when then-Secretary of Education Paige made additional allowances for newly emigrated students who have not yet mastered the English language. These modifications came as a result of hundreds of schools and LEAs protesting to their local districts (and elected officials). The LEA superintendents then protested to their state departments and often directly to the Secretary of Education's office. As these complaints reached a sufficient crescendo, the Secretary of Education almost inevitably modified federal policy and guidance.

Whether additional modifications will occur or not is an ongoing question. However, what is clear is that through NCLB, the president, Congress, and the federal government have attempted to reach through various levels of traditional U.S. educational organization to improve student achievement.

This effort then harkens back to other levels of the federal involvement figure. To assist teachers, schools, and school districts in achieving AYP, the federal government has moderately increased funding for IES, which in turn is funding a new generation of studies of "what works," to improve student achievement and has also funded a What Works Clearinghouse to provide "research-based" knowledge to educators on how to achieve the ambitious goals of NCLB. Almost three years after initial funding, the What Works Clearinghouse had only released one study (on middle school mathematics) on "what works" but schools are already being held accountable for results across other subject areas and grade levels.

However, the federal government is also funding a series of other initiatives, such as providing funds to schools (through states) to support the implementation of comprehensive school reform designs and funding a range of university-based pilot programs to improve the preparation and professional development of teachers and administrators.

A final point connects NAEP with NCLB. It would be theoretically possible for educators in any given state to focus their efforts narrowly on their state's new tests and raise scores on those tests without improving actual student achievement. Wary of such potential criticism, the president and Congress build a state-level check into NCLB. All states must now administer "State NAEP" on a periodic basis to a sample of students. If a state's scores on its statewide test rise dramatically but the state's NAEP scores do not reflect similar progress, the state will be asked to explain the discrepancy and educational progress will be questioned.

## CONCLUSION

Even before the ratification of the U.S. Constitution, the federal government was involved in decisions about the education of our young people. That role expanded during the twentieth century, and

President Bush's No Child Left Behind legislation marked a dramatic "ratcheting up" of federal involvement in the working of the typical U.S. school.

NCLB, IES, and other current initiatives represent a unique level of additional federal involvement in public school education. Educators are being told that the current administration's suggestions for re-funding of IDEA (federal support for special education) and career and technical education will mirror major provisions of NCLB, further advancing a federal role in U.S. education.

Necessarily, the effects of this ambitious agenda, either on research or on practice, have yet to be fully seen, and modifications of many aspects are likely. It is undeniable that during the dawning years of the twenty-first century, the U.S. government is working very hard to produce a more tightly linked system of education in the United States.

# 8

# Methodological Issues in the Study of Systemic Integration for Effective Reform

A topic that runs throughout this volume is the lack of research literature specifically devoted to the education of linguistically and culturally diverse students. In the most general terms, this is an equity issue imbued with methodological challenges. Generic effectiveness research asks, "What makes a school or district effective for all students?" Equity-oriented research asks: "What makes a school effective for particular subgroups of students who have been historically underserved?"

Many intertwined methodological issues are related to this topic. The most obvious one is sampling, which boils down to questions related to the disaggregation of school-level data. Other methodological issues include the use of mixed methods (both quantitative and qualitative), the measurement of the intervention, the need for multiple outcome measures, and validity considerations.

## A BRIEF HISTORY OF SAMPLING ISSUES

In Chapter 1, a case is made for the continued importance of the school level as the unit of change and analysis in educational reform literature. However, we have also consistently emphasized the education of racially and linguistically diverse students. The distinction between school-level analysis and data analyses disaggregated by subgroups has been addressed in several iterative stages over the past thirty years.

The initial "effective schools" research had an equity focus and involved case studies of schools serving primarily low-SES students in urban areas.[1] The original five correlates of effective schooling emerged from this research (e.g., Brookover 1985; Edmonds 1979; Lezotte and Bancroft 1985).

Later, contextually sensitive school effectiveness research examined differences in effective schools serving students from predominantly low-SES versus predominantly middle-SES backgrounds (e.g., Hallinger and Murphy 1986; Teddlie and Stringfield 1985, 1993). Some of the effective schools processes operating in these environments were similar, but several differential recommendations (for schools serving low-SES, as opposed to middle-SES students) also emerged from these studies. Equity-oriented research revealed school and classroom practices that were particularly beneficial for linguistically and culturally diverse students. These studies came from a variety of research areas (e.g., the ethnographic studies of the education of English language learners).

Currently, there is an increased emphasis on equity-related research that has been fueled by a number of factors. For instance, the increase in the number and variety of subgroups in public education in the United States has focused interest on their education. The NCLB legislation has, of course, focused even more attention on disaggregated data analysis. Research by the Center for Research on Education, Diversity and Excellence (CREDE) has also highlighted the importance of the education of linguistically and culturally diverse students over the past few years.

While effectiveness research is based on a pragmatist[2] philosophical foundation (e.g., Teddlie and Reynolds 2001), a number of scholars have been advocating for a transformative-emancipatory orientation (e.g., Mertens 1998, 2003). The pragmatist orientation focuses on the

[1] "School-effects research," which is another branch of SER concerned with the "scientific properties" of schooling, employs a quantitative approach that involves probability sampling.
[2] Pragmatism is a deconstructive paradigm that debunks concepts such as "Truth" or "Reality" and focuses instead on "what works" as the "truth" regarding the research questions under investigation. Pragmatism rejects the either/or choices associated with the paradigm wars, advocates for the use of mixed methods in research, and acknowledges that the values of the researcher play a large role in interpretation of results (Tashakkori and Teddlie 2003, p. 713).

discovery of "what works," while the transformative-emancipatory orientation seeks social justice, especially for marginalized subgroups in asymmetric power relationships, such as those that may exist in schools serving linguistically and culturally diverse students. This philosophical orientation obviously advocates for the use of disaggregated data.

The generalizability of effects across subgroups of students within schools (i.e., the differential effect) is directly related to the achievement gap between subgroups of students within schools. Unfortunately, most of the evidence on this effect is from Europe and is part of school-effects research that is concerned with the size of the effect, not with the properties of schools that have successfully dealt with equity issues related to ethnicity and linguistic differences, among other factors.

There is now general agreement that disaggregated data analysis by subgroups within schools is the preferred method for assessing the education of linguistically and culturally diverse students. These analyses allow researchers to determine the extent of the achievement gap among subgroups and to identify schools that have reduced or eliminated that gap. Case studies of those successful schools could be instrumental in developing best practices for reducing the achievement gap and more appropriately educating linguistically and culturally diverse students.

Although there is widespread agreement on these points, why is there still such a relative dearth of research related to the achievement gap and how to reduce it? This research requires schools to report disaggregated data by subgroups, and there are several reasons why this has not been a common practice:

- Many educators see the school as the unit of change and analysis and prefer to report school-level data only. The emphasis on comprehensive school reform has accentuated this tendency.
- Until the advent of NCLB, most state accountability systems focused on school-level performance almost exclusively, and this emphasis was reflected in the data that the schools reported.
- Many educators believe that it is very difficult to reduce the achievement gap and are concerned that their efforts will not prove successful; therefore, these educators are reluctant to report disaggregated data.

The current federal focus on subgroup analysis, like the rest of their educational research agenda, is almost exclusively quantitative in nature. Disaggregated data analysis from NCLB is designed to ascertain whether there is still an achievement gap, to determine its magnitude, and address it. There is not a corollary emphasis on qualitatively oriented case studies of schools that have narrowed the gap. While quantitative subgroup analyses are illuminating, they only tell part of the story. Researchers should be moving beyond the mere demonstration of the achievement gap, or its reduction, to how it is perpetuated or eliminated.

Other problems with disaggregated subgroup analysis within schools, while not sufficient to preclude the analyses, should be taken into consideration:

- Subgroup analyses often lead to problems with small sample size and large standard errors of measurement. Subgroup analyses with small numbers often lead to highly fluctuating results from year to year.
- Specific operational definitions of subgroup status need to be developed. Should a subgroup with 5 percent of the school's population be treated the same in quantitative and qualitative analyses as a subgroup with 40 percent of the school's population? How can generalizations be made across studies in which the percentages of linguistically and culturally diverse students vary greatly?
- What happens in mixed schools where a minority subgroup in the national population is the majority in the school? How does this affect the subgroup analyses or the manner in which they are presented?

## THE NEED FOR MIXED METHODS

A major thrust of NCLB is "scientifically based research," which results in "evidence-based" education or policy, that uses randomized controlled trials or experiments (e.g., Coalition for Evidence-Based Policy 2002; Fitz-Gibbon 1996; Slavin and Fashola 1998). Experimentation is now referred to as the "gold standard" for educational research, and the work of Donald T. Campbell and his colleagues is the core logic for the movement (e.g., Campbell and Stanley 1966;

Cook and Campbell 1979; Shadish, Cook, and Campbell 2002). No Child Left Behind scientifically based research emphasizes experiments using random assignment to condition, quantitative methods, numerical data analysis, internal validity, summative evaluations of programs aimed at determining cause and effect relations, and time- and context-free generalizations.

According to the Coalition for Evidence-Based Policy (CEBP), evidence-based research is a reaction to "decades of stagnation in American education" (CEBP 2002, p. i) and is aimed at the "widespread implementation of research-proven interventions, with quantifiable goals" (p. ii). Although it does not refer to the "paradigm wars"[3] (e.g., Gage 1989; Guba and Lincoln 1994; Tashakkori and Teddlie 1998), it is clear that evidence-based experimentalists prefer their approach as opposed to case study–oriented research, which emphasizes qualitative methods, analysis of narrative data, external validity (or transferability), formative evaluations of programs aimed at improving the interventions, and time- and context-bound generalizations.

Although widespread implementation of research-proven interventions aimed at the education of linguistically and racially diverse students is a desirable goal, this research area cannot be fully examined using only quantitative experimental approaches. There are at least two concerns about the experimental approach.

1. Experimental designs are not *practical* in some settings, especially in schools that serve a high proportion of disadvantaged students. It may be impossible to find true control schools, either because those schools refuse to serve as controls or because they are already receiving a range of other interventions. Multiple interventions obviously pose a threat to the internal validity of experimental designs.

2. There is also a potential problem with the generalizability of experimental results to other settings. This threat involves a volunteer effect with regard to schools assigned to the control condition. Because many schools do not like the "delayed

---

[3] The paradigm wars are somewhat like the cultural wars in the United States: Both have been recurring since the 1960s, and their reappearance is usually associated with a "salvo" (e.g., the publication of the first *Handbook of Qualitative Research* [Denzin & Lincoln 1994]; the current NCLB focus on experimentation) from one side or the other.

treatment" condition, those schools volunteering to be in experiments may not be representative of the entire school population because they are willing to take the chance that they will be assigned to the control condition. For example, consider an Accelerated Schools research project. Only certain schools would volunteer to be in the project (i.e., those who like the Accelerated Schools model). Then only a percentage of these volunteer schools would be willing to participate in the control condition. The generalizability of results from this sample of control schools is problematic.

In addition to these problems with experimental designs, there is also the concern that quantitatively oriented, randomized controlled trials cannot answer basic program developer questions about how his or her program works across a variety of multiethnic, multilingual settings. Quantitatively oriented experimental designs may not yield sufficient *process data* about what is actually going on in schools that are succeeding (or failing). Quantitative research is summative and addresses whether the treatment works to increase student achievement. Some experimentalists are not interested in how the treatment works in one school as opposed to another. Between-schools contextual differences are treated as "noise" that can hopefully be controlled by random assignment to condition.

In the meantime, results from extensive research indicate that "context matters" in terms of how schools become more effective and in terms of how educators "co-construct the realities of their interventions" (Datnow, Hubbard, and Mehan 2002). Program developers and evaluators are concerned that change processes cannot be adequately assessed with the experimental techniques alone because that approach does not adequately evaluate the effect of individual school contexts. Successful reform is complex and must be assessed in a variety of ways that include both quantitative and qualitative data and both experimental and case study approaches.

Mixed methods is a third methodological approach to the study of school reform in general and to the study of change in multilingual, multiethnic settings in particular (e.g., Brewer and Hunter 1989; Greene, Caracelli, and Graham 1989; Patton 2002; Tashakkori and Teddlie 1998, 2003). Mixed methods is "a type of research design in which quantitative and qualitative approaches are used in type of questions, research methods, data collection and analysis procedures, and/or in inferences" (Tashakkori and Teddlie 2003, p. 711). In the most thoroughly integrated of these designs, the two approaches are used in conjunction with one another from problem formulation through data analysis and inference.

Mixed methods are desirable for studying educational reform strategies in schools with various multicultural and multiethnic settings. The experimental approach can be used to test the basic hypothesis regarding whether the reform strategy is working across a representative sample of these schools. Simultaneously, the case study approach can be used to study a sample of schools purposefully selected to represent certain contextual conditions that are deemed relevant to how the reforms are actually implemented. The research team needs to translate back and forth constantly between the quantitative and qualitative methodologies (Tashakkori and Teddlie 2003).

### THE MEASUREMENT OF THE INNOVATION

A major issue in reform and other research on promising programs is fidelity of implementation. As noted in Chapter 5, a consistent finding throughout the comprehensive school reform literature is that the design team and the school/district staff have to co-construct the reform at the school site for it to be successful (e.g., Datnow, Hubbard, and Mehan 2002; Datnow and Stringfield 2000; Hubbard and Mehan 1999; Stringfield and Datnow 2002;). For any reform to succeed, multiple players (e.g., members of the design team, faculty members, the principal, district personnel) must work together toward an innovation that can work in a particular context. This is characterized as a mutual adaptation process to a particular shared environment or context.

Researchers have also identified a set of factors that lead to poor implementation. These factors include:

- A poor match or "fit" between the treatment and the school's characteristics.
- Lack of teacher "buy-in" to the innovation.
- School faculty not prepared or trained adequately to enact the treatment.

• Lack of monitoring of the implementation by the school leadership team or the design team, which may lead the faculty to conclude that no one cares about the treatment and that there will no accountability for failure to implement it properly. (See Chapter 5 for more details.)

This issue is important from a methodological perspective because the evaluation team must measure (a) the degree to which each of the components of the reform are being implemented and (b) the factors that might be impeding its implementation. This is a basic part of the evaluation design, both in terms of what is being implemented at the whole-school level and what is being put into practice for subgroups at the school.

This is an especially important issue in schools serving linguistically and culturally diverse students. The reform or "treatment" that students receive is not always the same across subgroups; as a matter of fact, disadvantaged students may receive less treatment because of the way that faculty members perceive students' "limitations." As noted earlier, Stringfield and colleagues (1998) concluded that students in some comprehensive school reform schools, who were classified as LEP or were perceived to be low in ability, were placed in separate classes where they received less of the reform than those students in regular classrooms. These students would probably benefit the most from the reforms, so it is unfortunate that they received diluted versions of them. The evaluation team should document how much of the reform each subgroup receives so that any inequalities are identified and redressed early in program implementation.

MULTIPLE OUTCOMES MEASURES FOR LINGUISTICALLY
AND RACIALLY DIVERSE STUDENTS

Outcome measures have been widely discussed in effectiveness research for the past twenty-five years (e.g., Good and Brophy 1986; Levine and Lezotte 1990; Reynolds and Teddlie 2000; Rutter 1983), with most authors commenting that multiple criteria for school effectiveness are needed. Critics have noted that schools may not have consistent effects across different criteria and that to use one criterion (typically academic achievement) is not adequate for ascertaining the true effectiveness status of a school.

The same conclusion can be made for studies of educational reform. Quantitative measures of student achievement are not enough, especially during the early months of program implementation when changes in achievement are not forthcoming. Other outcome measures (e.g., attitudinal measures, behavioral measures) related to the implementation should be collected, which is especially important in schools serving diverse students.

Some investigators working in school effectiveness research have used composite scores, which combine several indicators (e.g., attendance, dropout, suspension into one participation index) into one index (e.g., Crone et al. 1994; Crone et al. 1995; Kochan, Tashakkori, and Teddlie 1996). Again, it is essential that these attitudinal and behavioral indices be broken down by subgroups so that any differential effects for linguistically and culturally diverse students will be identified. These subgroups may show differential sensitivity to the treatment, especially with regard to attitudinal and behavioral indices, and documentation of these effects is important in understanding the true impact of the school reform.

There are several school monitoring systems with multiple data elements spread across the school, teacher, and student levels. These include (a) Marzano's (2003) system with eleven data elements; (b) the "ABC + Model for School Diagnosis, Feedback, and Improvement" (Teddlie, Kochan, and Taylor 2002), which crosses four types of data by four levels of analysis; and (c) ADAM (Academic Data Analysis and Management System), which is a data management system that uses the principles of effective schooling (Chrispeels 2002a). All of these systems can be used to create whole-school and subgroup analyses.

Reynolds and Teddlie (2000, p. 326) summarized school effectiveness research related to best practices for gathering multiple outcome measures. These have been adapted below to focus on subgroup analyses:

1. Use varied measures of the effectiveness of schooling, including academic achievement, attitudes (toward self and toward others), and behavior with scores broken down by important subgroups (e.g., cultural, linguistic subgroups).
2. Use measures that are sensitive to the mission of schools in the twenty-first century, especially those schools that serve

linguistically and culturally diverse students. For example, measures of perceived racism may be important indicators of the effectiveness of schooling in some contexts (e.g., Fitz-Gibbon 1996). "Learning to learn" or "knowledge acquisition" should be assessed.

3. Use composite variables where possible.
4. Use multidimensional matrices where possible, broken down by relevant subgroups.
5. Use student behavioral data, broken down by relevant subgroups, as extensively as possible.

## VALIDITY ISSUES RELATED TO STUDIES OF LINGUISTICALLY AND CULTURALLY DIVERSE STUDENTS

This section extends the discussion on "The Need for Mixed Methods" from an earlier section. Validity issues in mixed methods include the following:

- The internal validity of experimental or quasi-experimental designs used in mixed-methods research.
- The external validity of experimental or quasi-experimental designs used in mixed-methods research.
- The trustworthiness of results from case study designs used in mixed-methods research.
- The transferability of results from case study designs used in mixed-methods research.

A mixed-methods design for reform implementation research conducted in schools in multilingual, multiethnic settings might involve two stages, thereby constituting a sequential mixed-method study (Tashakkori and Teddlie 1998, 2003):

1. An experimental design stage in which basic hypotheses are tested regarding whether the reform strategy is working in a representative sample of schools.
2. A case study design stage conducted in a smaller set of purposefully selected schools that represent certain important contextual conditions (e.g., Kemper, Stringfield, and Teddlie 2003; Patton 2002) to ascertain how the various players co-construct the school reform under those different conditions.

There always is a tension between the demands of internal and external validity in experimental studies (e.g., Cook and Campbell 1979). Given a fixed budget as one increases internal validity (e.g., by controlling for contextual conditions between schools), one risks decreasing external validity, and vice versa. New terms have been introduced for internal and external validity throughout this section (i.e., contextually sensitive research focuses on external validity issues, while evidence-based research focuses on internal validity). These considerations are a continuation of the debates between Cronbach and Campbell (e.g., Cook and Campbell 1979; Cronbach 1982) on the relative merits of these two types of validity. As noted earlier, because context is important in any study of reform, external validity issues must also be emphasized.

For the case study design, issues of trustworthiness and transferability must be considered (e.g., Lincoln and Guba 1985; Tashakkori and Teddlie 1998). Trustworthiness is a global qualitative concept used as a substitute for the validity issues from quantitative research. Two of the criteria for trustworthiness are credibility (similar to internal validity) and transferability (similar to external validity). The credibility of qualitative results can be established by several techniques, including prolonged engagement, triangulation of data sources, and member checks. The credibility of the results from research conducted in multilingual, multiethnic settings may be examined by: (a) having multiple observers in the schools for lengthy periods of time assessing how the co-constructed realities develop; (b) using and triangulating multiple data sources (e.g., student, teacher, and design team member interviews, classroom and school observations, achievement test scores, results from authentic assessments); and (c) asking students from the relevant subgroups to read reports and confirm/deny/edit those reports.

Transferability in qualitative research concerns the generalizability of results, but this generalizability is highly constricted: it is from one specific sending context (where the research occurred) to a specific receiving context. In the Sunland County example (see Chapter 6), Stringfield and colleagues (1998) described in detail how one Core Knowledge sequence was adapted to a particular school (Wild Cypress Elementary), which had a certain kind of student body (91 percent Hispanic; 72 percent free and reduced lunch; 33 percent

LEP). The degree of transferability is an empirical matter, dependent on the degree of similarity between sending and receiving contexts. Transferability inferences cannot be made by someone who knows *only* the sending context.

## CONCLUSIONS REGARDING METHODOLOGY

This chapter began with a comment regarding the lack of research literature specifically devoted to the education of linguistically and culturally diverse students. After examining various methodological issues, we can now list the characteristics of a research project that would most adequately address that deficit. To study the reform implementation designed to positively affect the education of students in a multilingual, multiethnic setting properly, the ideal study would do the following:

- Use a mixed-methods design, preferably with experimental/quasi-experimental and case study components.
- Study multiple school contexts and multiple subgroups within those school contexts.
- Gather data on district, state, community, and other systemic linkages that might influence school-level reform efforts.
- Employ strong innovations that are consistently administered across subgroups (to the degree possible).
- Employ multiple outcome measures related to the education of linguistically and racially diverse students.
- Measure the implementation of the innovation in general and separately for relevant subgroups.
- Assess internal and external validity, trustworthiness, and transferability issues.
- Do subgroup analyses throughout.

A research team must be experienced and well funded to complete such studies successfully. Education research has evolved from simple studies of individuals to complex analyses of systems. These studies necessarily involve more time and money.

# 9

# Discussion and Conclusion

Our goal has been to develop a greater knowledge of research on educational reform at the school, district, state, design team, community, and federal levels. Our focus in particular has been on reform in multicultural, multilingual settings, though often research studies did not have this explicit focus and we needed to intuit the implications for these students in particular. Moreover, in reviewing studies, we tend to include only research that addressed reform in more than one of the levels noted. We were interested in examining the linkages between levels, or systemic integration, because a key assumption of current moves toward systemic reform is that such integration would result in school improvement. We attempt to conceptualize the educational system as an interconnected and interdependent policy system.

In this discussion section, we attempt to synthesize what we have learned thus far regarding systemic linkages in school reform and their role in improving the educational experiences of linguistic and racial minority students. We begin with a summary of the factors that appear to be important in any educational reform effort, whether generated at the school, district, community, or federal level. As will be clear, there are implications for actions at multiple levels in most of the factors.

KEY FACTORS IN EDUCATIONAL REFORM IN MULTICULTURAL,
MULTILINGUAL SETTINGS

A review of the studies discussed in this report reveal the following
factors as key in educational reform in multicultural, multilingual
settings. These include:

• **A carefully planned reform initiation process**

No matter where the reform originates, a careful initiation process
is key to establishing the buy-in among those most responsible for
carrying out the plans. The more participatory the reform initiation
process, as far as teachers are concerned, the more likely it is that
there will be support and enthusiasm for implementation. So, too,
a careful process in planning for reform also means that it is more
likely that a reform agenda will be well matched to the needs of the
particular context.

• **Support from leadership at multiple levels**

A successful reform effort requires at least three key levels of strong
leadership – district, principal, and teacher. When there is an absence
of support at one of these levels, or where there is turnover in key positions of leadership, the sustainability of the reform is often compromised as agendas and resources often shift quickly. Leadership also
needs to be distributed among board members, community members, superintendent, teacher leaders, universities, principals, and
students, if possible. Obviously, state-initiated reforms also require
reform from the state level; however, leadership at the other three
levels is critical to make reform happen.

• **High-quality professional development at multiple levels**

The studies reviewed here show that regardless of the systemic
level where reform began, sustained and high-quality professional
development was found to be integral to successful reform. Yet, it
was rare that teachers experienced high-quality training for reform,
regardless of where the reform initiated. In general, reform is likely
to be more successful when professional development efforts are
closely related to the content of classroom practice, are sustained over
time, and involve coaching, mentoring, and modeling. High-quality

professional development for teachers will become even more important with the emphasis on teacher quality in No Child Left Behind.
Professional development efforts most often target teachers, but they
should also engage principals, district office administrators, and
other key leaders.

- **Resources to support reform**

Change in education does not happen without resources. Available
resources may include but are not limited to district and school financial resources allocated to staffing, time, and resources or financial and
material resources within a community, as represented by the availability of jobs, social services, and corporate investment. However,
the resources needed to support reform in schools serving racially
and linguistically diverse students are critically important and often
need to come from governmental agencies, given that resources are
often not located in the communities served by the schools.

The present funding formulas and resource distribution structures
states and districts have established are not adequate for meeting the
requirement of systemic reform to ensure that all students are given a
high-quality education. Another key factor inhibiting improvement
efforts is that most states lack money to provide sufficient resources
for low-performing or needy schools.

- **Political will**

Politics and political struggles are inherent in most educational
reform efforts involving racially and linguistically diverse urban
school systems. Hence, for a reform effort to be successful in such contexts, there needs to be substantial political will among key players
because reform is not easy when it questions existing power arrangements within a school or educational system. Educational leaders
often need to fight battles within their communities for change to
occur.

- **Educational reform plans and policies need to focus specifically,
rather than peripherally, on the needs of culturally and linguistically diverse students**

Schools or systems serving racially and linguistically diverse students
often do not make improving the education of these students a focal
point of reform efforts. As a result, effective educational practices for

these students often are not a feature of reform plans. However, in cases where reforms have built on the assets of these students and focused on their educational needs, they have been more smoothly implemented.

- **Reform efforts need to call on individuals to address their own belief systems about teaching racially and linguistically diverse students**

A common barrier to reforming education for racially and linguistically diverse students is educators' lack of confidence that reforms can actually work. Teachers sometimes believe that these students are incapable of high achievement. When we review the literature, we seldom see instances of people confronting such beliefs when undertaking change efforts. Yet, professional development and opportunities for inquiry can help people change their beliefs. If educators are provided with tools to be able to help students be successful, they are more likely to view students' capabilities differently.

- **Capacity, capacity, capacity**

Capacity is key to educational reform. Capacity should exist across policy levels. Education reformers need capacity to solve problems, lead reform efforts, and strategize about new directions. Organizations engaged in reform, particularly schools, districts, and states, need ample capacity as collectives for reform to be successful. At the same time, reform efforts should focus on building capacity at all levels through professional development, group problem solving, and networking.

## THE SYSTEMIC LINKAGES THAT ARE *MOST* IMPORTANT IN SCHOOL REFORM

In addition to the tenets mentioned, we have also distilled a list of systemic linkages that seem the most important for school reform.

- **Accountability policies and systems are powerful linkages between the federal government, states, districts, and schools**

Federal and state accountability systems are salient linkages between the state as a policy domain and districts and schools. They are also an expression of existing state capacity to develop, interpret, and use data gathered from accountability systems to inform decision making. Accountability systems can both facilitate and interfere with school-improvement efforts. States and districts that have successfully improved classroom teaching and learning as measured on standardized assessments have increased their internal capacity to develop or choose, coordinate, and finance appropriate assessments; to establish content and performance standards; and to create support systems for low-performing schools.

In short, much needs to be learned about developing viable tests used as part of accountability systems, content and performance standards, coordinating these systems, and creating revenue to support these systems. These are areas greatly contested and ripe for future research. Accountability is not questioned, but how to hold adults in the educational system responsible for student learning is something that requires more thought and research.

Overall, the increased use of standardized tests in American education has meant that the federal government, states, districts, and schools are much more tightly linked than ever before, at least with concern for student outcomes. Although this has had its benefits, it has also led to the narrowing of curriculum and a relationship between policy levels that is more often characterized by tension, surveillance, and fear, rather than pressure and support. There are ways in which accountability systems are being used for productive learning purposes, and more research into settings where this has occurred is required.

- **Systems for using data effectively to inform decision making throughout the policy system**

State, district, and school personnel who understand how to read and interpret student performance and other data can more effectively use this information in their improvement efforts, particularly in creating viable feedback loops that lead to continuous improvement. States, districts, and schools can use different kinds of data to plan and implement improvement strategies, including research reports and other publications; information from other states, districts, or schools that have been more successful in their improvement efforts; student achievement results from benchmark and teacher-created assessments; and results from teacher surveys.

When central office staff use data to understand barriers to teaching and learning, to improve instruction, and to target where resources are most needed, their improvement efforts are more successful (Snipes, Doolittle, and Herlihy 2002). So, too, their linkages with schools tend to be more effective.

- **Linking present reform efforts with past reform efforts**

In general, when we look across various levels of the policy system, we do not see many instances of sustained improvement plans or strategies. An important linkage between systemic levels is the connection of present reform efforts with past reform efforts. Elmore and Burney (1998) use the term "continual improvement" in describing reform efforts that have continuity over time of core components, which have internal feedback loops so that reform leaders can make decisions based on the most current information and adapt reform strategies accordingly. To accomplish this kind of stability in reform requires coordination and planning across multiple policy domains and reform stakeholders (Clune 2001; Stone et al. 2001).

Sustainability of state policies is difficult because improvement strategies often change with leadership changes at various levels, thus creating not only turnover in leadership but also turnover in reforms (Cibulka and Derlin 1998), although Cuban (2003) has asserted that there has been quite a bit of consistency in educational policy from the federal level across the Clinton and Bush administrations. In general, states most successful in creating both depth and breadth of reform implementation have built on previous reforms that went back ten to fifteen years. In these instances, there was continuity rather than discontinuity between the earlier reform efforts and the current systemic reform efforts (Clune 1998).

- **Ideological linkages, or shared values, vision, and goals across reform stakeholders**

A school's ability to respond to any form of external performance-based accountability is determined by the degree to which individuals share common values and understandings about such matters as what they expect of students academically, what constitutes good instructional practice, who is responsible for student learning, and how individual students and teachers account for their own work and learning (Elmore and Fuhrman 2001).

The process of developing the vision should involve multiple stakeholders. Creating shared vision can mean that ideological chasms need to be bridged, particularly when working with a broad spectrum of reform stakeholders. When district leaders or state leaders initiate reforms that challenge individuals' existing belief systems, one of the most important linkages that people need to make is ideological. If the ideological chasms cannot be bridged, change is unlikely to occur. Teachers need to understand how district initiatives apply to their daily work (Massell and Goertz 2002). Likewise, district and school personnel need to believe that state mandates requiring all students be taught to higher standards are in fact possible to achieve and relevant to their population of students (Spillane 1999).

• **Relational linkages**

Robust, trusting professional relationships across policy levels, which we term "relational linkages," are essential to reform efforts (Bryk and Schneider 2002; Stein et al. 2002). Teachers are more likely to be receptive to external intervention when they trust and feel respected by the people providing professional development or introducing intervention strategies (Stein et al. 2002). Relational capacity in elementary schools, including high levels of "peer collaboration, teacher-teacher trust, and collective responsibility for student learning" (O'Day in press, p. 27, from Mintrop 2004), can lead to higher degrees of implementation, while schools with low "relational capacity" appear not to benefit from external pressure (Mintrop 2004).

Reform efforts can begin or end over informal conversations, or serendipitous encounters among reform stakeholders (Datnow, Hubbard, and Mehan 2002; Hamann 2002). Relational alliances and allegiances are potent linkages as the people who are brought together often share values, sense of purpose, and common ideas about the direction reforms might take. Bonds of personalism are significant as informal linkages that create unity and a common purpose across different groups (Rich 1996). These can both facilitate and impede improvement efforts (Hamann 2003). An obvious differentiation here concerns whether the effect of the relational linkage is on improvement rather than maintaining the status quo or practices such as nepotism, personalism, or patronage politics (Anyon 1997; Rich 1996; Stone 1998a).

- **Political alliances**

Political alliances are a powerful linkage for coordinating and aligning both human and financial resources across policy domains. Continuity in political will across multiple stakeholders and over time is essential for effective and sustained capacity building to improve teaching and learning. Robust and enduring political alliances create a critical mass necessary for determining the direction policy will take; what kinds of reforms and improvement efforts will be emphasized; how resources will be allocated and to whom they will go; how state accountability systems look, including the assessments that are used, the development of content standards, and the proficiency levels for performance standards; how district superintendents and school boards are chosen; how programs for English language learners are developed; and whether building capacity in low-performing schools is valued or whether sanctions are emphasized.

- **Resource partnerships**

Resource partnerships focus on bringing some form of human or material resources to states, districts, or schools in need of additional resources to support improvement efforts. Improving teaching and learning in schools requires financial resources to hire external partners capable of increasing leadership capacity and teacher content and pedagogical skill and knowledge; technological resources, books, teaching guides, and other material resources are often necessary as well. States, districts, and schools that have been more successful in bringing in outside assistance have relied on realigning funding sources and/or finding new sources of money that supported their improvement efforts. These can be partnerships with external partners, such as design teams, philanthropic organizations, businesses, or other community organizations or universities. Partnerships are particularly important for high-poverty districts or schools in both rural and urban areas to bring resources up to a level closer to what middle-class districts and schools enjoy by virtue of their locale and tax base.

- **Professional development and learning partnerships**

Learning partnerships focus on increasing the knowledge or skills of people in varying levels in the policy system. States and districts that have made the most significant inroads into improving teaching and learning in schools, as measured using results from state or district accountability systems and teacher or principal reports of implementation, have taken seriously their responsibility to learn what needs to be done to achieve improvement goals. In this way, the central office or the state leaders model the risk taking and learning for employees that can facilitate reform. Learning opportunities include both formal and informal educational sessions; visiting other states, districts, or schools that have been more successful in their improvement efforts; hiring outside experts or vendors to provide professional development; or one-shot conferences or sessions where people successful in a specific domain or skill share their knowledge or expertise with less-skilled others. The most promising professional development models are those that have highly qualified mentors providing the service; are site based, integrated into teachers' working days, while also offering more intensive summer institutes; meet teachers' developmental needs; and relate directly to how teachers can better meet the objectives set by state standards while also increasing subject area knowledge and improving teaching technique (Cohen and Hill 2002; Elmore and Burney 1997; Finnigan, O'Day, and Wakelyn 2003; Supovitz and Turner 2000).

- **Problem-solving partnerships**

Problem-solving partnerships focus on developing problem-solving and planning capacity in agencies and organizations. People working in state and district organizations responsible for designing, coordinating, and overseeing the improvement requirements of systemic reform are often faced with having to create infrastructures, funding formulas, and systems they have never before created. States, districts, and schools that have been more effective in developing sustainable improvement efforts have developed partnerships with outside experts to help them envision, plan, and implement improved learning and teaching in classrooms. Inherent in what these more successful states and districts have done is creating a habit of mind or orientation toward learning.

One particularly effective strategy is to structure alliances and establish forums across school sites and districts for discussion among principals and among teacher leaders. This allows them to share concerns related to reform and then move on to developing problem-solving strategies. Having a skilled facilitator present is also important to set conversation norms and rules, provide direction, keep people on task, and provide the knowledge so the process of shared problem solving no longer requires outside guidance or support.

- **District as mediator of federal and state policy directed at schools**

Districts can be key mediators of federal and state policies, as well as key initiators of reform policies themselves. When district leaders have a strong and articulated theory of change or clear and articulated directions for change, they can help buffer schools from fast-changing or inconsistent policies, while also coordinating the demands from multiple and possibly inconsistent accountability systems.

Districts that have begun to improve classroom teaching and student learning had several elements in place, in particular (a) stable leadership across the school board, district office, and school focused on one primary purpose – improving student opportunities for learning; (b) skillful and coordinated resource distribution; school leadership was networked with more expert others; (c) systemwide capacity was developed, including content and process knowledge, along with problem-solving and planning abilities; (d) material and human resources were provided; (e) crisis situations were minimal; a history of trust and cooperation existed; (f) school-level autonomy and/or authority was present, as was union support; (g) data use skills were developed and multiple sources of data were used to inform planning and decision making.

Aligning district standards, curriculum, and accountability systems internally and with state standards and accountability systems is a key linkage necessary to increasing collective district capacity because it helps to focus reform activities (Regional Educational Laboratory Network 2000). Some districts have developed standards and accountability systems that go beyond state systems (Hightower 2002a, 2002b). Doing this creates a buffer between schools and the political changes at the state level, while also focusing goals. These districts have specific, measurable long-term goals associated with deadlines and specific intermediate goals for each year of reform (Snipes, Doolittle, and Herlihy 2002, p. 44).

- **Link educational reform to social reconstruction of urban and rural communities**

In communities that have experienced a long history of economic divestment and white flight, urban renewal can be a necessary component to building the local tax base to provide more funding to schools, creating safe neighborhoods. Schools play an important role in urban economies, particularly those that have experienced enduring corporate divestment or sudden economic shifts. For example, in Detroit and Baltimore, the emergence of school systems as major employers was tied to the decline of manufacturing and heavy industry (Henig et al. 1999; Rich 1996; Stone 1998b; Stone et al. 2001).

Along with being a service that students receive, education and education systems create jobs, contracts, and career tracks – all things that represent financial security for people working in the educational system. The protection of jobs and career ladders is often at the heart of how education politics is organized (Stone 1998b). School districts generate millions of dollars for their local economies (Rich 1996). They serve a core function in the local political economy, as sources of city-wide economic development, community development or stability, and upward mobility for many people.

Each linkage identified as a positive, or effective, linkage can be used to maintain status quo practices or to usurp reform implementation. The human factor is the primary unpredictable element in each policy domain and in how linkages are or are not used. Nepotism is one example of "relational linkages" and "shared values" run amok. Similarly, in the United States, a weak district Title I director can focus on the least-likely-to-be-productive aspects of the No Child Left Behind Act and impede improved instruction in schools. Recent reform mandates necessitate building support for a new set of political arrangements that support excellence and equity in schools (Stone 1998). Transforming long-standing personal, social, and political arrangements in the education system is no small task and is likely to be a core factor in why reforms based on equity and excellence are difficult to implement.

## WHAT SYSTEMIC LINKAGES SEEM TO BE LEAST EFFECTIVE IN PRODUCING SUSTAINABLE SCHOOL REFORM?

When analyzing linkages that are not particularly effective, we need be clear that the presence of a linkage does not assure that resources or communication across policy domains are coordinated, high quality, or generally conducive to facilitating improved teaching and learning. Each of the linkages we identified in the previous section becomes an ineffective or counterproductive linkage when the resources that flow across it are low quality, inappropriate for the context in which they will be used, distributed without coordination, or are used toward goals negatively aligned with the stated purpose of the system. Likewise, if a linkage exists but is not used, it also becomes ineffective. For instance, learning partnerships are not effective when they are short term, lack mutual respect, or use inappropriate materials. Similarly, funding linkages that do not provide adequate operating expenses for high-quality education, and that do not allocate sufficient funds for personnel and other supporting resources are ultimately ineffective in bringing about improved teaching or learning. For example, grants may be available to schools to facilitate their improvement efforts, but if school or district personnel do not know about the grant sources, it becomes an ineffectual linkage for school reform. Similarly, if a start-up grant is of insufficient duration to lead to institutionalization of a change, the long-term effect is likely to be counterproductive.

- **Linkages between state-federal levels and local levels that are simply funding streams and no more**

Simply providing money can but does not necessarily improve capacity for improved teaching and learning. Low-capacity states, districts, and schools need outside expertise and other kinds of assistance to develop the skills necessary for supporting school improvement efforts (Hatch 2000). The key here is helping these organizations develop basic organizational and leadership capabilities, reduce nonproductive teacher turnover, create an orderly school climate, develop teacher pedagogic and content knowledge, and develop self-monitoring and continual learning capabilities. In some instances, improvement efforts also need to include repairing the actual physical

plant, or building safe, new schools with enough basic equipment for
students to learn and teachers to teach (Snipes, Doolittle, and Herlihy
2002; Cotton 1995; Taylor 1990; Reynolds and Teddlie 2000; Reynolds
et al. 2002). In short, capacity is built most naturally atop existing
capacity (Hatch 2000).

Private and government school reform seed money is often insufficient to sustain reform efforts in cities that lack a strong tax base and
vibrant local economies (Rich 1996). Schools and districts in areas that
generate low amounts of property tax are at a disadvantage compared
with their counterparts in more wealthy communities. These schools
often ask for grant money as a way to supplement an inadequate
budget, but once the grant money is gone, they are still left in conditions of poverty. In schools located in high-poverty areas, funding
formulas based on adequacy rather than equity seem promising as a
way to provide extra financial resources just to get schools and districts up to the per student spending amounts closer to those their
counterparts in more wealthy communities enjoy just by virtue of
their locale (Odden 1999; Odden and Clune 1998; Ladd and Hansen
1999).

- **Federal, state, and district rewards and sanctions that are not
  accompanied by capacity-building efforts**

Rewards and sanctions alone do not build organizational capacity
to support improved teaching and learning. They can be effective
as warnings to low-performing schools and function as a way to
alert them that changes need to be made in the school or district.
They can also warn schools and districts that adequately educate a
majority population that a specific minority group is not being adequately served. They are occasionally viewed as effective incentives
for successful teachers, schools, or districts, but research demonstrating long-term effects of such rewards are lacking. Of equal concern,
Clune (1998) and Finnigan, O'Day, and Wakelyn (2003) found that to
improve organizational capacity for teaching and learning, opportunities for professional development and learning that go both broad
and deep are necessary.

In instances where the risk of sanctions is high, teaching and learning are frequently compromised for several reasons. This includes
narrowing the curriculum; replacing the regular curriculum with

test prep material; losing teaching time to test preparation; or encouraging low-achieving students to drop out of school (Amrein and Berliner 2002; Hannaway 2003; Livingston and Livingston 2002; McNeil 2000; McNeil and Valenzuela 2001).

Results of state takeovers and reconstitution efforts for schools that have been sanctioned are mixed. On the positive side, they can help to eliminate nepotism within a school district's decision-making processes; improve a school district's administrative and financial management practices; or upgrade the condition of rundown school buildings (Rudo 2001). There is virtually no evidence, though, that state takeovers or reconstitutions actually improve teaching and learning in schools (Desimone et al. 2002; Rudo 2001).

Overall, educational reform in multicultural, multilingual settings is a complex enterprise that ideally involves a coordinated effort among stakeholders across levels of the system. However, the evidence reviewed here suggests it is well worth the effort, given the possible improvements in academic achievement that can result. At the same time, we still need to know much more about exactly which strategies at each level, particularly levels beyond the school where the research base is least strong, are most promising. Well-designed, systematic research studies are much needed to examine reform efforts at district, state, and federal levels.

# Bibliography

Acker-Hocever, M., and Touchton, D. (2001, April). *Principals' struggle to level the accountability playing field of Florida graded "D" and "F" schools in high poverty and minority communities*. Paper presented at the annual meeting of the American Educational Research Association, Seattle, WA.

Airasian, P. W. (1994). *Classroom assessment* (2nd ed.). New York: McGraw-Hill.

Amrein, A., and Berliner, D. (2002). High-stakes testing, uncertainty, and student learning. *Education Policy Analysis Archives, 10*(18). Retrieved February 23, 2004, from http://epaa.asu.edu/epaa/v10n18/.

Anderson, L. W. (1983). Policy implications of research on school time. *School Administrator, 40,* 25–28.

Anderson, S. (2003). The school district role in educational change: A review of the literature. Unpublished manuscript.

Anyon, J. (1997). *Ghetto schooling: A political economy of urban educational reform.* New York: Teachers College Press.

Armor, D., Conry-Oseguera, P., Cox, M., King, N., McDonnell, L., Pascal, A., Pauly, E., and Zellman, G. (1976). *Analysis of the school preferred reading program in selected Los Angeles minority schools.* Santa Monica, CA: RAND.

Ascher, C. (1985). *Raising Hispanic achievement* (ERIC/CUE Digest 26). New York: ERIC Clearinghouse on Urban Education (ED 256 842).

August, D., and Hakuta, K. (1998). *Educating language-minority children.* Washington, DC: National Academy Press.

Austin, G., and Holowenzak, S. P. (1985). An examination of 10 years of research on exemplary schools. In G. Austin and H. Garber (Eds.), *Research on Exemplary Schools*. Orlando, FL: Academic Press.

Bahktin, M. M. (1981). *The dialogical imagination: Four essays.* (C. Emerson & M. Holquist, Trans.), Austin, TX: University of Texas Press.

Baker, E. L. (1992). *Issues in policy, assessment, and equity.* Los Angeles: Center for Research on Evaluation, Standards, and Student Testing, University of

California at Los Angeles. (ERIC Document Reproduction Service ED 349 823).

Bamburg, J. D. (1994). *Raising expectations to improve student learning.* Oak Brook, IL: North Central Regional Educational Laboratory.

Bangert-Downs, R. L., Kulik, C. C., Kulik, J. A., and Morgan, M. (1991). The instructional effects of feedback in test-like events. *Review of Educational Research, 61,* 213–238.

Bascia, N. (1996). Caught in the crossfire: Restructuring, collaboration and the "problem" school. *Urban Education, 31*(2), 177–198.

Beck, S., and Allexsaht-Snider, M. (2001). Recent language minority education policy in Georgia: Appropriation, assimilation, and Americanization. In S. Wortham, E. Murillo, Jr., and T. Hamann (Eds.), *Education, Policy, and the Politics of Identity in the New Latino Diaspora.* Westport, CT: Ablex.

Benard, B. (1993). Fostering resiliency in kids: Protective factors in the family, school, and community. *Educational Leadership, 51*(3), 44–48.

Berends, M. (2000). Teacher-reported effects of New American Schools' designs: Exploring relationships to teacher background and school context. *Educational Evaluation and Policy Analysis, 22,* 65–82.

Berends, M., Bodilly, S., and Kirby, S. (2003). District and school leadership for whole school reform: The experience of New American Schools. In J. Murphy and A. Datnow (Eds.), *Leadership for school reform: Lessons from comprehensive school reform designs* (pp. 109–131). Thousand Oaks, CA: Corwin.

Berends, M., Chun, J., Schuyler, G., Stockly, S., and Briggs, R. (2001). *Challenges of conflicting school reforms: Effects of New American Schools in a high-poverty district* (MR-1483-EDU). Santa Monica, CA: RAND.

Bernie, R., and Stiefel, L. (1999). Concepts of school finance. In H. Ladd, R. Chalk, and J. Hansen (Eds.), *Equity and adequacy in education finance: Issues and perspectives* (pp. 7–34). Washington, DC: National Academy Press.

Bickel, W. E. (1998). The implications of the effective schools literature for school restructuring. In C. R. Reynolds and T. B. Gutkin (Eds.), *The handbook of school psychology* (3rd ed.) (pp. 959–983). New York: Wiley.

Billig, S., Perry, S., and Pokorny, N. (1999). School support teams: Building state capacity for improving schools. *Journal of Education for Students Placed At Risk, 4,* 231–240.

Blum, R., and Butler, J. (1987). *Onward to excellence: Teaching schools to use effective schooling and implementation research to improve student performance.* Portland, OR: Northwest Regional Educational Laboratory.

Bodilly, S. (1998). *Lessons from New American Schools' Scale-Up Phase: Prospects for bringing designs to multiple schools* (RAND research report). Retrieved February 23, 2004, from http://www.rand.org/publications/ MR/MR942/.

Bodilly, S. (2001). *New American Schools' concept of break-the-mold designs: How designs evolved over time and why* (RAND research report).

Retrieved February 23, 2004, from http://www.rand.org/publications/ MR/MR1288/.

Bodilly, S. J., and Berends, M. (1999). Necessary district support for comprehensive school reform. In G. Orfield and E. H. DeBray (Eds.), *Hard work for good schools: Facts not fads in Title I reform* (pp. 111–119). Boston: Civil Rights Project, Harvard University.

Borman, G., Hewes, G., Overman, L., and Brown, S. (2002). *Comprehensive School Reform and student achievement: A meta-analysis.* Baltimore: Center for Research on the Education of Students Placed At Risk, Johns Hopkins University.

Borman, G., Wong, K., Hedges, L. V., and D'Agostino, J. K. (1998). The longitudinal achievement of Chapter 1 students: Preliminary evidence from the Prospects study. *Journal of Education for Students Placed At Risk, 3,* 363–399.

Borman, K. M., Kromrey, J., Katzenmeyer, W., and Della Piana, G. (2000, April). *How do standards matter? Linking policy to practice in four cities implementing systemic reform.* Paper presented at the annual meeting of the American Educational Research Association, New Orleans, LA.

Bourdieu, P. (1986). The forms of capital. In J. Richardson (Ed.), *Handbook of theory and research for the sociology of education* (pp. 241–258). Westport, CT: Greenwood.

Brewer, J., and Hunter, A. (1989). *Multimethod research: A synthesis of styles.* Newbury Park, CA: Sage.

Brookover, W. B. (1985). *Can we make schools effective for minority students? Journal of Negro Education, 54,* 257–268.

Brookover, W. B., Beady, C., Flood, P., Schweitzer, J., and Wisenbaker, J. (1979). *Schools, social systems and student achievement: Schools can make a difference.* New York: Praeger.

Brookover, W. B., and Lezotte, L. W. (1979). *Changes in school characteristics coincident with changes in student achievement.* East Lansing: Institute for Research on Teaching College of Education, Michigan State University.

Brophy, J. E. (1982). Successful teaching strategies for the inner-city child. *Phi Delta Kappan, 63,* 527–530.

Brophy, J. E. (1986). Teacher influences on student achievement. *American Psychologist, 4,* 1069–1077.

Brophy, J. E. (1988). Educating teachers about managing classrooms and students. *Teaching and Teacher Education, 4,* 1–18.

Brophy, J. E. (1996). *Teaching problem students.* New York: Guilford.

Brophy, J. E., and Good, T. L. (1986). Teacher behavior and student achievement. In M. Wittrock (Ed.), *Third Handbook of Research on Teaching* (pp. 328–375). New York: Macmillan.

Brown, B. W., and Saks, D. H. (1986). Measuring the effects of instructional time on student learning: Evidence from the Beginning Teacher Evaluation Study. *American Journal of Education, 94,* 480–500.

Bryk, A., and Schneider, B. (2002). *Trust in schools: A core resource for improvement.* New York: Russell Sage Foundation.

Bryk, A., Sebring, P., Kerbow, D., Rollow, S., and Easton, J. (1998). *Charting Chicago school reform democratic localism as a lever for change*. Boulder, CO: Westview.

Byrnes, D., and Kiger, G. (1987). Structural correlates of school children's religious intolerance. *Educational Research Quarterly, 11*(3), 18–25.

Byrnes, D. A. (1988). Children and prejudice. *Social Education, 52*, 267–271.

Campbell, D. T., and Stanley, J. (1966). *Experimental and quasi-experimental design for research*. Chicago: Rand McNally.

Campbell, R. L., and Farrell, R. V. (1985). The identification of competencies for multi-cultural teacher education. *Negro Educational Review, 36*, 137–144.

Carnegie Forum on Education and the Economy. (1986). *A nation prepared: Teachers for the 21st century*. Washington, DC: Author.

Carnoy, M., Loeb, S., and Smith, T. L. (2000, April). *Do higher state scores in Texas make for better high school outcomes?* Paper presented at the annual meeting of the American Educational Research Association, New Orleans.

Cawelti, G. (2003). Lessons from research that changed education. *Educational Leadership, 60*(3), 18–21.

Center for Research on Education, Diversity, and Excellence. (2002). *The five standards for effective pedagogy*. Retrieved April 28, 2005, http:www.crede.ucsc.edu/standards/standards.html.

Chrispeels, J. H. (1992). *Purposeful restructuring: Creating a culture for learning and achievement in elementary schools*. London: Falmer.

Chrispeels, J. H. (2002a). The California Center for Effective Schools: The Oxnard school district partnership. *Phi Delta Kappan, 83*, 382–387.

Chrispeels, J. H. (2002b). An emerging conceptual and practical framework for implementing district-wide effective schools reform. *Journal for Effective Schools, 1*, 17–30.

Chrispeels, J. H., Castillo, S., and Brown, J. H. (2000). School leadership teams: A Process model. *School Effectiveness and Improvement, 11*, 20–56.

Chrispeels, J. H., and Martin, K. J. (2002). Four leadership teams define their roles within organizational and political structures to improve student learning. *School Effectiveness and Improvement, 13*, 327–365.

Christman, J. (2001). *Powerful ideas, modest gains: Five years of systemic reform in Philadelphia middle schools*. Philadelphia, PA: Consortium for Policy Research in Education, University of Pennsylvania, Graduate School of Education. Retrieved February 23, 2004, from http://www.cpre.org/Publications/children05.pdf.

Christman, J. R., and Rhodes, A. (2002). *Civic engagement and urban school improvement: Hard to learn lessons from Philadelphia*. Philadelphia, PA: Consortium for Policy Research in Education, University of Pennsylvania, Graduate School of Education. Retrieved February 23, 2004, from http://www.cpre.org/Publications/children07.pdf.

Chun, T., and Goertz, M. (1999). Title I and state educational policy: High standards for all students? In G. Orfield and E. DeBray (Eds.) *Hard work for good schools: Facts not fads in Title I reforms*. Cambridge, MA: Civil Rights Project, Harvard University.

Cibulka, J. G., and Derlin, R. L. (1998). Accountability policy adoption to policy sustainability: Reforms and systemic initiatives in Colorado and Maryland. *Education and Urban Society, 30*, 502–513.

Clune, W. (1998). *Toward a theory of systemic reform: The case of nine NSF statewide systemic initiatives* (Research monograph No. 16). Madison, WI: National Institute for Science Education.

Clune, W. (2001). Toward a theory of standards-based reform: The case of nine NSF statewide systemic initiatives. In S. Fuhrman (Ed.), *From the capital to the classroom: Standards-based reform in the United States* (pp. 13–39). Chicago: University of Chicago Press.

Coalition for Evidence-Based Policy. (2002). *Bringing evidence-driven progress to education: A recommended strategy for the U.S. Department of Education*. Washington, DC: Author.

Cohen, D., and Ball, D. (2001). Making change: Instruction and its improvement. *Phi Delta Kappan, 83*, 73–77.

Cohen, D., and Hill, H. (2001). *Learning policy: When state education reform works*. New Haven, CT: Yale University Press.

Coleman, J. S. (1988). Social capital in the creation of human capital. *American Journal of Sociology, 94*, S95–S120.

Collier, V. P. (1992). A synthesis of studies examining long-term language minority student data on academic achievement. *Bilingual Research Journal, 16*, 187–212.

Comer, J. P., Haynes, N. M., Joyner, E. T., and BenAvie, M. (1996). *Rallying the whole village: The Comer process for reforming education*. New York: Teachers College Press.

Consortium for Policy Research in Education. (1998). *States and districts and Comprehensive School Reform* (CPRE Policy Brief). Philadelphia, PA: Consortium for Policy Research in Education, University of Pennsylvania, Graduate School of Education. Retrieved February 23, 2004, from http://www.cpre.org/Publications/rb24.pdf.

Cook, T. D., and Campbell, D. T. (1979). *Quasi-experimentation: Design and analysis issues for field settings*. Boston: Houghton Mifflin.

Core Knowledge Foundation. (1998). *Core Knowledge Sequence: Content guidelines for grades K–8*. Charlottesville, VA: Core Knowledge Foundation.

Cotton, K. (1995). *Effective schooling practices: A research synthesis – 1995 update*. Portland, OR: Northwest Regional Educational Laboratory. Retrieved June 5, 2003, from http://www.nwrel.org/scpd/esp/esp95toc.html.

Creemers, B. P. M. (1994). *The effective classroom*. London: Cassell.

Creemers, B. P. M., and Reezigt, G. J. (1996). School level conditions affecting the effectiveness of instruction. *School Effectiveness and School Improvement, 7*, 197–228.

Creemers, B. P. M., and Scheerens, J. (1994). Developments in the educational effectiveness research programme. In R. J. Bosker, B. P. M. Creemers, and J. Scheerens (Eds.), *Conceptual and methodological advances in educational effectiveness research*. Special issue of *International Journal of Educational Research, 21*, 125–140.

Cronbach, L. J. (1982). *Designing evaluations of educational and social programs*. San Francisco: Jossey-Bass.

Crone, J., Lang, M., Franklin, B., and Halbrook, A. (1994). Composite versus component scores: Consistency of school effectiveness classification. *Applied Measurement in Education, 7*, 303–321.

Crone, L., and Teddlie, C. (1995). Further examination of teacher behavior in differentially effective schools: Selection and socialization processes. *Journal of Classroom Interaction, 30*, 1–9.

Crone, L. J., Lang, M. H., Teddlie, C., and Franklin, B. (1995). Achievement measures of school effectiveness: Comparison of model stability across years. *Journal of Applied Measurement, 8*, 365–377.

Cross, C. (2004). *Political education: National policy comes of age*. New York: Teachers College.

Cuban, L. (1989). At-risk students: What teachers and principals can do. *Educational Leadership, 46*(5), 29–32.

Cuban, L. (1993). Preface. In C. Teddlie and S. Stringfield (Eds.), *Schools make a difference: Lessons learned from a 10-year study of school effects* (pp. ix–xi). New York: Teachers College Press.

Cuban, L. (2003). *Why is it so hard to get good schools?* New York: Teachers College Press.

Cummins, J. (1986). Empowering minority students: A framework for intervention. *Harvard Educational Review, 56*, 18–36.

Dalton, S. (1998). *Pedagogy matters: Standards for effective teaching practice (Research Report No. 4)*. Washington, DC, and Santa Cruz, CA: Center for Research on Education, Diversity and Excellence.

D'Amico, L., Harwell, M., Stein, M., and den Heuvel, J. (2001, April). *Examining the implementation and effectiveness of a district-wide instructional improvement effort*. Paper presented at the annual meeting of the American Educational Research Association, Seattle, WA.

Darder, A., and Upshur, C. (1992). *What do Latino children need to succeed in school? A study of four Boston public schools* (Document No. 92-02). Boston: Boston Public Schools (ERIC Document Reproduction Service ED 344 951).

Darling-Hammond, L., and Ball, D. (1998). *Teaching for high standards: What policymakers need to know and be able to do*. Consortium for Policy Research in Education Joint Report Series. University of Pennsylvania, Graduate School of Education: CPRE Publications.

Darling-Hammond, L., Hightower, A., Husbands, J., LaFors, J., and Young, V. (2002, April). *Building instructional quality: Inside-out, bottom-up, and top-down: Perspectives on San Diego's school reform*. Paper presented at the annual meeting of the American Educational Research Association, New Orleans, LA.

Darling-Hammond, L., Hightower, A. M., Husbands, J. L., LaFors, J. R., Young, V. M., and Christopher, C. (2003, September). *Building instructional quality: "Inside-out" and "outside-in" perspectives on San*

*Diego's school reform.* Seattle, WA: Center for the Study of Teaching and Policy, University of Washington. Retrieved February 24, 2004, from http://depts.washington.edu/ctpmail/PDFs/InstructionalQual-09-2003.pdf.

Datnow, A. (2000). Power and politics in the adoption of school reform models. *Educational Evaluation and Policy Analysis, 22*(4), 357–374.

Datnow, A. (2005). The sustainability of comprehensive school reform in changing district and state contexts. *Educational Administration Quarterly, 41*, 121–153.

Datnow, A., Borman, G., and Stringfield, S. (2000). School reform through a highly specified curriculum: A study of the implementation and effects of the Core Knowledge Sequence. *Elementary School Journal, 101*, 167–191.

Datnow, A., Borman, G., Stringfield, S., Overman, L., and Castellano, M. (2003). Comprehensive school reform in culturally and linguistically diverse contexts: Implementation and outcomes from a four-year study. *Educational Evaluation and Policy Analysis, 25*, 143–171.

Datnow, A., and Castellano, M. (2001). Managing and guiding school reform: Leadership in Success for All schools. *Educational Administration Quarterly, 37*, 219–249.

Datnow, A., Hubbard, L., and Mehan, H. (2002). *Extending educational reform: From one school to many.* London: RoutledgeFalmer.

Datnow, A., and Kemper, E. (2002, March). *From statehouse to schoolhouse: The implementation of Comprehensive School Reform in the era of CSRD* (Report prepared as a deliverable to OERI, U.S. Department of Education for CRESPAR Project 4.2.). Baltimore: Center for Research on the Education of Students Placed At Risk, Johns Hopkins University.

Datnow, A., and Kemper, E. (2003). *Connections between federal, state, and local levels in the implementation of Comprehensive School Reform.* Unpublished manuscript.

Datnow, A., and Stringfield, S. (2000). Working together for reliable school reform. *Journal of Education for Students Placed At Risk, 5*, 183–204.

Davis, B. R. (1985). Effects of cooperative learning on race/human relations: Study of a district program. *Spectrum, 3*, 37–43.

Deal, T. E., and Peterson, K. D. (1990). *The principal's role in shaping school cultures.* Washington, DC: U.S. Department of Education.

Desimone, L. (2000). *Making Comprehensive School Reform work.* New York: ERIC Clearinghouse on Urban Education.

Desimone, L., Porter, A., Garet, M., Suk Yoon, K., and Birman, B. (2002). Effects of professional development on teachers' instruction: Results from a three-year long study. *Educational Evaluation and Policy Analysis, 24*, 81–113.

DeVries, D. L., Edwards, K. J., and Slavin, R. E. (1978). Biracial learning teams and race relations in the classroom: Four field experiments using Teams-Games-Tournament. *Journal of Educational Psychology, 70*, 356–362.

Diamond, J. (1997). *Guns, germs, and steel.* New York: Norton.

Dreeben, R. (1987). Closing the divide: What teachers and administrators can do to help black students reach their reading potential. *American Educator, 11*(4), 28–35.

Druian, G., and Butler, J. A. (1987). *Effective schooling practices and at-risk youth: What the research shows* (Topical Synthesis No. 1). Portland, OR: Northwest Regional Educational Laboratory (ERIC Document Reproduction Service ED 291 146).

Duncombe, W., and Yinger, J. (1999). Performance standards and educational cost indexes: You can't have one without the other. In H. Ladd, R. Chalk, and J. Hansen (Eds.), *Equity and adequacy in education finance: Issues and perspectives*, pp. 260–298. Washington, DC: National Academy Press.

Dyer, H. S., Linn, R. L., and Patton, M. J. (1969). A comparison of four methods of obtaining discrepancy measures based on observed and predicted school system means on achievement tests. *American Educational Research Journal, 6*, 591–605.

Edmonds, R. R. (1979). Effective schools for the urban poor. *Educational Leadership, 37*(10), 15–24.

Edmonds, R. R. (1981). Making public schools effective. *Social Policy, 12*, 56–60.

Education Commission of the States. (1999). *Comprehensive School Reform: Five lessons from the field*. Denver, CO: Author.

Elmore, R. (1993). The role of local districts in instructional improvement. In S. Fuhrman (Ed.), *Designing coherent education policy improving the system* (pp. 96–125). San Francisco: Jossey-Bass.

Elmore, R. (2002, April). *Stakes for whom?* Paper presented at the annual meeting of the American Educational Research Association, New Orleans, LA.

Elmore, R. F., and Burney, D. (1997). *School variation and systemic instructional improvement in Community School District #2, New York City*. Unpublished manuscript.

Elmore, R. F., and Burney, D. (1998). *Continuous improvement in Community District #2, New York City*. Unpublished manuscript.

Elmore, R., and Fuhrman, S. (2001). Holding schools accountable: Is it working. *Phi Delta Kappan, 83*, 67–72.

Epstein, J. L. (1997). *School, family, and community partnerships*. Thousand Oaks, CA: Corwin Press.

Erickson, F., and Shultz, J. (1982). *The counselor as gatekeeper*. New York: Academic Press.

Erlichson, B., and Goertz, M. (2001). *Implementing whole school reform in New Jersey: Year Two*. New Brunswick, NJ: Department of Public Policy and Center for Government Services, Rutgers, University of New Jersey.

Evans, L., and Teddlie, C. (1995). Facilitating change in schools: Is there one best style? *School Effectiveness and School Improvement, 6*, 1–22.

Fairman, J., and Firestone, W. (2001). The district role in state assessment policy: An exploratory study. In S. Fuhrman (Ed.), *From the capital to the classroom: Standards-based reform in the States* (pp. 124–147). Chicago: University of Chicago Press.

Fiedler, F. (1967). *A theory of leadership effectiveness*. New York: McGraw-Hill.

Fiedler, F. (1973). The contingency model and the dynamics of the leadership process. *Advances in Experimental Social Psychology, 11*, 60–112.

Fillmore, L. W., and Valadez, C. (1986). Teaching bilingual learners. In M. C. Wittrock (Ed.), *Handbook of research on teaching, third edition* (pp. 648–685). New York: Macmillan.

Finnigan, K., O'Day, J., and Wakelyn, D. (2003). *External support to schools on probation: Getting a leg up?* Philadelphia, PA: Consortium for Policy Research in Education, University of Pennsylvania, Graduate School of Education. Retrieved February 24, 2004, from http://www.cpre.org/Publications/Chicago.pdf.

Fitz-Gibbon, C. T. (1996). *Monitoring education: Indicators, quality and effectiveness*. New York: Cassell.

Flanagan, A., and Grissmer, D. (2001, February). *The role of federal resources in closing the achievement gaps of minority and disadvantaged students*. Brookings conference on the Black-White Test Score Gap, Washington, DC.

Foley, E. (1998). *Restructuring student support services: Redefining the role of the school district*. Philadelphia: Consortium for Policy Research in Education, University of Pennsylvania, Graduate School of Education. Retrieved February 23, 2004, from http://www.cpre.org/Publications/careport01.pdf.

Foley, E. (2001). *Contradictions and control in systemic reform: The ascendancy of the central office in Philadelphia schools*. Philadelphia: Consortium for Policy Research in Education, University of Pennsylvania, Graduate School of Education. Retrieved February 23, 2004, from http://www.cpre.org/Publications/childreno3.pdf.

Fuhrman, S., Goertz, M., and Duffy, M. (2002, April). *"Slow down, you move too fast": The politics of making changes in high-stakes accountability policies for students*. Paper presented at the annual meeting of the American Educational Research Association, New Orleans, LA.

Fullan, M. (1999). *Change forces: The sequel*. London: Falmer.

Fuller, J., and Johnson, E. (2001). Can state accountability systems drive improvements in school improvement for children of color and children from low-income homes. *Education and Urban Society, 33*, 261–263.

Gabelko, N. H. (1988). Prejudice reduction in secondary schools. *Social Education, 52*, 276–279.

Gage, N. (1989). The paradigm wars and their aftermath: A "historical" sketch of research and teaching since 1989. *Educational Researcher, 18*, 4–10.

Gallo, D. (1989). Educating for empathy, reason and imagination. *Journal of Creative Behavior, 23*, 98–115.

Garcia, E. E. (1988). Attributes of effective schools for language minority students. *Education and Urban Society, 2*, 387–398.

Garcia, E. E., and Gonzalez, R. (1995). Issues in systemic reform for culturally and linguistically diverse students. *Teachers College Record, 96*, 418–431.

Garfinkel, H. (1967). *Studies in ethnomethodology*. Englewood Cliffs, NJ: Prentice Hall.

Gettinger, M. (1984). Achievement as a function of time spent in learning and time needed for learning. *American Educational Research Journal, 21*, 617–628.

Gettinger, M. (1989). Effects of maximizing time spent and minimizing time needed for learning on pupil achievement. *American Educational Research Journal, 26*, 73–91.

Gewertz, C. (2002, August 7). Philadelphia lines up outside groups to run schools. *Education Week 21*(43), 1, 18, 19.

Gimmestad, B. J., and De Chiara, E. (1982). Dramatic plays: A vehicle for prejudice reduction in the elementary school. *Journal of Educational Research, 76*, 45–49.

Glaser, M. (1992). After the alternative elementary program: A promise of continued student success? *Urban Review, 24*, 55–71.

Goertz, M., Duffy, M., and Le Floch, K. C. (2001). Assessment and accountability systems in the 50 states: 1999–2000 (CPRE Research Report Series RR-046). Philadelphia, PA: Consortium for Policy Research in Education, University of Pennsylvania, Graduate School of Education. Retrieved February 23, 2004, from http://www.cpre.org/Publications/rr46.pdf.

Goldenberg, C. (1996). *Effective schooling for LEP students: The school domain*. Paper prepared for the Committee on Developing a Research Agenda on the Education of Limited English Proficient and Bilingual Students. Washington, DC: National Research Council.

Good, T. L. (1987). Two decades of research on teacher expectations: Findings and future directions. *Journal of Teacher Education, 38*(4), 32–47.

Good, T. L., and Brophy, J. E. (1986). School effects. In M. Wittrock (Ed.), *Third handbook of research on teaching* (pp. 570–602). New York: Macmillan.

Goodson, I. (2000). Social histories of educational change theory. *Journal of Educational Change, 2*, 45–63.

Grant, C. A., Sleeter, C. E., and Anderson, J. E. (1986). The literature on multicultural education: Review and analysis. *Educational Studies, 12*, 47–71.

Greene, J. C., Caracelli, V. J., and Graham, W. F. (1989). Toward a conceptual framework for mixed-method evaluation designs. *Educational Evaluation and Policy Analysis, 11*, 255–274.

Grissmer, D., and Flanagan, A. (1998). *Exploring rapid achievement gains in North Carolina and Texas*. Washington, DC: National Educational Goals Panel.

Grissmer, D., Flanagan, A., Kawata, J., and Williamson, S. (2000). *Improving student achievement: What state and NAEP test scores tell us*. Santa Monica, CA: RAND, MR-924-EDU.

Griswold, P. A., Cotton, K. J., and Hansen, J. B. (1986). *Effective compensatory education sourcebook, Volume I: A review of effective educational practices*. Washington, DC: U.S. Department of Education (ERIC Document Reproduction Service ED 276 787).

Grossman, F. K., Beinashowitz, J., Anderson, L., Sakurai, M., Finnin, L., and Flaherty, M. (1992). Risk and resilience in young adolescents. *Journal of Youth and Adolescence, 21,* 529–550.

Guba, E. G., and Lincoln, Y. S. (1994). Competing paradigms in qualitative research. In N. K. Denzin and Y. S. Lincoln (Eds.), *Handbook of qualitative research* (pp. 105–117). Thousand Oaks, CA: Sage.

Guthrie, J., and Rothstein, R. (1999). Enabling "adequacy" to achieve reality: Translating adequacy into state school finance distribution. In H. Ladd, R. Chalk, and J. Hansen (Eds.), *Equity and adequacy in education finance: Issues and perspectives* (pp. 209–260). Washington, DC: National Academy Press.

Hall, G. E., Rutherford, W. L., Hord, S. M., and Huling, L. L. (1984). Effects of three principalship styles on school improvement. *Educational Leadership, 41,* 22–29.

Hall, P. M., and McGinty, P. J. W. (1997). Policy as the transformation of intentions: Producing program from statutes. *Sociological Quarterly, 38,* 439–467.

Hallinger, P., and Murphy, J. (1986). The social context of effective schools. *American Journal of Education, 94,* 328–355.

Hamann, E. (2002, April). *The politics of bilingual education, Latino student accommodation, and school district management in Southern Appalachia.* Paper presented at the annual meeting of the American Educational Research Association, New Orleans, LA.

Hamann, E. (2003). *The educational welcome of Latinos in the New South.* Westport, CT: Praeger.

Hamann, E., and Lane, B. (2002). *"We're from the state and we're here to help": State-level innovations in support of high school improvement.* Providence, RI: Education Alliance for Equity in the Nation's Schools, Brown University.

Hamann, E., Zuliani, I., and Hudak, M. (2002, April). *English Language Learners, comprehensive school reforms, and state departments of education: An unbridged dichotomy.* Paper presented at the annual meeting of the American Educational Research Association, New Orleans, LA.

Haney, W. (2000). The myth of the Texas miracle in education. *Education Policy analysis archives, 8.* Retrieved April 15, 2001, from http://epaa.asu.edu/epaa/v8n41.

Hannaway, J. (2003). Accountability, assessment, and performance issues: We've come a long way, or have we? In W. L. Boyd and D. Miretzky (Eds.), *American educational governance on trial: Change and challenges* (pp. 20–37). Chicago: University of Chicago Press.

Hargreaves, D. H., and Hopkins, D. (1991). *The empowered school: The management and practice of developing planning.* London: Cassell.

Harwell, M., D'Amico, L., Stein, M., and Gatti, G. (2000). *Professional development and the achievement gap in Community School District #2.* Pittsburgh, PA: University of Pittsburgh, HPLC Project, Learning Research and Development Center.

Hatch, T. (2000). What happens when improvement programs collide. *Phi Delta Kappan, 81,* 10.

Helsby, G. (1999). *Changing teachers' work*. Buckingham, United Kingdom: Open University Press.

Henig, J., Hula, R., Orr, M., and Pedescleaux, D. (1999). *The color of school reform: Race, politics, and the challenge of urban education*. Princeton, NJ: Princeton University Press.

Herman, R., Aladjem, D., McMahon, P., Masem, E., Mulligan, I., O'Malley, A., Quinones, S., Reeve, A., and Woodruff, D. (1999). *An educators' guide to schoolwide reform*. Washington, DC: American Institutes for Research.

Hess, F. (1999). *Spinning wheels: The politics of urban school reform*. Washington, DC: Brookings Institution Press.

Hightower, A. (2002a). San Diego's big boom: Systemic instructional change in the central office and schools. In A. Hightower, M. Knapp, J. Marsh, and M. McLaughlin (Eds.), *School districts and instructional renewal* (pp. 76–94). New York: Teachers College.

Hightower, A. (2002b). *San Diego's big boom: District bureaucracy supports culture of learning* (Research Report). Seattle, WA: Center for the Study of Teaching and Policy, University of Washington. Retrieved February 23, 2004, from http://depts.washington.edu/ctpmail/PDFs/SanDiego-AH-01-2002.pdf.

Hill, H., Cohen, D., and Moffitt, S. (1999). Instruction, poverty, and performance. In G. Orfield and E. DeBray (Eds.), *Hard work for good schools: Facts not fads in Title I reforms*. Cambridge, MA: Civil Rights Project, Harvard University.

Hill, P., Campbell, C., and Harvey, J. (2000). *It takes a city getting serious about urban school reform*. Washington, DC: Brookings Institution Press.

Hopkins, D. (2002). The Aga Khan Foundation school improvement initiative: An international change perspective. In S. E. Anderson (Ed.), *Improving schools through teacher development: Case studies of the Aga Kahn Foundation Projects in East Africa* (pp. 271–296). Lisse, The Netherlands: Swets & Zeitlinger.

Horn, J. (2000a). *A case study of the Humphreys County (Mississippi) School District and its role as a partner in the NSF-supported Delta Rural Systemic Initiative (RSI)*. Evaluation Report. Kalamazoo, MI: Western Michigan University, Evaluation Center. Paper retrieved May, 15, 2002, from http://www.wmich.edu/evalctr/rsi/humphreys.html.

Horn, J. (2000b). *A case study of Rockcastle County (Kentucky) School District and its role as a partner in the NSF-supported Appalachian Rural Systemic Initiative*. Prepared for the NSF Rural Systemic Initiatives Evaluation Study. Kalamazoo, MI: Western Michigan University, Evaluation Center. Retrieved September 15, 2002, from http://www.wmich.edu/evalctr/rsi/rockcastle.html.

Jennings, J. (2000). Title I: Its legislative history and its promise. *Phi Delta Kappan, 81*(7), 516–522.

Kearns, D., and Anderson, J. (1996). Sharing the vision: Creating New American Schools. In S. Stringfield, S. Ross, and L. Smith (Eds.), *Bold plans for school restructuring* (pp. 9–23). Mahwah, NJ: Lawrence Erlbaum.

Kemper, E., Stringfield, S., and Teddlie, C. (2003). Mixed methods sampling strategies in social science research. In A. Tashakkori and C. Teddlie (Eds.) *Handbook of mixed methods in social behavioral research* (pp. 273–296). Thousand Oaks, CA: Sage.

Kirby, S., Berends, M., and Naftel, S. (2001). *Implementation in a longitudinal sample of New American Schools: Four years into scale-up.* Santa Monica, CA: RAND. Retrieved February 23, 2004, from http://www.rand.org/publications/MR/MR1413/.

Klein, S., Hamilton, L., McCaffery, D., and Stecher, B. (2000). What do test scores in Texas tell us? *Education Policy Analysis Archives, 8*(41). Retrieved February 23, 2004, from http://epaa.asu.edu/epaa/v8n49/.

Knapp, M. S., Turnbull, B. J., and Shields, P. M. (1990). New directions for educating the children of poverty. *Educational Leadership, 48*(1), 4–8.

Kochan, S. E., Tashakkori, A., and Teddlie, C. (1996, April). *You can't judge a high school by test data alone: Constructing an alternative indicator of secondary school effectiveness.* Paper presented at the annual meeting of the American Educational Research Association, New York.

Kushman, J., and Yap, K. (1999). What makes the difference in school improvement? An impact study of Onward to Excellence in Mississippi schools. *Journal of Education for Students Placed At Risk, 4,* 277–298.

Ladd, H. and Hansen, J. (Eds.) (1999). *Making money matter: Financing America's schools.* Washington, DC: National Academy Press.

Land, D. (2002). *Local school boards under review: Their role and effectiveness in relation to students' academic achievement.* CRESPAR technical report 56 Baltimore: Center for Research on the Education of Students Placed At Risk, Johns Hopkins University.

Lareau, A. (1989). *Home advantage.* New York: Falmer.

Lasky, S. (2001, January). *School change, power, moral purpose and teachers' emotions in Ontario.* Paper presented at the annual meeting of the International Congress for School Effectiveness and Improvement (ICSEI), Toronto, Ontario.

Lasky, S., and Foster, L. (2003, August). *An ecological model for analyzing policy implementation.* Paper presented as part of the International Center for Educational Change Seminar Series, Ontario Institute for Studies in Education, University of Toronto, Ontario.

Lee, V. E., and Smith, J. B. (1993). Effects of school restructuring on the achievement and engagement of middle-grade students. *Sociology of Education, 66,* 164–187.

Levin, H. (1987). New schools for the disadvantaged. *Teacher Education Quarterly, 14*(4), 60–83.

Levine, D. U., Levine, R. F., and Eubanks, E. E. (1985). Successful implementation of instruction at inner-city schools. *Journal of Negro Education, 54* (3), 313–332.

Levine, D. U., and Lezotte, L. W. (1990). *Unusually effective schools: A review and analysis of research and practice.* Madison, WI: The National Center for

Effective Schools Research and Development. (ERIC Document Reproduction Service ED 330 032).

Lezotte, L. (1989). School improvement based on the effective schools research. *International Journal of Educational Research, 13*, 815–825.

Lezotte, L. W., and Bancroft, B. (1985). Growing use of effective schools model for school improvement. *Educational Leadership, 42*(3), 23–27.

Lightfoot, S. (1983). *Good high schools: Portraits of character and culture.* New York: Basic Books.

Lincoln, Y. S., and Guba, E. G. (1985). *Naturalistic inquiry.* Beverly Hills, CA: Sage.

Lindle, J. (1999). Hasn't anyone else done this right? A field note on the political realities and perceptions in modifying Kentucky's high stakes accountability system. Paper presented at the annual meeting of the American Educational Research Association, Montreal.

Linn, R., Baker, E., and Betebanner, D. (2002). Accountability systems: Implications of requirements of the No Child Left Behind Act of 2001. *Educational Researcher, 31*(6), 3–17.

Lipka, J. (1991). Toward a culturally based pedagogy: A case study of one Yup'ik Eskimo teacher. *Anthropology and Education Quarterly, 22*, 203–223.

Livingston, D. R., and Livingston, S. M. (2002). Failing Georgia: The case against the ban on social promotion. *Education Policy Analysis Archives, 10*(49). Retrieved February 23, 2004, from http://epaa.asu.edu/epaa/v10n49.

Longoria T., Jr. (1998). School politics in Houston: The impact of business involvement. In C. Stone (Ed.), *Changing urban education* (pp. 184–198). Lawrence: University Press of Kansas.

Lucas, T., Henze, R., and Donato, R. (1990). Promoting the success of Latino language-minority students: An exploratory study of six high schools. *Harvard Educational Review, 60*, 315–340.

Lumpkins, B., Parker, F., and Hall, H. (1991). Instructional equity for low achievers in elementary school mathematics. *Journal of Educational Research, 84*, 135–139.

Lusi, S. (1997). *The role of state departments of education in complex school reform.* New York: Teachers College Press.

Luthar, S. S. (1991). Vulnerability and resilience: A study of high-risk adolescents. *Child Development, 62*, 600–616.

Mac Iver, M., and Farley, L. (2003). *Bringing the district back in: The role of the central office in improving instruction and student achievement* (Report No. 65). Baltimore: Center for Research on the Education of Students Placed at Risk, Johns Hopkins University.

Madaus, G., and Clarke, M. (2001). The adverse impact of high-stakes testing on minority students: Evidence from one hundred years of test data. In G. Orfield and M. Kornhaber (Eds.), *Raising standards or raising barriers: Inequality and high-stakes testing in public education* (pp. 85–107). New York: Century Foundation Press.

Madaus, G. F., Kellaghan, T., Rakow, E. A., and King, D. J. (1979). The sensitivity of measures of school effectiveness. *Harvard Educational Review, 49,* 207–230.

Madden, N. A., Slavin, R. E., Karweit, N. L., Dolan, L. J., and Wasik, B. A. (1993). Success for All: Longitudinal effects of a restructuring program for inner-city elementary schools. *American Educational Research Journal, 30,* 123–148.

Malen, B., Croninger, R., and Muncey, D. (2002). Reconstituting schools: "Testing" the "theory of action." *Educational Evaluation and Policy Analysis, 24,* 113–133.

Marco, G. L. (1974). A comparison of selected school effectiveness measures based on longitudinal data. *Journal of Educational Measurement, 11,* 225–233.

Marsh, J. (2002). How districts relate to states, schools, and communities: A review of emerging literature. In A. Hightower, M. Knapp, J. Marsh, and M. McLaughlin (Eds.), *School districts and instructional renewal,* (pp. 25–41). New York: Teachers College.

Marzano, R. J. (2003). *What works in schools: Translating research into action.* Alexandria, VA: Association for Supervision and Curriculum Development.

Marzano, R. J., Pickering, D. J., and Pollock, J. E. (2001). *Classroom instruction that works: Research-based strategies for increasing student achievement.* Alexandria, VA: Association for Supervision and Curriculum Development.

Massell, D. (1998). *State strategies for building capacity in education: Progress and continuing challenges* (CPRE Research series RR-41). Philadelphia, PA: Consortium for Policy Research in Education, University of Pennsylvania, Graduate School of Education. Retrieved February 23, 2004, from http://www.cpre.org/Publications/rr41.pdf.

Massell, D., and Goertz, M. (2002). District strategies for building instructional capacity. In A. Hightower, M. Knapp, J. Marsh, and M. McLaughlin (Eds.), *School districts and instructional renewal* (pp. 43–61). New York: Teachers College.

May, H., Supovitz, J., and Lesnick, J. (2004). *The impact of America's Choice on writing performance in Georgia: First year results.* Philadelphia: Consortium for Policy Research in Education, University of Pennsylvania. Retrieved March 30, 2005, from http://www.cpre.org/Publications/AC-09.pdf.

McDonald, D., and Keedy, J. (2002). Principals conceptualize the development of teacher leaders: A cross-case study of shared leadership in high-poverty Kentucky schools. In J. Chrispeels (Ed.), *Learning to lead together: The promise and challenge of sharing leadership* (pp. 219–255). Thousand Oaks, CA: Sage.

McGregor, J. (1993). Effectiveness of role playing and antiracist teaching in reducing student prejudice. *Journal of Educational Research, 86,* 215–226.

McHugh, B., and Spath, S. (1997). Carter G. Woodson Elementary School: The success of a private school curriculum in an urban public school. *Journal of Education for Students Placed At Risk, 2,* 121–136.

McIntyre, E., and Kyle, D. (2002). *Nongraded primary programs: Possibilities for improving practice for teachers.* Practitioner Brief No. 4. Center for Research on Education, Diversity, and Education. Retrieved, December 1, 2002, from http://crede.ucsc.edu/products/print/pract_briefs/pb4.shtml.

McLaughlin, M., and Talbert, J. (2002). Reforming districts. In A. Hightower, M. Knapp, J. Marsh, and M. McLaughlin (Eds.), *School districts and instructional renewal* (pp. 173–193). New York: Teachers College.

McLaughlin, M. W. (1990). The Rand change agent study revisited: Macro perspectives, micro realities. *Educational Researcher, 19,* 11–16.

McLaughlin, M. W., and Talbert, J. E. (1993). *Contexts that matter for teaching and learning.* Stanford, CA: Center for Research on the Context of Secondary School Teaching, Stanford University.

McMillan, J. H. (2000). *Basic assessment concepts for teachers and administrators.* Thousand Oaks, CA: Corwin.

McNeil, L. (2000). *Contradictions of school reform: Educational costs of standardized testing.* New York: Routledge.

McNeil, L., and Valenzuela, A. (2001). The harmful impact of the TAAS system of testing in Texas: Beneath the policy rhetoric. In G. Orfield and M. Kornhaber (Eds.), *Raising standards or raising barriers: Inequality and high-stakes testing in public education* (pp. 127–151). New York: Century Foundation Press.

Mehan, H., Hertweck, A., and Meihls, J. L. (1986). *Handicapping the handicapped: Decision making in students' educational careers.* Stanford, CA: Stanford University Press.

Menken, K. (2000). *Do the models fit? Towards comprehensive school reform for English language learners.* Washington, DC: National Clearinghouse for Bilingual Education, Center for the Study of Language and Education. Retrieved July 2, 2001, from http://www.ncbe.gwu.edu/ncbepubs/tasynthesis/framing/4models.htm.

Merrick, R. M. (1988). *Multicultural education: A step toward pluralism.* South Bend: Indiana University at South Bend. (ERIC Document Reproduction Service ED 302 451).

Mertens, D. M. (1998). *Research methods in education and psychology: Integrating diversity with quantitative and qualitative approaches.* Thousand Oaks, CA: Sage.

Mertens, S. (2003). Mixed models and the politics of human research. In A. Tashakkori and C. Teddlie, (Eds.), *Handbook of mixed methods in social and behavioral research* (pp. 135–166). Thousand Oaks, CA: Sage.

Midgley, C., Feldlaufer, H., and Eccles, J. S. (1989). Student/teacher relations and attitudes toward mathematics before and after the transition to junior high school. *Child Development, 60,* 981–992.

Minorini, P., and Sugarman, S. (1999). School finance litigation in the name of educational equity: Its evolution, impact and future. In H. Ladd, R. Chalk, and J. Hansen (Eds.), *Equity and adequacy in education finance: Issues and perspectives* (pp 34–72). Washington, DC: National Academy Press.

Mintrop, H. (2004). High-stakes accountability, state oversight, and educational equity. *Teachers College Record, 106*, 2128–2145.

Moore, H. A. (1988). Effects of gender, ethnicity, and school equity on students' leadership behaviors in a group game. *Elementary School Journal, 88*, 515–527.

Mortimore, P., Sammons, P., Stoll, L., Lewis, D., and Ecob, R. (1988). *School matters: The junior years.* Somerset, England: Open Books (Reprint, Paul Chapman: London, 1995).

Murphy, J., and Hallinger, P. (1989). Equity as access to learning: Curricular and instructional treatment differences. *Journal of Curriculum Studies, 21*, 129–149.

National Commission on Education. (1995). *Success against the odds.* London: Routledge and Kegan Paul.

New American Schools. (1997). *Bringing success to scale: Sharing the vision of New American Schools.* Arlington, VA: Author.

Newman, F., Smith, B., Allensworth, E., and Bryk, A. (2001). *School instructional program coherence: Benefits and challenges.* Research report for the Consortium on Chicago School Research. Chicago: Consortium on Chicago School Research. Retrieved February 23, 2004, from http://www.consortium-chicago.org/publications/pdfs/p0d02.pdf.

Northwest Regional Educational Laboratory. (1998). Catalog of school reform models: First edition. Portland, OR: Author.

Nye, B. A., Boyd-Zaharias, J., Fulton, B. D., and Wallenhorst, M. P. (1992). Smaller classes really are better. *American School Board Journal, 179*(5), 31–33.

Oakes, J. (1985). *Keeping track: How schools structure inequality.* New Haven, CT: Yale University Press.

Oakes, J., Quartz, K. H., Ryan, S., and Lipton, M. (2000). *Becoming good American schools: The struggle for civic virtue in educational reform.* San Francisco: Jossey-Bass.

Oakes, J., and Wells, A. (1996). *Beyond the technicalities of school reform: Lessons from detracking schools.* Los Angeles: University of California at Los Angeles, Graduate School of Education and Information Studies.

Oakes, J., Wells, A. S., Jones, M., and Datnow, A. (1997). Detracking: The social construction of ability, cultural politics, and resistance to reform. *Teachers College Record, 98*, 482–510.

O'Day, J. (2002). Complexity, accountability, and school improvement. *Harvard Educational Review, 72*, 293–329. Retrieved February 23, 2004, from http://gseweb.harvard.edu/~hepg/oday.html.

O'Day, J., and Gross, B. (1999, April). *One system or two? Title I accountability in a context of high stakes for schools in local districts and schools.* Paper presented at the annual meeting of the American Educational Research Association, Seattle, WA.

O'Day, J. A., and Smith, M. S. (1993). Systemic reform and educational opportunity. In S. Fuhrman (Ed.), *Designing coherent education policy: Improving the system* (pp. 250–312). San Francisco: Jossey-Bass.

Odden, A. (1999). *Improving state school finance systems: New realities cre-ate need to re-engineer school finance structures* (Occasional paper series). Philadelphia: Consortium for Policy Research in Education, University of Pennsylvania, Graduate School of Education. Retrieved February 23, 2004, from http://www.cpre.org/Publications/op-04.pdf.

Odden, A., and Clune, W. (1998). School finance systems: Aging structures in need of repair. *Educational Evaluation and Policy Analysis, 20*, 157–177.

Padron, Y., Waxman, H., and Rivera, H. (2002). Issues in educating Hispanic students. In S. Stringfield and D. Land (Eds.), *Educating at-risk students* (pp. 66–89). Chicago: Chicago University Press.

Pate, G. S. (1981). Research on prejudice reduction. *Educational Leadership, 38*, 288–291.

Pate, G. S. (1988). Research on reducing prejudice. *Social Education, 52*, 287–289.

Patton, M. Q. (1990). *Qualitative research and evaluation research methods* (3rd ed.). Newbury Park, CA: Sage.

Pine, G. J., and Hilliard, A. G. (1990). Rx for racism: Imperatives for America's schools. *Phi Delta Kappan, 71*, 593–600.

Placier, M., Hall, P., McKendall, S. B., and Cockrell, K. (2000). Policy as trans-formation of intentions: Making multicultural education policy. *Educational Policy, 14*(2), 259–289.

Porter, A., and Chester, M. (2001). *Building a high-quality assessment and accountability program: The Philadelphia example.* Paper presented at a Brook-ings Institution Conference, Washington, DC.

President's Task Force on Education. (1964). Report of the President's Task Force on Education. Unpublished report. Department of Health, Educa-tion, and Welfare, Washington, D.C.

Ralph, J. H. and Fennessey, J. (1983). Science or reform: Some questions about the effective schools model. *Phi Delta Kappan, 64*, 692.

Regional Educational Laboratory Network. (2000). *Implementing education reform: Strategies used by states, districts, and schools.* Aurora, CO: Mid-Continent Research for Education and Learning.

Resnick, L., and Glennan, T. (2002). Leadership for learning: A theory of action for urban school districts. In A. Hightower, M. Knapp, J. Marsh, and M. McLaughlin (Eds.), *School districts and instructional renewal* (pp. 160–173). New York: Teachers College.

Resnick, L., and Harwell, M. (2000, June). *Instructional variation and student achievement in a standards-based education district.* (CSE Technical Report 522). Los Angeles: University of California, Graduate School of Educa-tion and Information Studies, National Center for Research on Evaluation, Standards, and Student Testing, Center for the Study of Evaluation.

Reyes, M. D. (1992). Challenging venerable assumptions: Literacy instruction for linguistically different students. *Harvard Educational Review, 62*, 427–445.

Reynolds, D. (1976). The delinquent school. In P. Woods (Ed.), *The process of schooling*. London: Routledge.

Reynolds, D., Creemers, B., Stringfield, S., Teddlie, C., and Schaffer, E. (2002). *World class schools: International perspectives on school effectiveness.* London: RoutledgeFalmer.

Reynolds, D., and Teddlie, C. (2000). The future agenda for school effectiveness research. In C. Teddlie and D. Reynolds (Eds.), *The international handbook of school effectiveness research* (pp. 322–343). London: Falmer.

Reynolds, D., Teddlie, C., Creemers, B., Scheerens, J., and Townsend, T. (2000). An introduction to school effectiveness research. In C. Teddlie and D. Reynolds (Eds.), *The international handbook of school effectiveness research* (pp. 3–25). London: Falmer.

Rich, W. (1996). *Black mayors and school politics: The failure of reform in Detroit, Gary and Newark.* New York: Garland.

Rich, Y. (1987). The potential contribution of school counseling to school integration. *Journal of Counseling and Development, 65,* 495–498.

Richardson, V. (Ed.). (2002). *Handbook of research on teaching.* (4th ed.). Washington, DC: American Educational Research Association.

Robinson, G. E. (1990). Synthesis of research on the effects of class size. *Educational Leadership, 47*(7), 80–90.

Rogers, M., Miller, N., and Hennigan, K. (1981). Cooperative games as an intervention to promote cross-racial acceptance. *American Educational Research Journal, 18,* 513–516.

Rosenshine, B. (1983). Teaching functions in instructional programs. *Elementary School Journal, 83,* 335–351.

Ross, S. M., Alberg, M., and Nunnery, J. (1999). Selection and evaluation of locally developed versus externally developed schoolwide programs. In G. Orfield and E. H. Debray (Eds.), *Hard work for good schools: Facts not fads in Title I reform* (pp. 147–158). Cambridge, MA: Harvard University, Civil Rights Project.

Rowan, B. (1984). Shamanistic rituals in effective schools. *Issues in Education, 2,* 76–87.

Rowan, B. (2001, March). *The ecology of school improvement: Notes on the school improvement industry in the U.S.* Paper presented at the conference on Social Geographies of Educational Change, Barcelona, Spain.

Rowan, B., Bossert, S. T., and Dwyer, D. C. (1983). Research on effective schools: A cautionary note. *Educational Researcher, 12*(4), 24–31.

Rudo, Z. (2001). *Corrective action in low-performing schools and school districts.* Austin, TX: Southwest Educational Developmental Laboratory.

Ruiz-Primo, M., Li, M., and Shavelson, R. (2002). *Looking into students' science notebooks: What do teachers do with them?* CSE Technical Report. Los Angeles: Center for the Study of Evaluation, National Center for Research on Evaluation, Standards, and Student Testing, Graduate School of Education and Information Studies, University of California at Los Angeles.

Rumberger, R. W., and Douglas, W. J. (1992). The impact of racial and ethnic segregation on the achievement gap in California high schools. *Educational Evaluation and Policy Analysis, 14,* 377–396.

Russon, C., Horn, J., and Oliver, S. (2000). *Gila River indicant community (Arizona) and its role as a partner in the NSF-supported UCAN Rural Systemic Initiative (RSI).* Prepared for the NSF Rural Systemic Initiatives Evaluation Study, The Evaluation Center, Western Michigan University, Kalamazoo. Retrieved September 15, 2002, from http://www.wmich.edu/evalctr/rsi/gila_river.htm.

Rutter, M. (1983). School effects on pupil progress: Research findings and policy implications. In L. Shulman and G. Sykes (Eds.), *Handbook of teaching and policy* (pp. 3–41). New York: Longman.

Rutter, M., Maughan, B., Mortimore, P., and Ouston, J., with Smith, A. (1979). *Fifteen thousand hours: Secondary schools and their effects on children.* London: Open Books and Boston: Harvard University Press.

Saldate, M., IV, Mishra, S. P., and Medina, M., Jr. (1985). Bilingual instruction and academic achievement: A longitudinal study. *Journal of Instructional Psychology 12*, 24–30.

Sammons, P., Hillman, J., and Mortimore, P. (1995). *Key characteristics of effective schools: A review of school effectiveness research.* London: International School Effectiveness and Improvement Centre, University of London.

Sammons, P., Mortimore, P., and Thomas, S. (1993, September). *Do schools perform consistently across outcomes and areas?* Paper presented at annual conference of the British Educational Research Association, Oxford.

Sarason, S. (1997). Revisiting the creation of settings. *Mind Culture and Activity, 4*, 175–182.

Scheerens, J. (1992). *Effective schooling: Research, theory and practice.* London: Cassell.

Scheerens, J., and Bosker, R. (1997). *The foundations of educational effectiveness.* Oxford: Pergamon.

Schmidt, M., and Datnow, A. (2002, April). *How teachers make sense of comprehensive school reform within their state policy contexts.* Paper presented at the annual meeting of the American Educational Research Association, New Orleans, LA.

Shadish, W. R., Cook, T. D., and Campbell, D. T. (2002). *Experimental and quasi-experimental designs for general causal inference.* Boston: Houghton Mifflin.

Shavelson, R., Baxter, G., and Pine, J. (1992). Performance assessments: Political rhetoric and measurement reality. *Educational Researcher, 21*(4), 22–27.

Sizer, T. R. (1984). *Horace's compromise.* Boston: Houghton Mifflin.

Slavin, R. E. (1985). Cooperative learning: Applying contact theory in desegregated schools. *Journal of Social Issues, 41*(3), 43–62.

Slavin, R. E. (1987). Grouping for instruction: Equity and effectiveness. *Equity and Excellence, 23*, 31–36.

Slavin, R. E. (1988). Synthesis of research on grouping in elementary and secondary schools. *Educational Leadership, 46*(1), 67–77.

Slavin, R. E. (1990). Achievement effects of ability grouping in secondary schools: A best-evidence synthesis. *Review of Educational Research, 60*, 471–499.

Slavin, R. E. (1994). Quality, appropriateness, incentive, and time: A model of instructional effectiveness. *International Journal of Educational Research, 21*, 141–157.

Slavin, R. E. (1998, Fall). Far and wide: Developing and disseminating research-based programs. *American Educator*. Retrieved February 23, 2004, from http://www.aft.org/edissues/rsa/guide/change/slavin.htm.

Slavin, R. E., and Fashola, O. (1998). *Show me the evidence* Thousand Oaks, CA: Corwin.

Slavin, R. E., Karweit, N., and Madden, N. A. (Eds.). (1989). *Effective programs for students at risk*. Boston: Allyn & Bacon.

Slavin, R. E., Karweit, N., and Wasik, B. (1994). *Preventing early school failure*. Needham Heights, MA: Allyn & Bacon.

Slavin, R. E., Leavey, M., and Madden, N. A. (1982). *Effects of student teams and individualized instruction on student mathematics achievement. Attitudes and behaviors*. Baltimore: Johns Hopkins University.

Slavin, R. E., and Madden, N. A. (1989). What works for students at risk: A research synthesis. *Educational Leadership, 46*(5), 4–13.

Slavin, R. E., and Madden, N. A. (1998). *Scaling up: Lessons learned in the dissemination of Success for All*. Baltimore: Johns Hopkins University, Center for Research on the Education of Students Placed At Risk.

Slavin, R. E., and Madden, N. A. (1999). *Effects of bilingual and English as a Second Language adaptations of Success for All on the reading achievement of students acquiring English*. Baltimore: Johns Hopkins University and Success for All Foundation. Retrieved February 23, 2004, from http://www.successforall.net/resource/research/bilingualesl.htm.

Slavin, R. E, Madden, N., Dolan, L., and Wasik, B. (1996). *Every child, every school: Success for All*. Thousand Oaks, CA: Corwin.

Smith, L., Ross, S., McNelis, M., Squires, M., Wasson, R., Maxwell, S., Weddle, K., Nath, L., Grehan, A., and Buggey, T. (1998). The Memphis Restructuring Initiative: Analysis of activities and outcomes that affect implementation success. *Education and Urban Society, 30*, 296–325.

Smylie, M., and Wenzel, S. (2003). *The Chicago Annenberg Challenge: Successes, failures, and lessons for the future*. Chicago: Consortium on Chicago School Research. Retrieved June 10, 2003, from http://www.consortium-chicago.org/publications/p62.html.

Snipes, J., Doolittle, F., and Herlihy, C. (2002). *Foundations for success: Case studies of how urban school systems improve student achievement*. Washington, DC: Council of the Great City Schools.

Snyder, J. (2002). New Haven Unified School District: A teaching quality system for excellence and equity. In A. Hightower, M. Knapp, J. Marsh, and M. McLaughlin (Eds.), *School districts and instructional renewal* (pp. 94–111). New York: Teachers College.

Solano-Flores, G., and Trumbull, E. (2003). Examining language in context: The need for new research and practice paradigms in the testing of English-language Learners. *Educational Researcher, 32*, 3–13.

Spillane, J. (1996). School districts matter: Local educational authorities and state instructional policy. *Educational Policy, 10,* 63–87.

Spillane, J. (1999). State and local government relations in the era of standards-based reform: Standards, state policy instruments, and the local instructional policy making. *Educational Policy, 13,* 546–572.

Spillane, J. (2000). *District leaders' perceptions of teacher learning* (CPRE Occasional Paper Series OP-05). Philadelphia, PA: Consortium for Policy Research in Education, University of Pennsylvania, Graduate School of Education. Retrieved February 23, 2004, from http://www.cpre.org/Publications/op-05.pdf.

Spillane, J. (2001). Challenging instruction for "all students": Policy, practitioners, and practice. In S. Fuhrman (Ed.), *From the capital to the classroom: Standards-based reform in the United States* (pp. 217–242). Chicago: University of Chicago Press.

Spillane, J., and Jennings, N. (1997). Aligned instructional policy and ambitious pedagogy: Exploring instructional reform from the classroom perspective. *Teachers College Record, 98,* 449–481.

Stein, M., and D'Amico, L. (2002). District as professional learning community. In A. Hightower, M. Knapp, J. Marsh, and M. W. McLaughlin (Eds.), *School districts and instructional renewal: Opening the conversation* (pp. 61–76). New York: Teachers College Press.

Stein, M. K., Hubbard, L., and Mehan, H. (2002, April). *Reform ideas that travel far afield: The two cultures of reform in New York City's District #2 and San Diego.* Paper presented at the annual meeting of the American Educational Research Association, New Orleans, LA.

Stein, M. K., Leinhardt, G., and Bickel, W. (1989). Instructional issues for teaching students at risk. In R. E. Slavin, N. L. Karweit, and N. A. Madden (Eds.), *Effective programs for students at risk* (pp. 145–194). Boston: Allyn & Bacon.

Stone, C. (1998a). Civic capacity and urban school reform. In C. Stone (Ed.), *Changing urban education* (pp. 250–277). Lawrence: University Press of Kansas.

Stone, C. (1998b). Introduction: Urban education in political context. In C. Stone (Ed.), *Changing urban education* (pp. 1–23). Lawrence: University Press of Kansas.

Stone, C., Henig, J., Jones, B., and Pierannuzi, C. (2001). *Building civic capacity: The politics of reforming urban schools.* Lawrence: University Press of Kansas.

Stringfield, S. (1999). The phoenix rises from its ashes...doesn't it? In J. Freiberg (Ed.), *School climate: Measuring, improving and sustaining healthy learning environments* (pp. 186–207). London: Falmer.

Stringfield, S. (2000). A synthesis and critique of four recent reviews of whole school reform in the United States. *School Effectiveness and School Improvement, 11,* 259–269.

Stringfield, S., and Datnow, A. (2002). Systemic support for schools serving students placed at risk. In S. Stringfield and D. Land (Eds.), *Educating at-risk students* (pp. 269–288). Chicago: National Society for the Study of Education.

Stringfield, S., Datnow, A., Borman, G., and Rachuba, L. (1999). *National evaluation of Core Knowledge Sequence implementation: Final report*. Baltimore: Center for Social Organization of Schools, Johns Hopkins University.

Stringfield, S., Datnow, A., Ross, S. M., and Snively, F. (1998). Scaling up school restructuring in multicultural, multilingual contexts: Early observations from Sunland County. *Education and Urban Society, 30*, 326–357.

Stringfield, S., Millsap, M. A., Herman, R., Yoder, N., Brigham, N., Nesselrodt, P., Schaffer, E., Karweit, N., Levin, M., and Stevens, R. (with Gamse, B., Puma, M., Rosenblum, S., Beaumont, J., Randall, B., and Smith, L.). (1997). *Urban and suburban/rural special strategies for educating disadvantaged children. Final report*. Washington, DC: U.S. Department of Education.

Stringfield, S., and Ross, S. (1997). A "reflection" at mile three of a marathon: The Memphis Restructuring Initiative in mid-stride. *School Effectiveness and School Improvement, 8*, 151–161.

Stringfield, S., and Teddlie, C. (1991). School, classroom, and student level indicators of rural school effectiveness. *Journal of Research in Rural Education, 7*(3), 15–28.

Stringfield, S., Teddlie, C., and Suarez, S. (1985). Classroom interaction in effective and ineffective schools: Preliminary results from phase III of the Louisiana School Effectiveness Study. *Journal of Classroom Interaction, 20*(2), 31–37.

Supovitz, J. A., and Turner, H. (2000). The influence of standards-based reform on classroom practices and culture. *Journal of Research in Science teaching, 37*, 963–980.

Supovitz, J., and Weathers, J. (2004). *Dashboard lights: Monitoring implementation of district institutional reform strategies*. Philadelphia: Consortium for Policy Research in Education, University of Pennsylvania. Retrieved March 30, 2005, from http://www.cpre.org/Publications/pdf/snapshotstudy.pdf.

Swisher, K. (1990). Cooperative learning and the education of American Indian/Alaskan Native students: A review of the literature and suggestions for implementation. *Journal of American Indian Education, 29*, 36–43.

Tashakkori, A., and Teddlie, C. (1998). *Mixed methodology: Combining the qualitative and quantitative approaches*. Thousand Oaks, CA: Sage.

Tashakkori, A., and Teddlie, C. (Eds.). (2003). *Handbook of mixed methods in social and behavioral research*. Thousand Oaks, CA: Sage.

Taylor, B. O. (Ed.). (1990). *Case studies in effective schools research*. Madison, WI: National Center for Effective Schools Research and Development.

Teddlie, C. (1994). Integrating classroom and school data in school effectiveness research. In D. Reynolds et al. (Eds.), *Advances in school effectiveness research and practice* (pp. 111–132). Oxford: Pergamon.

Teddlie, C. (2003). The KEYS case study in Mississippi: A failed "graft" of one school reform onto another. In B. Portin, L. Beck, M. Knapp, and J.

Murphy (Eds.), *Self reflective renewal in schools: Local lessons from a national initiative* (pp. 129–146). Westport, CT: Praeger.

Teddlie, C., Kirby, P., and Stringfield, S. (1989). Effective versus ineffective schools: Observable differences in the classroom. *American Journal of Education, 97*, 221–236.

Teddlie, C., Kochan, S., and Taylor, D. (2002). The ABC+ model for school diagnosis, feedback, and improvement. In A. J. Visscher and R. Coe (Eds.), *School improvement through performance feedback* (pp. 75–114). Lisse, The Netherlands: Swets & Zeitlinger.

Teddlie, C., Lang, M. H., and Oescher, J. (1995). The masking of the delivery of educational services to lower achieving students. *Urban Education, 30*, 125–149.

Teddlie, C., and Meza, J. (1999). Using informal and formal measures to create classroom profiles. In J. Freiberg (Ed.), *School climate: Measuring, improving and sustaining healthy learning environments* (pp. 48–64). London: Falmer.

Teddlie, C., and Reynolds, D. (2000). *The international handbook of school effectiveness research*. London: Falmer.

Teddlie, C., and Reynolds, D. (2001). Countering the critics: Responses to recent criticisms of school effectiveness research. *School Effectiveness and School Improvement, 12*, 41–82.

Teddlie, C., and Stringfield, S. (1985). A differential analysis of effectiveness in middle and lower socio-economic status schools. *Journal of Classroom Interaction, 20*(2), 38–44.

Teddlie, C., and Stringfield, S. (1993). *Schools make a difference: Lessons learned from a 10-year study of school effects*. New York: Teachers College Press.

Teddlie, C., Stringfield, S., and Reynolds, D. (2000). Context issues within school effectiveness research. In C. Teddlie and D. Reynolds (Eds.), *The international handbook of school effectiveness research* (pp. 160–185). London: Falmer.

Tharp, R. G., Estrada, P., Dalton, S. S., and Yamauchi, L. A. (2000). *Teaching transformed: Achieving excellence, fairness, inclusion and harmony*. Boulder, CO: Westview.

Tharp, R. G., Lewis, H., Hilberg, R., Bird, C., Epaloose, G., Dalton, S. S., Youpa, D. G., Rivera, H., Riding In-Feathers, M., and Eriacho, W. (1999). Seven more mountains and a map: Overcoming obstacles to reform in Native American schools. *Journal of Education for Students Placed At Risk, 4*(1), 5–25.

Tikunoff, W. J. (1985). *Applying significant bilingual instructional features in the classroom*. Bilingual Education Research Series. Rosslyn, VA: National Clearinghouse for Bilingual Education (ERIC Document Reproduction Service ED 338 106).

Togneri, W., and Anderson, S. E. (2003). *Beyond islands of excellence: What districts can do to improve instruction and achievement in all schools*. Washington, DC: Learning First Alliance and the Association for Supervision and Curriculum Development.

U.S. Department of Education. (1999). *CSRD in the field: Fall 1999 update.* Washington, DC: Author.

U.S. Department of Education. (2000). *Guidance on the Comprehensive School Reform Demonstration Program.* Washington, DC: Author. Retrieved February 23, 2004, from http://www.ed.gov/programs/compreform/guidance/guidance2002.pdf.

Valenzuela, A. (1999). *Subtractive schooling: U.S. American-Mexican youth and the politics of caring.* Albany: State University of New York Press.

Valverde, L. A. (1988). Principals creating better schools in minority communities. *Education and Urban Society, 20,* 319–326.

Venezky, R. L., and Winfield, L. F. (1979). *Schools that succeed beyond expectations in teaching reading (Tech. Rep. No. 1).* Newark: University of Delaware, Studies in Education.

Virgilio, I., Teddlie, C., and Oescher, J. (1991). Variance and context differences in teaching at differentially effective schools. *School Effectiveness and School Improvement, 2,* 152–168.

Walberg, H. J., and Genova, W. J. (1983). School practices and climates that promote integration. *Contemporary Educational Psychology, 8,* 87–100.

Wang, M., Haertel, G., and Walberg, H. (1997). *What do we know.* Philadelphia: Temple University, Laboratory for Student Success.

Warring, D., Johnson, D. W., Maruyama, G., and Johnson, R. (1985). Impact of different types of cooperative learning on cross-ethnic and cross-sex relationships. *Journal of Educational Psychology, 77,* 53–59.

Watson, N., Fullan, M., and Kilchner, A. (2002, April). *The role of the district: Professional learning and district reform.* Paper presented at the annual meeting of the American Educational Research Association, New Orleans, LA.

Waxman, H., Wang, M. C., Anderson, K. A., and Walberg, H. J. (1985). Synthesis of research on the effects of adaptive education. *Educational Leadership, 43*(1), 26–29.

Weber, G. (1971). *Inner city children can be taught to read: Four successful schools.* Washington, DC: Council for Basic Education.

Wenzel, S. A., Smylie, M. A., Sebring, P. B., Allensworth, E., Gutierrez, T., Hallman, S., Luppescu, S., and Miller, S. R. (2001). *Development of the Chicago Annenberg Schools: 1996–1999* (Research report for the Consortium on Chicago School Research). Chicago: Consortium on Chicago School Research. Retrieved February 23, 2004, from http://www.consortium-chicago.org/publications/pdfs/p0b05.pdf.

Wilde, J., Thompson, B., and Herrera, R. M. (1999). *Guide: Comprehensive school reform models addressing the needs of English language learners.* Retrieved January 15, 2000, from: http:www.cesdp.nmhu.edu/CSRD-Guide/backgrnd.htm.

Wimpelberg, R., Teddlie, C., and Stringfield, S. (1989). Sensitivity to context: The past and future of effective schools research. *Educational Administration Quarterly, 25*(1), 82–107.

Yakimowski, M. (2004). *No Child Left Behind: A focus on accountability.* Baltimore: Baltimore City Public Schools System.

Yonezawa, S., and Datnow, A. (1999). Supporting multiple reform designs in a culturally and linguistically diverse school district. *Journal of Education of Students Placed At Risk, 4,* 101–126.

Yonezawa, S., and Stringfield, S. (2000). *Special Strategies for Educating Disadvantaged Students follow-up study: Examining the sustainability of research based school reforms.* Baltimore: Johns Hopkins University, Center for Research on the Education of Students Placed At Risk.

# Index

*2712*
*gift*